CATALONIA REBORN

How Catalonia Took On the Corrupt Spanish State
and the Legacy of Franco

CHRIS BAMBERY and GEORGE KEREVAN

Luath Press Limited

EDINBURGH

www.luath.co.uk

First published 2018

ISBN: 978-1-912147-38-0

The authors' right to be identified as author of this book under the
Copyright, Designs and Patents Act 1988 has been asserted.

The paper used in this book is recyclable. It is made from low chlorine pulps
pro   duced in a low energy, low emission manner from renewable forests.

Typeset in 11 point Sabon by Lapiz

Printed and bound by Bell & Bain Ltd., Glasgow

Contents

Map

Image: Shutterstock

Timeline

Classical Age – Fertile Catalan coastal region emerges as key link in Phoenician, Greek, Carthaginian and finally Roman Mediterranean trading empires.

8th–11th centuries – Islamic rule in most of Spain but Catalan border lands remain contested after Charles Martel defeats Arab-Berber armies at Poitiers, in 732 AD.

801 – Franks occupy Barcelona, creating a buffer between Charlemagne's Empire and Muslim Spain. Catalan monasteries become major cultural centres transmitting knowledge between Christian and Muslim worlds.

870 – Wilfred the Hairy, Count of Gerona and Barcelona, unites four Catalan feudal counties, creating powerful state straddling the Pyrenees. Inward migration creates free peasantry and agricultural boom.

988 – Count Borrell II refuses to renew oath of loyalty to the Frankish kings. Feudal Catalonia declares de facto independence.

1023–76 – Under Ramon Berenguer I, the county of Barcelona acquires a dominant economic and political position in the area.

12th century – First mention of the term Catalonia.

1137 – Catalonia and Kingdom of Aragon to the south-west unite through marriage to become the Crown of Catalonia and Aragon, though Catalan autonomy remains intact. Over the next three centuries, Catalan empire spreads across the Western Mediterranean to Sicily and Sardinia.

1359 – The Generalitat of Catalonia established, with a president and what is considered one of Europe's earliest parliaments.

1469 – King Ferdinand of Catalonia and Aragon marries Queen Isabella of Castile, uniting the two Spanish monarchies. But Catalonia retains self-rule, with its own political institutions, courts and laws.

1474 – First printed book in Catalan.

1640–1659 – War of the Reapers: Catalan peasants rise up against the monarchy amid anger over taxation and being forced to station and provision troops fighting against France. Strengthens tradition of popular Catalan resistance to external rule.

1659 – Spain and France sign the Treaty of the Pyrenees and Catalonia loses the northernmost part of its territory.

1705 – War of the Spanish Succession: Fearful of a French Bourbon king on the Spanish throne, the Catalans ally themselves with England in defence of their traditional autonomy.

1713 – Tory government in Great Britain resolves to end the Spanish war and signs the Treaty of Utrecht. It wins trade concessions and territory, including Gibraltar. Abandoned, Catalonia keeps fighting.

1714 – Barcelona falls to the Bourbons after a 14-month siege, on 11 September – thereafter celebrated as National Day in Catalonia. Generalitat abolished and Catalan language suppressed.

1796–1814 – French Revolutionary and Peninsula War. Napoleon at first restores Catalan independence but then annexes Catalonia to France. With end of wars, absolutism renewed under Ferdinand VII.

19th century – With the loss of its American colonies, Spain enters a century of economic decline. The exception is Catalonia, where rapid industrialisation creates a new, militant working class and triggers a cultural and linguistic renaissance, reviving Catalan nationalism.

1833 – First steam-driven textile mill in Barcelona. Burned down two years later by striking workers.

1873 – First Spanish Republic declared, committed to liberalism, modernisation and federalism. Overthrown by the army the following year. Bourbons restored.

1888 – Founding (in Barcelona) of Spanish Socialist Party (PSOE) and General Workers' Union (UGT). Universal exhibition in Barcelona.

1898 – Catalan business hurt when Spain loses Cuba. Reinforces desire of Catalan middle class for more political and economic autonomy.

1895–1906 – Zenith of Catalan Modernist architecture.

1901 – Formation of middle class Catalan Regionalist League, supporting autonomy not independence.

1909 – Working class uprising in Barcelona ('Tragic Week') triggered by opposition to sending Catalan conscripts to colonial war in Morocco.

1910 – Anarchist CNT founded in Barcelona.

1914 – Limited self-government returned to Catalonia under the leadership of Enric Prat de la Riba.

1917 – General strike in Barcelona.

1923 – Miguel Primo de Rivera imposes a military dictatorship in Spain. Catalan self-government and language supressed yet again.

1931 – With the collapse of the de Rivera dictatorship, Spain becomes a republic (again). An autonomous Catalan government, the Generalitat, is created under the leadership of Francesc Macia and the new Republican Left of Catalonia (ERC). Spain enters period of intense instability.

1934 – Following election of a right-wing Spanish government, new Catalan president, Luis Companys, declares independence. But this breakaway is suppressed by the army and Companys is jailed. Leftist rising in Asturias also supressed. Spain divided between left and right.

1936 – Popular Front government elected in Spain. Catalan autonomy restored under freed Companys. Franco mounts a military coup, which fails in Catalonia due to popular action. Spanish Civil War begins.

1937 – Communists and Spanish Republican government repress Catalan left-wing opposition of POUM and CNT. Andreu Nin murdered.

1939 – Barcelona occupied by Francoist forces. Catalan language banned in public, Catalan newspapers, books and culture suppressed. Thousands executed, hundreds of thousands flee into exile.

1940 – Lluis Companys executed by firing squad at Montjuic Castle.

1947 – First signs of popular resistance to Franco when Catalan used (illegally) in public at religious celebrations at Monserrat.

1951 – Tram boycott in Barcelona forces concessions from regime.

1954 – Josep Tarradellas elected Catalan President in exile.

1960s – Catalan economy revives with start of mass tourism and increasing industrialisation. Barcelona attracts large numbers of migrants from other Spanish regions. Growing cultural and political opposition to the Dictatorship led by students at Barcelona University.

1960 – Franco's visit to Barcelona met with civil disobedience.

1962 – New strike wave leads to creation of Communist-led unions, the Commissions Obreres.

1974 – Regime executes Salvador Puig Antich, despite world-wide pleas for clemency. Mass resistance to the Dictatorship in Catalonia.

1975 – Franco dies. Juan Carlos 1 declared king.

1977 – First, limited democratic elections are held in Spain. One million Catalans demonstrate on 11 September. New regime allows Josep Tarradellas to return from exile.

1979 – New Statute of Autonomy for (devolved) Catalonia finally approved. Catalonia is defined as a 'nationality' but not a nation.

1980 - Moderate, regionalist Convergència i Unió (CIU), led by Jordi Pujol, wins the first of many elections to new Catalan parliament.

1981 – Failed military coup frightens Spanish governments into limiting autonomy for Catalonia and Basque Lands. Sets scene for later friction.

1992 – Olympics hosted in Barcelona.

2003 – Left-wing victory in Catalan elections. Massive demonstrations against Iraq War in Barcelona. Demands for greater Catalan autonomy.

2006 – New Statute of Autonomy is approved by Catalan Parliament, by the Spanish Parliament and by a referendum in Catalonia. This settlement is opposed by the Spanish right and the Popular Party.

2008 – Global banking crisis and collapse of the Spanish property bubble triggers mass unemployment in Spain and Catalonia.

2010 – Spain's highly politicised Constitutional Court, in judgement on a case brought by the Popular Party, waters down the new Statute of Autonomy. For the first time since Franco's death, there is a majority in Catalonia for independence.

2011 – The 15-M anti-austerity movement erupts across Spain. In Barcelona, anti-austerity and nationalist sentiments combine, undermining the traditional autonomist leadership of the CIU.

2012 – In response to the anti-austerity protests, Catalan President Artur Mas asks for negotiations on a new fiscal pact with Spain. Madrid refuses. A major independence demonstration brings 1.5 million people on to the streets of Barcelona in protest. Under pressure, Mas calls for an independence referendum. Catalan National Assembly founded.

2013 – Nearly two million people link hands across Catalonia calling for independence – possibly the largest demonstration in European history. Artur Mas asks Spanish Prime Minister Mariano Rajoy to discuss a referendum. Madrid snubs the request.

2014 – The Catalan Government holds a consultative referendum on independence. Over 80 per cent of the 2.25m votes cast favour the independence option.

2015 – Pro-independence parties win a clear majority in fresh election to the Catalan Parliament. Under pressure from the far-left CUP party, Artur Mas is replaced by Carles Puigdemont as Catalan President.

2017 –

1 October: With Madrid still refusing negotiations, the Catalan Parliament holds a second independence referendum. Despite savage Spanish police attacks on polling stations, 2,020,000 voters (91.96 per cent) answer 'Yes', while 177,000 say 'No'. Puigdemont asks Madrid to enter a dialogue brokered by the EU. The Spanish Government and the EU both reject these overtures.

3 October: General strike across Catalonia in protest at Guardia Civil brutality on referendum day. Over 700,000 demonstrate in Barcelona. TV broadcast by King Filipe fails to condemn police action.

16 October: Two prominent independence leaders – Jordi Sanchez of the Catalan National Assembly and Jordi Cuixart of Omnium Cultural – arrested and imprisoned on charges of sedition.

27 October: Catalan Parliament votes to declare an independent Catalan Republic. Immediately, Spanish Senate invokes Article 155 of the constitution and imposes direct rule over Catalonia. Prime Minister Rajoy dissolves

Catalan Parliament. Puigdemont and Catalan ministers escape into exile in Belgium.

7 December: Over 50,000 Catalans come to Brussels in solidarity with Puigdemont and to demand the EU intervenes in Catalonia. EU ignores.

21 December: Pro-independence parties win narrow majority in election.

2018 –

January 2018 – Three jailed Catalan independence leaders – Oriol Junqueras, Jordi Sànchez and Jordi Cuixart – file a complaint with the United Nations, saying their imprisonment in Spain breaks international law.

March 2018 – The pro-independence majority in the Catalan parliament are unable to elect Jordi Sànchez as president after the Spanish Supreme Court refused to free him from prison so he could attend the session.

A third attempt to elect a new president collapses after a proposal to install Jordi Turull was defeated by 65 votes against 64.

Spain's Supreme Court plans to try 13 Catalan independence leaders on charges of rebellion.

April 2018 – Carles Puigdemont arrested by German police after crossing the border en route to Belgium after Spain secured a European arrest warrant while he was visiting Finland. A German court releases him on bail saying the charge of violent rebellion was inadmissible.

Seven activists from the grassroots Committees for the Defence of the Republic are arrested following their campaign of non-violent civil disobedience.

Hundreds of thousands take to the streets of Barcelona on Sunday 15 April to demand freedom for Catalan political prisoners under the slogan 'Us Volem a Casa' ('We want you home').

May 2018 – Jordi Cuixart, Jordi Sànchez, Oriol Junqueras, Joaquim Forn, Dolors Bassa, Carme Forcadell, Raul Romeva, Josep Rull and Jordi Turull remain in Spanish prisons; Carles Puigdemont is in exile in Germany awaiting trial; Clara Ponsati awaits a Scottish court decision on the validity of the European Arrest Warrant; and Meritxell Serret, Antoni Comín and Lluís Puig remain in Belgium.

List of Abbreviations and Glossary

Alianza Popular (People's Alliance). Right-wing party founded by Manuel Fraga in 1977; precursor of Partido Popular.

ANC: **Assemblea Nacional Catalana** (Catalan National Assembly). Grassroots civic association organization that seeks political independence of Catalonia and Catalan-speaking areas from the Spanish state. The ANC has its origins in the Conferència Nacional per l'Estat Propi (National Conference for Our Own State), held in April 2011 in Barcelona. Formed officially in March 2012, with Carme Forcadell as President. Famous for holding mass demonstrations.

Carlism. Traditionalist, right-wing movement seeking the establishment of a separate line of the Bourbon dynasty to Spanish throne. Focal point for peasant and regionalist opposition, especially in Basque lands, defending local autonomist rights. Carlism was a significant force from 1833 until the end of the Franco regime. Today, a fringe movement.

Catalunya en Comú-Podem. Left-wing electoral coalition comprising Podem (Catalan branch of Podemos) and Catalunya en Comú, a local grouping organised by Barcelona mayor Ada Colau. Also includes Iniciativa per Catalunya-Verds (ICV), the continuation of the former Catalan communist PSUC. Confusingly, during 2015–2017, Catalunya en Comú-Podem ran under the name Catalunya Sí Que Es Pot.

CIU: **Convergència i Unió** (Convergence and Union). Pro-autonomy, centre-right electoral alliance comprising Democratic Convergence of Catalonia and smaller Democratic Union of Catalonia. Founded in 1978, dissolved in 2015. Under Jordi Pujol, CIU ran autonomous Catalan government for 23 years until 2003, favouring maximum devolution inside Spain rather than independence. Return to power in 2010 as part of a series of increasingly pro-independence coalitions. Dominant force in Catalan politics for most of post-Franco era.

CCOO: **Comisiones Obreras** (Workers' Commissions). Trade union body originally founded in 1960s by the Spanish Communist Party and liberal Catholic workers' groups. Illegal under Franco, the Commissions entered and subverted the state-controlled 'vertical unions'. Today the largest trades union federation in the Spanish state.

CEDA: **Confederatión Espanola de Derechas Autónomas** (Spanish Confederation of Autonomous Right-wing Groups). Amalgam of right-wing parties formed in 1933 to oppose Spanish Republican government. In the 1933 Cortes election, CEDA won a plurality of seats, precipitating a period of intense political stability. Defeated by the Republicans and left in the 1936 Cortes election, CEDA adherents supported the subsequent military uprising. Franco ordered CEDA dissolved in 1937.

CNT: **Confederación Nacional del Trabajo** (National Confederation of Labour). Confederation of anarcho-syndicalist labour unions, founded in Barcelona in 1910 by an amalgamation of earlier anarchist groups. Dominant force in Catalan working class up to the Civil War.

Ciudadanos (Citizens' Party). Spanish neo-liberal, anti-independence party launched in Catalonia in 2006 and later extended to the rest of the Spanish state.

Ciutadans (Citizens' Party). Catalan branch of Ciudadanos.

Convergència Democràtica (Democratic Convergence). Leading Catalan autonomist party now re-named PDeCAT. The largest constituent of the old CIU coalition. Led by Jordi Pujol than Artur Mas.

CUP: **Candidatura d'Unitat Popular** (Popular Unity Candidacy). Far-left party in Catalonia that favours independence from Spain. Traditionally, the CUP has focused on municipal politics, and is organised around autonomous local assemblies that run in local elections.

ERC: **Esquerra Republicana de Catalunya** (Republican Left of Catalonia). Left-wing Catalan party favouring independence for all the Catalan-speaking lands. Founded in 1931 by the union of Estat Català (Catalan State), led by Francesc Macià, and the Catalan Republican Party, led by Lluís Companys.

ETA: **Euskadi Ta Askatasuna** (Basque Homeland and Liberty). Radical Basque nationalist party founded in 1959, espousing independence and armed struggle.

Falange Española (Spanish Phalanx). In its final 1937 incarnation, the Falange was designated the sole legal political party during the Franco era. Created in 1934 as a merger of two earlier extremist groups, under the leadership of José Antonio Primo de Rivera. Originally, the Falange had an explicitly fascist and corporatist political ideology, though under the Franco regime it brought inside its ranks a variety of right-wing, monarchist, Carlist and Catholic-conservative elements. Officially dissolved in 1977 but many self-styled Falangist splinter groups continue to function.

GAL: **Grupos Antiterroritas de Liberación** (Anti-terrorist Liberation Groups). Illegal, para-military death squads created by Spanish government officials to wage secret war against ETA, 1983–1987.

Generalitat de Calalunya. Name traditionally given to the prevailing Catalan government.

Guardia Civil (Civil Guard). Spanish state para-military security force founded in 1844. Under military discipline with officers drawn from Spanish army.

Herri Batasuna (Popular Unity). Basque political coalition which supported armed struggle of ETA. Later used electoral name of Euskal Herritarrok (Basque Citizens).

ICV: **Iniciativa per Catalunya Verds** (Initiative for Catalonia Greens). Merger of PSUC, the former Catalan Communists, and Green Party.

IU: **Izquierda Unida** (United Left). Left-wing coalition formed in 1986 but dominated by PCE. Effectively now the modern incarnation of the PCE.

Junts per Catalunya (Together for Catalonia). Electoral front created by Puigdemont's PDeCAT to fight December 2017 Catalan election. Excluded the ERC but included independent figures such as Jordi Sánchez, the President of the ANC.

Junts pel Sí (Together for Yes). Electoral front formed pro-independence parties in 2015 Catalan election, led by Artur Mas. Included Democratic Convergence and ERC.

Lliga Regionalista de Catalunya (Regionalist League of Catalonia). Usually referred to simply as the Lliga. Conservative, monarchist, right-wing Catalanist party founded in 1901 to represent interests of Catalan business and middle class. Dominant force in Catalan politics till dictatorship of Primo de Rivera. After Civil War, many prominent Lliga supporters opted to make their peace with Franco's regime.

Òmnium Cultural. A civic association that defends and promotes the Catalan language and culture. Established in 1961 under the Franco regime when the public and institutional use of Catalan was illegal. Played a key role since 2012 in organising pro-independence demonstrations. Òmnium president, Jordi Cuixart, was remanded in custody in September 2017, charged with sedition against Spain.

Opus Dei (God's Work). Founded by the Spanish priest Josemaria Escriva de Balaguer in 1928 and eight years later it backed Franco's rebellion against the Spanish Republic. By the 1960s many members of Opus Dei were ministers in the Franco regime championing the need to modernise the Spanish economy, combining a technocratic outlook with Catholic fundamentalism.

PCE: **Partido Comunista de España** (Communist Party of Spain). Founded in 1921, after a split in PSOE. Traditionally Stalinist and pro-Moscow. Dominant opposition to Franco after Civil War but went into decline with fall of the dictatorship. From 1936, organised separately in Catalonia as PSUC. Since 1986, the PCE in the Spanish state operates as Izquierda Unida.

PDeCAT: **Partit Demòcrata Europeu Català** (Catalan European Democratic Party). Centre-right party founded in 2016 by Artur Mas. Direct successor to the now-defunct Democratic Convergence of Catalonia. Also known as Catalan Democratic Party. Under Artur Mas and Carles Puigdemont, PDeCAT embraced a pro-independence stance, breaking with the pro-devolution, Catalanist stance of its predecessor party.

PNV: **Partido Nacionalista Vasco** (Basque Nationalist Party). In Basque: Euzko Alderdi Jeltzalea (EAJ). Traditional, conservative leading party representing Basque autonomy, founded in 1895.

Podemos ('We Can!'). Spanish centre-left, populist party founded in 2014, in the aftermath of the 15-M protests against austerity. Main leader: Pablo Iglesias. Opposed to Catalan independence.

POUM: **Partido Obrero de Unificación Marxista; Catalan: Partit Obrer d'Unificació Marxista** (Workers' Party of Marxist Unification). A Spanish revolutionary Marxist but anti-Stalinist party, formed in 1935 by merger of the fusion of the Trotskist Izquierda Comunista de España (Communist Left of Spain) and the mainly Catalan Bloc Obrer i Camperol (Workers and Peasants' Bloc). Led by Andreu Nin and Joaquim Maurín. Famously, the writer George Orwell served with the POUM militia.

PP: **Partido Popular** (People's Party). Dominant, post-Franco right-wing party in Spain, founded in 1989.

PSC: **Partit dels Socialistes de Catalunya** (Socialist Party of Catalonia). Catalan branch of the main Spanish Socialist Party, the PSOE, in the post-Franco era. The PSC governed Catalonia in a coalition with ERC and ICV, from 2003 to 2010.

PSOE: **Partido Socialista Obrera Español** (Socialist Workers' Party). Main Spanish socialist party, founded in 1879. Formed post-Franco governments under Felipe González (1982–1996) and José Luis Zapatero (2004–2011).

PSUC: **Partit Socialista Unificat de Catalunya** (Unified Socialist Party of Catalonia). Formed in July 1936 through the unification of the Catalan PSOE and the Catalan Communists in the PCE. Effectively a Stalinist take-over of the local PSOE. Post-Franco, the new, social democratic PSOE created its own Catalan branch, the PSC. With the fall of the Soviet Union, the rump PSUC merged with the Greens, as the IVC.

SCC: **Societat Civil Catalana.** Created in April 2014, the SCC is a civic society organisation opposing Catalonia independence.

UCD: **Union del Centro Democratico** (Union of the Democratic Centre). Short-lived alliance of ex-Francoists and Christian Democrats, founded in 1977 under leadership of Adolfo Suárez. Won elections in 1977 and 1979 before collapsing in wake of PSOE election victory in 1982.

UGT: **Unión General de Trabajadores** (General Union of Workers). A major Spanish trade union, historically affiliated with the PSOE. Founded in 1888 by Pablo Iglesias Posse.

Chapter One: Birth of a Republic

To the people of Catalonia and to all the peoples of the world... Despite the violence and the repression with the intent to impede the celebration of a peaceful and democratic process, the citizens of Catalonia have voted by a majority in favour of the constitution of the Catalan Republic... The constitution of the Republic is a hand held out to dialogue...
Catalan Declaration of Independence, 27 October 2017

ON THE AFTERNOON of Friday 27 October 2017, at 3.25pm, in the salmon pink Palau del Parlament in the heart of Barcelona's Ciutadella Park, the Second Catalan Republic was born. Even a month before, Catalonia hardly registered in global political consciousness. Now, seemingly from nowhere, a popular revolution had erupted in Western Europe for the first time since World War Two – albeit an insurgency based on peaceful mass resistance to Spanish rule. By 70 votes in favour, ten against and two unfathomable abstentions, Catalan MPs legislated a new state into being.

But the true authors of this new Republic were not the Catalan President Carles Puigdemont and his coalition of centre-right European Democrats and left-wing Republicans, trading under the banner of *Junts pel Sí*, or Together for Yes. Rather it was the Catalan people themselves – in their literal millions – who had marched, demonstrated, organised, protested, gone on strike and finally voted in two successive referendums to secure self-determination. Even this final vote in the Palau del Parlament had been in doubt until tens of thousands of people had taken to the streets of Barcelona chanting 'Declare the Republic!' and 'We are millions, we are our institutions!'.

Such a mass intervention from below is rare enough in this elite-dominated age and deserves fully the title of revolution. Perhaps only in the final days of the old German Democratic Republic, back in 1989, have we seen an equivalent mass movement on the streets, able to impose its will on historical events. This book will tell the story of the Catalan political revolution of October 2017, of its individual participants and protagonists. But its chief dramatis personae are the tens of thousands of excited Catalans who waited expectantly in Ciutadella Park that Friday afternoon to witness the birth of their new Republic announced to the world.

Birth of the Catalan Republic, Crisis of the Spanish State

The weather was balmy, in stark contrast to the torrential rain on referendum day only four weeks earlier, when many in this same crowd had their heads split open by baton-wielding Spanish Guardia Civil bent on closing polling stations. How they cheered when the final vote was announced. Win or lose, nothing now would or could be the same for insurgent Catalonia, or for a querulous and divided Spanish state, and certainly not for a crisis-ridden, myopic European Union desperate to ignore this fresh problem on its doorstep.

The Catalan parliament building, where these events were unfolding, is soaked in history. Construction began in 1717, a bare three years after Catalonia lost its independence to Spain. Philip V – first in the long and detested Bourbon line that runs down to the present incumbent, Felipe VI – required an arsenal to dominate Barcelona. The result was the gigantic, star-shaped fortress of the Ciutadella – the largest military fortification in Europe. Swathes of Barcelona had to be demolished to make room for what became a hated symbol of Spanish occupation. By chance, during the chaotic liberal uprisings against the Bourbons in the mid-19th century, the fortress walls were destroyed. Seizing an opportunity, the wily Barcelona bourgeoisie turned the Ciutadella into an urban park and zoo. But they kept the main arsenal building, which ended up as the Municipal Art Museum. With the downfall of the dictatorship of Primo de Rivera and the emergence of a democratic Spanish Republic in 1931, Catalonia declared independence. The new, autonomous Catalan parliament lacked a home. It found one instantly in that elegant Ciutadella art gallery, soon remodelled with an intimate hemicycle debating chamber.

But Catalan history was to take another turn. When Franco's victorious fascist army occupied Barcelona in January 1939, expunging Catalan freedoms and language, the debating chamber of the Palau del Parlament was literally bricked up and left to gather cobwebs. After the dictator's belated death in 1975, the bricks were taken down. The entombed Palau del

Parlament once again became the citadel of Catalan democracy and hopes for self-determination.

Those hopes were soon dashed. For post-Franco Spain turned out to be a pseudo democracy. The transition from Francoism to parliamentary democracy involved no purge of the state apparatus nor any attempt to come to terms with the legacy of the Spanish Civil War and the repression which followed. Instead, the ruling Francoist elite created only a semblance of democratic institutions following the dictator's death, in order to to gain access to the European Union. The result was the unique 1978 Spanish constitutional settlement: a political compromise that granted a degree of popular democratic representation and a degree of autonomy for Spain's constituent regions and nations, while preserving as much of the old, authoritarian order as possible.

As a result, the bulk of the nation's wealth and banking system remained in the hands of a narrow oligarchy centred on Mariano Rajoy's Popular Party (PP), the direct political heirs of the old Falangists and Francoists. This web of corruption between bankers and politicians reached its zenith during the great financial bubble of the early 21st Century. Billions were borrowed and spent by giant Spanish construction companies to build a new generation of toll highways around Madrid. These were funded by cheap bank loans underwritten by the Spanish state (i.e. PP politicians in Madrid). At the same time, illegal cash donations flowed into the coffers of the dominant, right-wing Popular Party. With the Bank Crash of 2008, many of these vanity construction projects went bankrupt, leaving the Spanish taxpayer (including the Catalan taxpayer) to foot the bill. The declaration of the Catalan Republic was a repudiation of this corrupt system.

As we will see in later chapters, Spain is structured very differently from the more mature European capitalist economies to its north. The Franco regime had fostered state capitalism in its drive to catch up with the rest of Europe. With the end of the dictatorship, a corrupt, conservative Popular Party elite deliberately engineered the transfer of these public industries and banks into the private ownership of a clique of its friends and allies, in return for illegal funding of the party's operations. Spanish capitalism (much like post-Soviet Russia) became dominated by a narrow circle of oligarchs, operating through private conglomerates funded by bank debt. Once Spain entered the Eurozone, and with global interest rates at rock bottom, the door was open to a gigantic property and speculation bubble. When the bubble burst in 2008, the Spanish economy imploded. Out of this economic and social crisis, the modern Catalan independence movement was born.

In May 2011, popular resistance to austerity, in particular to mass youth unemployment, touched off a spontaneous protest that occupied city squares across the Spanish state: the so-called 15-M Movement. By-passing existing political parties, the participants organised themselves via Facebook and Twitter, in the manner of the Tunisian and Egyptian activists of the Arab Spring. 15-M had major political repercussions. The crisis led to the emergence of new populist political parties: *Podemos* on the left and *Ciudadanos* ('Citizens') on the Blairite centre-right. It shattered the traditional Socialist Party (PSOE) leaving Spain virtually ungovernable. A series of inconclusive elections left a minority PP government clinging to power in Madrid. In Catalonia, the traditional centre-right 'autonomist' governing coalition – Convergència i Unió, Convergence and Union (CIU) – imploded as a result of corruption scandals and the rise of a left-wing, anti-austerity independence movement.

For decades after the fall of Franco, the Catalan secessionist movement was a political minority, motivated largely by cultural and language demands. Austerity changed that. Today 72 per cent of those supporting the Catalan Republic say they are left-wing as compared to 40 per cent who voted No. Polls also suggest that a majority of those supporting independence do so because they want to transform society and the economy. True, the language issues remain important; the Spanish Constitutional Courts continue to strike down laws that protect the Catalan mother tongue. And there is a wing of the Catalan middle class, led by Puigdemont's Partit Demòcrata Europeu Català (European Democrats, PDeCAT), that resents Madrid for its high taxes. Since the days of Franco, Madrid has used the Catalan economy as a milch cow to fund the rest of Spain, much as London kept hold of Scotland in order to use North Sea oil earnings to fund its trade deficit. But the desire of those crowds gathering in front of the Palau del Parlament on 27 October was less about high taxes and more about social change and the Catalan Republic that could bring it about.

That inevitably meant rupture with the Spanish state. Yet even on that fateful Friday afternoon there were those in the leadership of the independence movement who were still hesitating to take that final step in breaking with Spain. In the ornate corridors of the Palau del Parlament – modelled on the Paris Opera Garnier – the pro-independence coalition led by Puigdemont, an ex-journalist and former mayor of Girona, found itself caught between two opposing forces. On the one side, there was the intransigence of the ultra-conservative Spanish government that still refused any form of dialogue with the Catalans. On the other side, there was the mass movement and the desire of an animated people to remake Catalan society. Puigdemont's inclination was to continue to play cat and mouse with Madrid, hoping that the EU would force the Spanish state towards compromise. Even at the last minute on that decisive Friday, Puigdemont wanted to delay announcing the Republic and call fresh elections instead. But a revolt from within his own party forced his hand. Even the rank and file of the PDeCAT, which sits with the British Liberal Democrats in the European Parliament, had been pushed by the mass movement towards calling the Republic.

Few had ever expected Puigdemont to press on with the 1 October referendum in the face of Spanish legal and paramilitary threats. Ultimately, pressure from below gave him no room for manoeuvre. True, he showed unexpected skill in keeping his multi-party, multi-class, pro-independence coalition together long enough to hold 1-0 and declare the Republic. But as we shall see, Puigdemont's short-term perspectives, and naivety in believing that the EU would eventually intervene, meant that there was no planning for what to do the day after the Republic was declared. Puigdemont's empiricism and opportunism would have dangerous consequences. There is an old adage that those who make a revolution half way invariably dig their own graves – politically if not always literally. But on that dramatic Friday, Puigdemont had run out of ways of fending off the inevitable declaration of the Republic. Reason: Rajoy and the PP government in Madrid had initiated the legal process to impose direct rule on Catalonia, the so-called Article 155.

Rajoy triggers Article 155 and direct rule

The PP, created in 1989 as a political home for the various dissident factions of the old Francoist apparatus, remained the champion of Spain's economic oligarchy. Under the dull technocrat Mariano Rajoy, the PP had found a new lease of life as a devout servant of Germany's pro-austerity drive to save the Euro (and, in passing, save Germany's profligate banking system). Germany and the EU reciprocated by turning a blind eye to anything Rajoy did internally to recentralise the Spanish state. If that meant turning a blind EU eye to Spanish corruption or the repression of self-determination in Catalonia, so be it. Bequeathed a free hand by the EU, Rajoy made use of the surge in support for Catalan independence to bolster the fading popularity of the PP by playing the unionist card. This had many advantages. As well as diverting attention from the corruption trials engulfing the party, taking a hard line against Catalan sovereignty boosted PP support in other regions of the Spanish state, united the party's disaffected base, helped recover ground from Ciudadanos (its main competitors on the right), put Pedro Sánchez's 'new' Socialist Party (PSOE) under pressure, and moved the political debate away from the economy.

Rajoy chose to make the Catalans a political scapegoat rather than confront the existential crisis of the 1978 post-Franco regime. But that had always been the default position of the PP: to revert to Spanish nationalism and centralism to paper over the cracks in the economy and society. This should have been clear to the Catalan government in Barcelona. For the PP was acting on behalf of a narrow, interlocking financial elite of private investors and landed aristocracy whose personal wealth had become inextricably bound up with the fortunes of the Spanish state. Reform of the 1978 constitutional set-up was intrinsically linked to sweeping this elite away. In essence opposing Catalan sovereignty was key to protecting the '78 Regime.

Thus it was that in Madrid a separate drama unfolded on 27 October. In the Spanish Senate a vote was taking place to suspend the elected Catalan Parliament and impose direct rule. That morning, Rajoy made a speech outlining why he wanted direct rule. There was still time to offer some form of dialogue with Catalonia. Surely an agreed referendum taking place, as in Scotland, might defuse the crisis? But from the point of view of Rajoy and the PP, any compromise with Catalonia was impossible by definition. Lacking any sense of irony, Rajoy mocked the very idea of 'dialogue' in his argument for triggering 155:

> The word dialogue is a lovely word. It creates good feelings. Dialogue is widely practised in Spain. Our Constitution and our laws are the product of dialogue. But dialogue has two enemies: those who abuse, ignore and forget the laws, and those who only want to listen to themselves, who do not want to understand the other party.[1]

Rajoy's 45-minute speech was frequently interrupted by applause from excited PP senators. There was nothing new in his arguments: 'In Catalonia, there has been an attempt to ignore the laws, disregard them, repeal them, violate them, any term is valid.' He warned that Spain was faced with an 'exceptional situation', and claimed that 'Article 155 is not against Catalonia but to avoid the abuse of Catalonia'. He was followed by a line of senators either heaping unionist scorn on the Catalans or else (from the PSOE and the former Communists) trying to explain why they were helping the PP bludgeon Catalan self-determination into the ground. This non-debate was stretched out deliberately as the PP manoeuvred to time the inevitable triggering of 155 for the period after the Catalan Parliament had declared the Republic.

The most dramatic moment in the 155 debate came when Jokin Bildarratz, a senator representing the Basque Nationalist Party (PNV), remarked in passing that 'the Basque nation exists'. Instantly, incensed PP senators shouted back, 'No it doesn't exist!' The Senate chamber erupted into pandemonium as the PP revealed its concept of a unitary Spain – one where there is no room for different nations and cultures to co-exist. The PP senators seemed oblivious to the fact that the Basque regional premier Iñigo Urkullu had spent the previous 72 hours trying to persuade his Catalan counterpart, Carles Puigdemont, to opt for regional elections over a unilateral declaration of independence. Urkullu's involvement was not altruistic. PNV support in the Spanish *Cortes* provides the PP government with the necessary votes to pass its the budget. In exchange, the Basque administration has negotiated extra powers and extra funding from Madrid. However, the Catalan conflict has strained this cynical arrangement to the limit. The PNV finds itself propping up a Spanish unionist government which is suppressing Catalan democratic rights. It was little wonder Urkullu felt impelled to try and defuse the crisis before it spilled into Basque politics. The spectacle of boorish PP senators chanting that the Basque nation did not exist reveals the extent to which the Catalan crisis has exposed the fragile legitimacy enjoyed by the 1978 Spanish regime.

The chamber debates the Republic

Back in Barcelona, the moment had come. After Rajoy's belligerent speech, there was now no turning back. After lunch, the debate on declaring the Republic opened in the chamber of the Palau del Parlament, with Carme Forcadell presiding in the Speaker's Chair. Forcadell is deceptive. She may be slight and always a bit nervous, but she is the daughter of a peasant farmer – and Catalonia's rebellious peasantry have always been the heart of the nation's unique historic identity. Before her election to parliament in 2015, Forcadell had led the main civic independence movement, the ANC. Now she was under indictment by the Spanish Constitutional Court for having allowed independence and the 1-o referendum to be discussed, far less voted on. She was facing 30 years in prison for her commitment to democracy.

The large delegation of Catalan mayors who were present for the debate broke into loud chants of 'Independence! Independence!' when the live feed from the debating chamber of the Palau del Parlament finally appeared on the television screens. The debate was both emotional and angry, as might be expected. In the Catalan chamber, members do not speak from their seats but come to a lectern that faces the hemisphere, like an actor addressing the audience. The chamber is quite intimate. The parties supporting independence sat to the left of the person addressing them, while the Unionist parties were to the right. The speeches were short. There was little flowery language.

The most vitriolic and choleric voice in the debate was that of Carlos Carrizosa, of the Ciudadanos. The voice of the Spanish professional middle class and liberal parts of big business, Ciudadanos lacked the political guts to try and reform the creaking 1978 Spanish constitution that keeps the corrupt PP in power. Instead, it took out its frustrations on the Catalan independence movement, the one force willing to take on the PP and the economic oligarchy it protects. A frenzied Carrizosa railed at the ranks of pro-independence deputies, calling them totalitarians:

> You have driven us to social confrontation, you have divided Catalan society, you have ruined it, and that is why you are going to pass into history, Mr Puigdemont.[2]

But for Carles Riera (of the far left CUP) a declaration of independence was 'the best path for social transformation' and 'the construction of a free, feminist and socialist society'. He summed up: 'We will be a refuge, for all of those who want a better world.'[3]

Finally, it was time to vote. The opposition deputies from the PP, Ciudadanos and the Catalan Socialist Party (the local PSOE) ostentatiously quit the chamber in protest. As a gesture, the PP unionists left behind Spanish flags draped on their seats. Parliamentary lawyers then issued a formal warning that a vote on independence could be declared illegal by the Constitutional Court. To protect pro-independence deputies from being charged with rebellion, it was decided to hold a secret ballot. The ballot box was placed on Speaker Carme Forcadell's table in preparation for the vote.

Forcadell then read out the preamble to the independence motion. This 'declarative' preamble was not part of the motion itself but a political justification of what was about to happen. The text is addressed to 'the people of Catalonia and to all the peoples of the world'. It begins by stressing the historical continuity of the nation and its democratic heritage:

> The Catalan nation, its language and its culture have one thousand years of history. For centuries, Catalonia has endowed and enjoyed its own institutions which have exercised self-government in full... Parliamentarianism has been, during periods of liberty, the pillar upon which these institutions have sustained themselves...[4]

The document then stresses the attempts, post-Franco, to reach a political accommodation for legitimate Catalan aspirations within the Spanish state. Unfortunately, it concludes, 'the Spanish state has responded to that loyalty with the denial of the recognition of Catalonia as a nation' and since the 2008 economic crisis with a 'recentralisation' that has led to 'a profoundly unjust economic treatment, and linguistic and cultural discrimination'. In other words, Catalonia is more oppressed than ever. The 2006 revision to the internal Statute of Autonomy 'would have been the new stable and lasting marker of a bilateral relationship between Catalonia and Spain', but this was vetoed.

The last straw was the 'brutal police operation of a military nature and style orchestrated by the Spanish state' against voters during the 1 October referendum. However, despite the violence and the repression, 'the citizens of Catalonia have voted by a majority in favour of the constitution of the Catalan Republic' thus providing a mandate for independence. The historic document concludes by pointing to the tasks of the new state: 'The Catalan Republic is an opportunity to correct the current democratic and social deficits, and to build a more prosperous, more just, more secure, more sustainable society with greater solidarity.'

In the Catalan fashion, deputies were called by the speaker one by one to vote. Despite the secret poll, many held up their ballot paper to the cameras. At 3.25pm Catalan independence was passed, by 70 votes in favour to 10 against, plus two recorded abstentions. Another 53 deputies representing the main unionist parties abstained by virtue of not being in the chamber for the vote. In the words of the declaration, Catalonia was now 'an independent, sovereign, legal, democratic, socially-conscious state'. The leaders of the independence movement – Puigdemont, Forcadell, and Oriol Junqueras of the ERC – shook hands. They were overseen by the ghosts of all those who had gone before them in the Palau del Parlament, not least Lluís Companys, the murdered president of the first Catalan Republic.

Response to independence – Back to the streets

The response to the historic declaration of Catalan independence was not long in coming. While the crowds outside the Palau del Parlament broke into cheers and song, the Spanish Senate immediately ratified Rajoy's application for Article 155. There were 214 votes for, 47 against, and just one abstention. Big business was also quick to declare its view. Spain's main business association, the CEOE, issued a statement rejecting the 'illegal' decision of the Catalan parliament. Others tried to steer a middle course between Spanish unionism and repression on the one hand, and the unilateral declaration of independence on the other. In a long Facebook post, Barcelona Mayor Ada Colau showed her opposition to both the independence declaration in the Catalan parliament and Article 155 in the Senate: 'Not in my name. No to 155 and UDI'.

Abroad, prompted by a massive diplomatic effort engineered by the Rajoy government, country after country issued statements reaffirming support for the 'unity' of the Spanish state, a mantra that sounded more like a religious confession than any serious attempt to grapple with the European and global consequences of the crisis. Donald Tusk, the EU Council President, immediately tweeted to the world; 'For the EU nothing changes. Spain remains our only interlocutor. I hope the Spanish government favours force of argument, not argument of force'. The latter plea, which went largely unnoticed, suggested the EU was petrified that Spanish repression might get out of hand, now Article 155 had been triggered. But that did not stop Tusk giving diplomatic cover to Madrid's bid to close down a democratically elected Catalan parliament.

Only in Scotland was there anything like a positive response to the Catalan UDI. Hard on the vote in the Palau del Parlament, the External Affairs secretary of the Scottish Government, Fiona Hyslop, issued a carefully worded statement which began:

> We understand and respect the position of the Catalan Government. While Spain has the right to oppose independence, the people of Catalonia must have the ability to determine their own future. Today's Declaration of Independence came about only after repeated calls for dialogue were refused.[5]

Hyslop went on to demand both Madrid and the European Union engage in negotiations with Catalonia.

Meanwhile, in the chamber, President Puigdemont addressed several hundred supporters. He said: 'In the days ahead we must keep to our values of pacificism and dignity. It's in our, in your, hands to build the Republic.' Those gathered then erupted into the Catalan anthem 'Els Segadors' (The Reapers) and chants of 'Liberty!'

But now there was to be a strange absence. The crowds waiting expectantly outside the Palau del Parlament expected Puigdemont and the other leaders of the movement to appear before them. This was the 'balcony' moment when the people and their leaders would celebrate the public declaration of their new Republic. But the crowds who had created a revolution were destined to wait in vain. There would be no 'balcony' moment, no speeches to the Catalan people as there had been at the time of the declaration of the First Catalan Republic in 1931. Puigdemont, having led them to the declaration of the new state, simply disappeared from public view, leaving Catalans bemused and confused. This was an omen of things to come.

For the unilateral declaration of independence that Friday afternoon was not the launch of a new state with a functioning government. Within hours Madrid had taken control of the Catalan administration without any palpable resistance. Within days, Puigdemont had fled to Belgium. He issued no orders to the mass movement, leaving people demoralised and unsure what to do next. Meanwhile, Rajoy filled the political vacuum by calling fresh Catalan elections scheduled for 23 December. After the heady days of 27 November, Catalonia faced a great anti-climax. What had gone wrong?

Here we arrive at the final theme of this book. Momentous as was Friday 27 October 2017 in the long and turbulent history of Catalonia, we should not romanticise a single day's events. For the Catalan revolution is a process in which 27 October was but one weigh station. Driven from below by a mass movement unprecedented in 21st century Europe, the Catalan independence movement is transcending being a mere political challenge to the Spanish 1978 regime. By overflowing these democratic boundaries, the Catalan struggle for self-determination. This is its significance for the rest of Europe and the world.

The modern Catalan independence movement – in distinction to contemporary populist and racist movements in Eastern Europe – is progressive in nature. At root, the upsurge in Catalonia is best understood as a rebellion against the authoritarian nationalism of the Spanish state. It is driven by a popular desire to reform and democratise the authoritarian and (despite its 'devolved' aspects) centralist Spanish regime, to defend Catalan language and culture, and to oppose the austerity policies imposed by Madrid. As we will see in later chapters, Catalan independence is not – and never was – a project of the Catalan bourgoisie. The latter have always, in the final resort, preferred staying with authoritarian Spain, the better to protect their material interests. Today, the left social democratic Esquerra Republicana de Catalunya, or Republican Left of Catalonia (ERC), has become the most popular pro-independence party. The anti-capitalist Candidatura d'Unitat Popular, or Popular Unity (CUP), won ten seats in 2015 Catalan elections as well as capturing a raft of mayoralties. CUP's parliamentary bargaining power enabled it not only to make the *Junts pel Sí* coalition hold the 1-0 referendum, but also to force the Catalan government to ban evictions and close migrant detention centres.

As a result, the Catalan political crisis cannot be resolved within the boundaries of the present, repressive Spanish state. Equally, it will not be resolved without the independence movement making a thorough balance sheet of the October referendum. The vacuum that emerged at the very moment the Republic was declared on 27 October exposed the political limitations of Puigdemont and the PDeCAT wing of the independence struggle. Yet within days the mass movement began to revive despite the failure of the parliamentary leadership. The Committees for the Defence of the Referendum, which had emerged spontaneously in response to the Guardia Civil raids and attacks on polling stations, soon took up the challenge of organising public protests over the jailing of government ministers. The Republic of 27 October was indeed alive and kicking – not in the gilded splendour of the Palau del Parlament, but in streets and squares across Catalonia.

The birth pangs of that Peoples' Republic, the parallel crisis of the neo-Francoist 1978 Spanish regime, and the pivotal role played by the mass movement of ordinary Catalans struggling for democratic and social change constitute the theme of this book. Where the story finally ends will be determined on the streets.

Chapter Two: Catalonia, the Unknown Nation

'What is Catalan?'
'Why, the language of Catalonia – of the islands, of the whole of the Mediterranean coast down to Alicante and beyond. Of Barcelona. Of Lerida. All the richest part of the peninsula.'
'You astonish me. I had no notion of it. Another language, sir? But I dare say it is much the same thing – a putain, as they say in French.'
'Oh no, nothing of the kind – not like at all. A far finer language. More learned, more literary. Much nearer the Latin. And by the by, I believe the word is patois, sir, if you will allow me.'

Aubrey and Marurin dialogue, from *Master and Commander* by
Patrick O'Brian

BARCELONA IS ONE of the truly great cities of the world. Every year some eight million visitors flock to it for its architecture, its culture and its food. Others travel to the beach resorts of the Costa Brava and the Costa Dorada, to the north and south of the city. The more intrepid might go mountaineering or hillwalking in the Pyrenees to the north or skiing in winter. Yet many are unaware (at least until the current independence struggle made the global headlines) that they are in one of the oldest nations in Europe – Catalonia. The language and culture of Catalonia are as distinct from Spain as are Scotland's from England or Quebec's from English-speaking Canada.

Non-Catalans are equally unaware of just how many contemporary Catalans they might know and how passionate they are about their native land. There is Pep Guardiola, the FC Barça hero who is a staunch advocate of Catalan independence, even standing as a candidate for the pro-independence coalition *Junts pel Sí*. The Catalan tenor José Carreras is adamant: 'I am pro-independence and I am very patriotic. Sometimes you have to express how you feel, even if it could cause you problems in some situations.' Gerard Piqué, Barcelona defender and husband of Colombian pop star Shakira, is also in favour of Catalan self-determination, making it a point to march in the annual *Diada*, Catalonia's National Day.

Catalonia's recent cultural contribution to the world has been astonishing. The opera singer Montserrat Caballé was born in Barcelona in 1933. Pau Casals, arguably one of the best world's greatest-ever cellists, had to go into exile from his native Catalonia during the Civil War. The surrealist painter Salvador Dali was a native and devotee of Figueres. Picasso, though born in Malagá, moved to Barcelona when he was seven and adopted it as his home. He learned Catalan and his early paintings are redolent with motifs of rural Catalan life. His friend and fellow artist, Joan Miró described himself as an 'internationalist Catalan'. A Miró tapestry at the World Trade Centre was the most important work of art lost during the 11 September attacks in New York. More prosaically, Bacardi rum was founded by a Catalan: Facund Bacardí i Massó from Sitges.

Catalonia is a proud but welcoming nation. Since 1978, following the end of the dictatorship of General Francesco Franco, who ruled all Spain with an iron fist from his victory in the Spanish Civil War in 1939 until his death in 1975, Catalonia has enjoyed self-government in many matters. But the Spanish Government in Madrid has kept crucial powers – economic, military and diplomatic – under its own control. Indeed, in recent years it has tried to take many powers back. In the last decade, the demand for independence has grown in Catalonia – from only a small minority favouring a break away at the start of this century to something approaching a majority now. To understand Catalonia's position within the Spanish state, past and present, its democratic deficit and the bitter scars left by a fascist dictatorship, it is necessary to look back.

Firstly, the language is important. The Irish writer Colm Tóibín has lived in Barcelona and says this of his sometime home:

> On the positive side is that it's not hard to become Catalan. And if you look at the last 150 years, Catalans seem in general to import every generation. For example, a lot of factory workers, whose children become Catalans. It's not a matter of blood. It's not a matter of religion. It is merely a matter of speaking the language and living here with a view to permanence. But I suppose what people really do mind is the business of, if there are three people in the room and one speaks only Spanish and the other two speak Catalan and Spanish, the Catalans will talk Spanish to the Spaniard but every time they turn towards each other, they'll move back into Catalan. That drives Spaniards nuts. It's one of the things that... 'why can't they'. It's always 'why can't they...'[6]

But Catalans could not always speak their language in public or study it at school or university. Antoni Mas grew up under the Franco regime and recalled that his family spoke Catalan only at home because the police would act if they heard it being spoken in public. 'We couldn't speak Catalan in school... they would beat you,' Antoni recalled. Despite that he was not intimidated, and, in 1972, aged 20, together with two friends he began publishing an underground Catalan magazine, aided by sympathetic local priests. 'I was very young and without fear of anything,' he says of those years, the dying years of the regime but a time when its use of repression remained vicious.

Fresh in Antoni's memory is the suggestion of José Ignacio Wert, the Education Minister in the Spanish Government from 2011 until June 2016, that Catalan children needed to be 're-Spanishised'. Antoni's memory of repression under Franco was brought alive in 2015 when Pedro Morenés, the Spanish defence minister, stated that the army would not intervene in Catalonia, but only as long as 'everybody does their duty'.[7]

After Franco died there was a concerted attempt by the Spanish ruling elite and the main political parties to argue that people should put the Civil War behind them. To smooth the transition to democracy, Spain passed an amnesty law pardoning political crimes committed in the past – the so-called *Pacto del Olvido* (Pact of Forgetting). The bitter legacy of the dictatorship was scarcely spoken about. But a new generation, at the beginning of the 21st century, began to demand answers as to what happened to those who were on the losing side, particularly regarding the fate of grandparents, great-grandparents and relatives who were among the missing. Those taken away by Franco's forces and executed, and whose bodies were dumped in mass graves. The Association for the Recovery of Historical Memory (ARMH), has documented 114,226 cases of men and women buried in mass graves around Spain. 'There are at least 3,000 mass graves. We're not even sure exactly how many, but it's a lot,' said Emilio Silva, head of the AMRH.[8]

The scale of those buried in mass graves is staggering: 'Historical memory activists say that the remains of more than 100,000 Spanish victims of Franco from during and after the civil war still lie in unmarked graves, an estimate supported by many historians. Amnesty International says that Spain has the second-highest number of such graves in the world, after Cambodia.'[9]

Yet the current ruling People's Party, while not itself Francoist, has its roots in that regime and has systematically blocked attempts to uncover the graves. Other examples leave a bad taste in the mouths of Catalans, and many Spaniards: it recently emerged that the PP government of José María Aznar gave the Francisco Franco Foundation €150,000 between 2000 and 2003.

The Catalan government has gone far further than its counterpart in Madrid in trying to trace the missing and commemorate those who fought to defend the legitimate governments of both Spain and Catalonia which Franco wanted removed. That reflects the fact that most Catalans opposed the Generalissimo. Yet when democracy came to Spain there was no purge of Franco supporters by the state apparatus. The judges, army officers, senior civil servants and police chiefs kept their jobs. Their children and grand-children often took the same jobs. Catalans recall that the head of Franco's secret police in Barcelona, a man renowned for torturing political prisoners, kept his job after his chief died.

The corruption that existed in the Francoist regime was inherited by the new democratic Spain, where it is endemic. This is resented by the Catalans, who fear that it will infect their political order. It has already infected the royal family. King Juan Carlos was Franco's designated heir, but he was forced to abdicate following a corruption scandal involving his daughter and son-in-law. Since then more dirty washing has been exposed involving the royals.

Meanwhile human rights groups have catalogued cases of torture and the denial of freedom of assembly and expression by the state. Much of this flows from attempts to crush the terror campaign of the Basque nationalist group, ETA. In its 2016-17 report on Spain, Amnesty International states:

> The offence of 'glorifying terrorism' continued to be used to prosecute people peacefully exercising their right to freedom of expression. New cases of torture and other ill-treatment, exces-sive use of force and collective expulsions by police officials were reported.

One case it highlights involved the prosecution of a high court judge:

> In April [2017], the Minister of the Interior urged the General Council of the Judiciary to take measures against José Ricardo de Prada, a National High Court judge. He had participated in a round table organised by the City Council of Tolosa, Guipúzcoa, in the Basque Country, where he expressed agreement with the concerns of international human rights organisations regarding

the barriers to effective investigation of torture cases in Spain. In addition, the Prosecutor's Office supported a request by the Association of Victims of Terrorism that he should be removed as a member of a court in two criminal trials because of his alleged bias.[10]

Spain remains a Castilian state, Castile being the biggest and dominant region, centred on Madrid, the capital. When a Socialist government decided to go ahead with Spain's first high speed rail link it was built to connect Madrid and Seville, not Barcelona. When the French and Catalan governments proposed extending France's high-speed TGV rail link to Barcelona and then on to Valencia, creating a Mediterranean corridor stretching to Marseilles, Madrid preferred a railway linking the southern port of Algeciras to Madrid. This would continue on to France over the central Pyrenees, climbing to 1000 metres and requiring 55 kilometres of tunnels. Hardly economically or environmentally sustainable.

Catalans make up 16 per cent of the Spanish population, pay 22 per cent of the taxes received by the Spanish government, but receive only eight per cent of investment. According to the respected economist and Catalan MEP Ramon Tremosa-i-Balcells:

> Under both the dictatorship and democracy the level of public investment by the state in Catalonia has always been clearly below the Spanish average. When officials in Madrid haggle over infrastructure projects that Catalans need in order to prosper, they know very well what they are doing; without this infrastructure future economic growth will not be possible, and so the Catalan language and culture, the Catalan nation as a whole, will fall back into decline, because the economy will have done so already.[11]

In 2007 and 2008, because of an economic bubble built on an unsustainable property boom with banks handing out mortgages for the asking, the Spanish economy collapsed, ushering in years of austerity. Spain's politicians and elite were heavily involved in this casino and once more stories of corruption abounded. Yet they did not pay the price, but ordinary Spanish citizens had to meet the bill. Catalans resent their taxes being used to clean up a mess they did not create.

The narrative from Madrid and from the European Union is that the Spanish economy is the success story of Europe, the fastest growing in the

EU, averaging around 3 per cent a year. In 2018, it is projected that it will grow 2.5 per cent. Unemployment has fallen from 28 per cent to just over 17 per cent. The Spanish Prime Minister, Mariano Rajoy, puts this down to the success of his austerity years. But youth unemployment remains the second highest in the EU, at 37 per cent, while living standards are still not back to the level of 2008.

Meanwhile examples of Castilian dominance abound. In 2001, King Juan Carlos stated:

> Our language was never one of imposition, but one of encounter; no one was ever obliged to speak Castilian.[12]

This is simply untrue, and he knows it because he was Franco's designated heir and trained under him all through the 1960s in preparation for succeeding the Generalissimo. He must have been very aware that Catalans were banned from speaking their language in public. The Spanish Parliament insists that only Spanish be spoken there, and not Catalan, Galician or Basque. Except for the brief period of the First Spanish Republic in the 1870s there have been no Catalan prime ministers of Spain. Contrast that with the number of Scots who have been Prime Minister of the United Kingdom, even after devolution.

So vivid memories of repression, the needs of the language and economics drive the growing support for independence. But to truly understand the re-birth of Catalonia, we need to step back in time because history shapes the present. And that is certainly the case in Spain and Catalonia.

When was Catalonia? When was Spain?

All nations have a founding myth. Or at least a seminal moment when the nation emerged fully-clothed on to the historical stage. For Spanish nationalists, this moment was the morning of 19 October 1469, when a wedding took place in the Castilian city of Valladolid. It was held in secret because the brother of the bride would have prevented it by force. The Bishop of Toledo had rescued her from house arrest and brought her under armed protection to Valladolid. The bridegroom had travelled through hostile territory disguised as a merchant. The couple were cousins and cousins were banned from marrying. But the Bishop produced a letter of special permission from the Pope. It was an expedient forgery.

The couple were 18-year-old Isabella, heiress to the throne of Castile, and 17-year-old Ferdinand, heir to the crown of Aragon, a kingdom centred on Catalonia. This was the birth of Spain and it seemed to offer partnership between the peoples of Castile and Aragon. The town councillors of Barcelona wrote to their fellows in Seville, the great Atlantic port in Andalusía, that 'Now... we are brothers'.[13] They would soon learn that they were mistaken.

For Spanish nationalists this Union of the Crowns of Castile and Aragon marks the creation of the nation and its Golden Age. So much so, that when General Franco became head of state after the Spanish Civil War, he attempted to identify his regime with the so-called glory days of Ferdinand and Isabella. He even adopted their coat of arms with the imperial eagle as his regime's own.

According to Spanish nationalist iconography, Ferdinand and Isabella would create for the first time a unified Spain on the Iberian peninsula, expel Moorish and Jewish influence, establish a common Catholic culture with a little help from the Inquisition, finance Columbus to 'discover' the Americas, and begin the foundation of a gigantic empire on the other side of the Atlantic. This Spanish Empire would then transform the arid Iberian plateau into the richest and most powerful kingdom in all Europe. It was no wonder that Ferdinand would become the model for Machiavelli's book on statesmanship, *The Prince*. Writing in 2001, the noted Spanish historian Núñez Seixas argued:

> Intellectuals close to the Popular Party still insist on the historical foundation of Spain as the outcome of the Christian kingdoms' fight against the Muslims during the Middle Ages, while also emphasising the role played by the so-called Catholic Monarchs at the end of the fifteenth century, the unifying agency of the Spanish monarchy – which is supposed to be the essence of the nation – and the intrinsically Catholic nature of the Spanish nation, whose moment of glory was the discovery and conquest of America.[14]

In this version of history, Catalonia has never been independent because it was always part of the Kingdom of Aragon, regardless of the fact that Catalan was its language and Barcelona its capital. In October 2012, Spain's Minister of Education, Culture and Sport, Esperanza Aguirre, Countess of Murillo and Bornos, and a leading figure in the ruling Popular Party, announced that:

> Catalonia has never been independent... wake up, read about true history, not history invented by nationalists... Spain is a

great nation with 3000 years of history. This is what children should learn.[15]

Aside from the loud echo from the Franco years in these remarks, the Countess was 100 per cent wrong. The stark historical truth is that the union of the Castilian and Aragonese monarchies did not create a unified Spanish state, language, culture or economy. Quite the reverse. Catalan autonomy actually increased over the next two centuries, only being extinguished by force in 1714. Thereafter, Catalans maintained a spirit of rebellion against Madrid. Despite the personal Union of the Crowns under Ferdinand and Isabella, Castile and Aragon (especially Catalonia) remained constitutionally distinct political entities, retaining separate councils of state and parliaments. The UK equivalent is the 1603 Union of the Crowns under King James I and VI, which left Scotland and England entirely separate jurisdictions – politically, legally and economically.

A free peasantry

Economics lay at the heart of Catalan exceptionalism. Catalonia was, and remains, principally, a Mediterranean power, while Castilian Spain looked to the Americas. When Christopher Columbus opened the sea route to the Americas, Europe's trade and economic centre of gravity shifted to the Atlantic Ocean, undermining Catalonia's importance. Aragonese and Catalan power in the Mediterranean would continue for centuries, but the Spanish-Castilian state concentrated its focus on the conquest of territories in the Americas. In 1493, Pope Alexander VI (Rodrigo Borgia, a Catalan) formally approved the division of the 'unexplored' world between Spain and Portugal. This was not a Catalan enterprise. Castile and Aragon would remain separate states and economies until 1716 in spite of a shared crown. The newly-established colonies in the Americas and the Pacific were administered as appendages of Castile. As late as 1778, Seville was the only Spanish-mainland port authorised to trade with the Americas. Catalans, as subjects of the Crown of Aragon, had no right to trade directly with the Castilian-ruled Americas. The traders of Barcelona found that they were not regarded as brothers or partners after all.

The new Spain would be characterised by religious intolerance and persecution, and by a Castilian military ideology bequeathed by the re-conquest of its lands from the Muslims. The union that created today's Spain was not one of equals, but it was one of contrasts. The Inquisition was alien to

Catalonia, but Ferdinand imported it, and the Jewish population fled. Castilian demands for racial and religious purity were at odds with the Mediterranean multi-culturalism that had created Catalonia and still underpins its modern society.

Catalonia was shaped by its geography. The eastern Pyrenees may look like a natural boundary on the map, but they were easily traversed by passes open even in the depths of winter. In fact, the River Ebro to the south forms the natural boundary of Catalonia, with the Mediterranean coast offering a direct window to the world. Catalonia was in essence a frontier society linking Iberia and North Africa to France and Central Europe by land and mountain pass; and linking Western Europe to the Eastern Mediterranean and Middle East through its seaports. As a result, the people of Catalonia can claim many ancestors: Pyreneans, Iberians, Celts, Greeks, Romans, Visigoths, Arabs and Muslims. Later still, in the 19th and 20th centuries, would come migrants from Southern Spain, and in the 20th and 21st centuries people from Africa, Asia and Eastern Europe, fleeing war, climate change and famine or simply seeking economic security.

Catalan soil is fertile, profiting from the rainfall flowing off the Pyrenees and the ocean climate. Interior Castilian Spain, on the other hand, because of its high elevation, is semi-arid, with barely 40 per cent of the land suitable for cultivation. As a result, land ownership in Castilla-La Mancha, Extremadura, Murcia and particularly Andalusia, was and is still dominated by big *latifundio* estates owned by a decadent (and often absentee) aristocracy. These Castilian *latifundios* traditionally depended on landless, illiterate labourers to work the land. But in Catalonia, with its better soil and frontier culture, a free peasantry emerged that owned or rented the land it tilled. This free peasantry would play a pivotal role in creating a more economically dynamic society – and, crucially, helping to create the social foundation of a unique Catalan community.

Catalonia's separate nationhood and resistance to incorporation into Castilian Spain can be traced back to the history, peculiar form and resilience of its peasantry. Catalonia was ever a frontier region, first between Islamic Spain and Christian Europe, and then, in later medieval times, between the absolutist monarchies of France and Spain. Frontier regions are, by their nature, hard to control from wherever is vying to be the political centre. And a free peasantry is more willing to defend itself. Catalonia, on Spain's northeast Mediterranean coast, has a climate and geography that permits diversified agriculture, giving rise to the material conditions in which a free peasantry could flourish. This had political repercussions: between 1462 and 1486 Catalan peasants mounted the most successful peasants' war of the Middle Ages. As a result, they achieved the formal abolition of feudal servitude and – crucially – direct control of their land. This prosperous economic base underpinned the power of local Catalan princes and supported a rich merchant class in Barcelona.

Only as late as 1714 would Catalonia lose its de facto independence and its local political institutions as a result of being on the wrong side of the War of Spanish Succession. However, social and economic gains in the countryside were not lost. Catalonia retained a distinct, native yeoman peasantry capable both of agricultural innovation, and of defending its language and culture. In the course of the 17th and 18th centuries, Catalonia was to follow England in introducing market capitalism into agriculture, boosting productivity and output through owner cultivation and land consolidation.

The peasantry was also to play a pivotal role in the politics of Catalonia. This is symbolised in a famous series of paintings by the renowned Catalan surrealist Joan Miró, entitled *Head of a Catalan Peasant*. This sequence was painted in the mid-1920s just as the Spanish aristocrat and military dictator Primo de Rivera was initiating a fresh wave of repression. Rivera banned the public display of Catalan symbols. The peasant depicted by Miró is bearded and pipe-smoking and – most ostentatiously – wears the traditional red snail-shaped cap, the *barretina*. The cap is a Catalan sign of liberty and defiance, first made famous by the Sans-Culottes of the French Revolution. Miró made it the most prominent symbol in this group of paintings – a deliberate political statement. But more so did ordinary Catalan peasants by wearing it.

A separate Catalan state and political culture

Discussion of the emergence of nationality has been dominated in recent decades by the notion that nations are in some sense 'imagined' communities conjured up at specific moments to serve the ideological purpose of a given political class or interest group. This is too simplistic, if not misleading. Nations are indeed constructs, but the construction is the result of titanic class, political and economic conflicts. An historic nationality is forged (or not forged) in the heat of these struggles. Catalonia is not the fictional and ideological construct of modern Catalan nationalism. Rather, over a long period of time, a Catalan national entity emerged directly as a result of real conflicts – struggles for political leadership and control over territory. These gave birth to institutions, constitutions, legal systems, and social processes that crystallised into a material entity we know as Catalonia.

The foundation of this process in the Catalan case lies in the early Middle Ages with the first faltering steps towards a separate Catalan polity. As the Moors were pushed south of the Pyrenees by the Frankish knights of the new Holy Roman Empire, the Catalan frontier land took on new importance. The Carolingian Kings encouraged colonisation of the newly-cleared but still dangerous lands. Peasants who moved or returned there could own the land they were given after they had worked it for 30 years. Under Carolingian rule, Barcelona assumed new importance, not least because Tarragona, the major Roman city, remained under Muslim control. Faced with repeated Muslim incursions, Charlemagne divided his new territory into six counties, administered by a vassal Count. Of the six, Barcelona was on the front line and it was there that the greatest number of troops were stationed.

These Counts made a habit of rebelling against Carolingian authority, but those who remained loyal were compensated with rebel lands. In this way the imaginatively-named Wilfred the Hairy, the 12th Count of Barcelona, also became Count of Urgell, Cerdanya, Girona, Besalú and Ausona – the core of modern-day Catalonia – on 11 September 878 CE. This date in the calendar is now celebrated every year as *La Diada Nacional de Catalunya*, though the first celebration only took place in 1886. Legend has it that as he lay dying on the battlefield ten years later, Wilfred dipped his fingers in his wound and drew four bloody lines on the ground – now the flag of Catalonia. Ironically, 11 September also marks the day in 1714 when the forces of the Spanish king, Philip V, took Barcelona, ending Catalan autonomy.

The new feudal Catalonia survived and exerted its own autonomy, while owing titular allegiance to the Holy Roman Emperor of the day. Catalonia was in fact one of the earliest and most complete feudal kingdoms, along with France and England. Its power soon extended from Narbonne in France to the River Ebro. Perpignan and Montpellier were incorporated, becoming seats of learning based on knowledge inherited from the Muslims, who had preserved Greek and Roman literature. Agricultural output and the population increased. By the 11th century a more centralised Catalan state emerged, one of the first of its kind in the medieval world. Catalonia was ready to extend its influence out across the Mediterranean.

Matters were different in turbulent Castile. Wealth was acquired primarily by the conquest of Moorish controlled-territory. The Castilian monarchs parcelled these conquests into great *latifundio* estates awarded to a tiny number of reliable grandees or the church. In Catalonia, confronted by a strong peasantry, the nobility had less land, and therefore less wealth. The ruling Duke of Barcelona, Ramon Berenguer 1 (1023–1076), found himself having to broker a political and economic balance between the crown, the nobility, the rising merchant class of Barcelona and the free peasantry.

Ramon achieved this by drafting the first full compilation of feudal law in Western Europe, the so-called *Ustages*. This was, in effect, the creation of a feudal constitution, delineating but limiting the powers and rights due each of the feudal classes – a Catalan Magna Carta. While hardly democratic, the *Ustages* gave all free men the same legal status, meaning in theory that free peasants were equal to the nobility. A key development was that disputes had to be negotiated and resolved before an adjudicator, in local courts (*Corts*). The free peasants seized on this to protect their status from noble attempts to enserf them. When that failed, resistance was common.

Under the reign of Peter the Great (1276–1285), the Catalan feudal courts extended their control to the monarchy. In Barcelona in 1283, Peter was forced to agree to hold a General Court once a year, with representation from the feudal estates. The king himself stated: *...si nós i els successor nostres volem fer alguna constitució o estatut a Catalunya, els sotmetrem a l'aprovació i consentiment dels Prelats, dels Barons, dels Cavallers i dels Ciutadans...* Translated: 'if we and our successors want to make a constitution or statute in Catalonia, we will submit them for the approval and consent of the prelates, barons, knights and citizens'.[16]

Henceforth, the Catalan King and the *Corts* shared sovereignty – forcing the Crown to negotiate over important decisions. The *Corts* was made up of representatives of the nobility, the bishops and the urban bourgeoisie. Its main function was to approve money required by the king, particularly for war, imposing its conditions before reaching a formal agreement, as would come into being in England a little later. In order to ensure that this deal was adhered to, the *Generalitat de Catalunya* was created, made up of three representatives from each group. It would be wrong to hold this up as a model of popular sovereignty or democracy yet it represented a tradition on which the Catalans could draw, and which separated Catalonia from absolutist Castile.

In 1150, the Dukes of Barcelona married into the neighbouring, and much poorer, monarchy of Aragon in 1150, thereby becoming kings in their own right. The two areas retained separate institutions, laws and forms of government. Sparsely populated Aragon needed Catalonia to prevent its conquest by Castile. Although the royal title gave precedence to Aragon for cosmetic reasons within the confederated realm, the population and wealth of Catalonia meant that the latter dominated the arrangement.

In the early 13th century, Catalonia began to carve out a Mediterranean Empire, starting with the conquest of the Balearic Islands. It would continue with the acquisition through marriage of Sicily and the Kingdom of Naples, the conquest of north-eastern Sardinia and the seizure of territory in southern Greece from the Byzantine Empire. From Barcelona Catalans traded with Venice, Tunis, Alexandria and Constantinople (Istanbul). Catalan armies also helped Aragon conquer Valencia from the Muslims.

These conquests were very much a Catalan affair, carried out by Catalan nobles, merchants and royal officers. The Catalans created an empire long before Castile. Such conquests involved, as all do, bad deeds. When a Catalan fleet took Menorca from the Muslims it slaughtered the inhabitants or sold them off as slaves. Alghero in Sardinia retains a Catalan dialect today because the Catalans killed or drove off the locals when they captured and settled it. In 2005 a Catalan Minister visited Greece on behalf of the government to issue an apology for the sacking of the monasteries on the Athos peninsula 700 years before.

Out of this trading empire, Catalonia acquired new export markets. This had a profound impact on the local economy. Catalonia turned increasingly to producing finished woollen cloth. From its ports, ships would sail to Syria and Egypt to trade cloth and coral for spices, to Sicily to trade cloth for wheat and to Genoa to trade cloth for alum and woad, even though the Genoese were the Catalans' bitterest rivals. This period would be seen by future Catalan nationalists as a Golden Age culturally as well as economically. Medieval Catalan literature would be reckoned one of the finest in Europe.[17]

But this Golden Age, if it was one, was about to come to a juddering halt. The 14th century brought the Black Death, economic collapse and endemic wars. Castile was gripped by a civil conflict which became an extension of the Hundred Years War between England and France. This coincided with an economic downturn which hit Catalonia hard at a time when it was facing fierce competition from the Italian city state of Genoa. Barcelona's banks crashed and trade dried up. Between 1365 and 1497 the population of Catalonia fell by over a third.

Conquest

As in other parts of Europe, the economic crisis of the 14th and 15th centuries brought peasant uprisings and conflict as the nobility tried to re-impose stricter feudal control over the land. In 1462 and 1485 there were *remenças* revolts as the peasants rebelled against feudal service. The revolts in Catalonia have been described as 'the best organised and most successful, despite the lack of support from the urban classes, in all of Europe'.[18] In fact, they ended serfdom in Catalonia.

These upheavals in Catalonia explain why Ferdinand was so keen on the marriage to Isabella. And from the north came another reason for this dynastic match. French kings would long look with a greedy eye on Catalonia. For Ferdinand, union with Castile meant that its united forces could match the French. The Spanish crown was not able to enforce the Castilian model on Catalonia, Aragon and Valencia until 1714. It not only had to recognise the safeguards put in place regarding the Crown, but had to increase them. Thus, the strange situation would develop in the 16th century that the Spanish king's powers were greater in his Italian possessions than in autonomous Catalonia.

The myth that is Spain would take a further twist. Ferdinand and Isabella were in fact the last native dynasty ever to rule in Iberia as their sole male heir, John, died in 1497. On Ferdinand's death in 1516, the crown passed to the Germanic Hapsburgs in the person of Charles of Ghent, a native of Flanders! Charles V, as he would become, would eventually rule over an empire which included all the Iberian Peninsula, the Low Countries and Burgundy, Milan, Naples and Sicily, and the Americas – including, of course, autonomous Catalonia. Because of Castile's imperial wealth, Charles based himself there. Yet his remained a loose imperial confederation, with separate laws, taxes and customs in its different regions. However Spain's revenues and consequent military power made it the most formidable power in Europe. The 16th and 17th centuries were Castilian Spain's Golden Age (*Siglo de Oro*) as represented by the art of Vélaquez, El Greco, Ribera and Zurbarán.

Meanwhile, Catalonia was ruled nominally by Viceroys sent from Madrid who tried to circumvent the local *Corts*. The Hapsburg rulers in Madrid had two main grievances against Catalonia: it would not meet their growing financial demands, nor would it conscript badly-needed troops. With the rise of Protestantism, Spain faced a rebellion in its rich Dutch colonies which proved to be long, costly and unsuccessful. Its effect was not dis-similar to America's war in Vietnam in the 1960s and 1970s: it bankrupted the country and ended in political humiliation. The Netherlands was the richest Hapsburg possession and its loss was a body blow to Spain, coming as it did when the flow of wealth from the Americas was slowing.

The final saga in this long chapter was the Thirty Years War (1618–1648) fought between Hapsburg Spain and Austria on the one side and, eventually, France, Sweden, Holland and the German Protestant states on the other. The war ravaged Germany, setting it back decades, but it also beggared Spain. By 1624 the Spanish King demanded that Catalonia conscript 16,000 men to replace his army's mounting losses. He travelled to Barcelona to convene the Corts to try and win its agreement. It refused and the King left under cover of night.

In 1639 the French invaded Catalonian territory to the north of the Pyrenees, capturing the fortress of Sales, near Perpignan. The Spanish side began a siege which would last six months and ordered their Viceroy in Barcelona to raise men and supplies to aid its recapture, over-riding the Corts and Catalan law. Though the fortress fell, the besieging army suffered heavy losses, and many Catalans deserted, increasing Madrid's bad temper with Catalonia. The Catalans, from the nobility to the peasantry, resented bitterly the overriding of their ancient rights, the way Spanish troops had been billeted on them and the human and material cost of the war.

When the Spanish administration decided that the army would stay billeted in Catalonia till the next spring, when the war would resume, and made clear that it wished to convene a meeting of the Corts to water down Catalonia's autonomy, the response was a nationwide revolt. It began in the countryside. In Empordà peasants attacked and killed royal officials, some who had taken refuge in a convent. The Bishops of Vic and Barcelona led some 3000 peasants from the Vallès region of central Catalonia in a march on Barcelona on 22 May 1640. The city was full of labourers looking for work at the time of Corpus Christi, a traditional hiring time for the harvest. Most carried a sickle in their belt. They sacked the Viceroy's palace, forcing him to flee to Barcelona harbour in search of a ship but he was eventually hunted down and beaten to death on the beach. The rebellion became known as the Reapers War, the *Guerra dels Segadors* – another iconic page in Catalan resistance to Castilian rule. Demonstrators in Barcelona on 27 October 2017, when the Second Catalan Republic was declared, would chant 'Els Segadors!' once again.

Madrid reacted by mobilising an army to march on Barcelona. Pau Claris, a cleric elected to preside over meetings of the *Generalitat*, responded by declaring Catalonia an independent republic, albeit under the protection of France. A combined Catalan and French force then defeated the Spanish army on Montjuïc, overlooking Barcelona, but Claris died shortly thereafter, possibly poisoned. Meanwhile Portugal, under Spanish rule since the reign of Philip II, took the opportunity to rise in revolt, seizing its own independence. Madrid, realising it could not keep fighting on so many fronts, finally accepted Dutch independence too.

It remains curious that modern-day Spanish politicians claim that Spain's unity is permanently indivisible but ignore the fact that three provinces of the Empire declared independence in the 1640s – the Netherlands, Catalonia and Portugal. Two succeeded, Catalonia did not. Madrid was now free to wreak vengeance on the Catalans. Spanish armies advanced on Barcelona, which was besieged and finally starved into submission. Then Spain negotiated a peace treaty with Paris in 1659, whereby France gained Roussillon, Conflent, Vallespir and part of Cerdanya. The Catalans were not consulted. Their ancient country had now been partitioned.

In 1700 the last Hapsburg King of Spain died without offspring. So began another round of dynastic warfare as Europe fought over Spain's decaying political carcass and the economic assets it brought with it. The two rising merchant capitalist states, Britain and newly independent Holland, feared that France would gain control of Spain and its vast American empire. So tactically they supported the Austrian contender to the throne. Seizing its opportunity, Catalonia negotiated a treaty with Britain whereby the latter would support independence in return for a Catalan rebellion against Spain. But perfidious Albion betrayed Catalan hopes. In 1713, under the Treaty of Utrecht, the British made peace with Spain in return for possession of Gibraltar, which they had captured with the aid of Catalan troops, and exclusive control of the slave trade in Spain's American colonies. In recompense, London dropped support for Catalan independence.

By the summer of 1714 all of Catalonia was under Spanish military occupation except Barcelona, which was under siege and blockaded by the Spanish navy. The local population mobilised in support of the defenders, bringing them provisions and rocks to throw at the Spanish. At the last moment, on the last day of fighting, a radical lawyer, Rafael de Casanovas, raised the banner of Saint Eulalia, Barcelona's patron saint, and led a counter attack. It was to no avail. Barcelona surrendered, unconditionally, on 11

September 1714. On that day Catalan autonomy was ended for over two centuries. Its historic *Corts* and separate laws were abolished. The chroniclers of the era spoke of 'the end of the Catalan nation'.[19] The aim of the triumphant Bourbons was precisely that: to erase Catalan identity entirely in an act of deliberate ethnic cleansing. There were to fail spectacularly, as we shall see in the next chapter.

In January 1716 Philip V issued the Decree of *Nueva Planta*, abolishing Catalonia's legislative, financial and legal sovereignty, and imposing his own absolutist control. From now on the Crown appointed three authorities to rule Catalonia: a captain general with political and military control, the Royal Audience which was the highest court, and the Superintendency in charge of collecting taxes. The *Nueva Planta* decrees have never been repealed. In contrast, the Basque Country was allowed to keep its separate statutes and charters. The Spanish state also took on a new, more absolutist form, but it was too late for a thorough rationalisation:

> Spain, under the Government of the Bourbons, was about to be centralised and Castilianised; but the transformation occurred at a time when Castile's economic hegemony was a thing of the past. Instead, a centralised Government was arbitrarily imposed on the wealthier peripheral regions, to be held there by force – the force of an economically retarded Castile.[20]

But what had been the most powerful state in Europe in the 16th century entered decline in the 17th century and by the 18th century was no longer regarded as a serious power within Europe. Its very nature meant the Spanish state could not arrest that decline.

Does history matter?

Does history matter or is it a dustbin to be plundered to justify contemporary demands? It certainly seemed to matter on *La Diada*, on 11 September 2014, when a staggering 1.6 million Catalans linked hands in a gigantic human chain, stretching 250 miles from one end of the country to the other, in a call for independence. They were not there because of Wilfred the Hairy. A good many of the participants, as either new immigrants or the children of immigrants to Catalonia, had probably never heard of him. Possibly more had heard of Catalonia's loss of de facto independence in 1714, just as Scots bemoan the gerrymandered Act of Union of 1707. Regardless, they would not have been holding hands in their millions but for the continuity of Catalan history. A history that was tempered in the long struggle for peasant, worker and national rights; and in the fight to maintain Catalan institutions, language and culture from eclipse by Castilian Spain.

Catalonia is a contemporary social and economic fact. If Catalonia were its own sovereign country, its 7.5 million residents would make it the 99th most populous in the world. The gross domestic product of the region – $314 billion – would rank it as the 34th largest economy, with a GDP exceeding that of Portugal, Hong Kong, and Egypt, to name but a few. Its GDP per capita, at $35,000, is greater than that of South Korea, Israel, and Italy. As those 1.6 million Catalans linked hands in September 2014, they were linking hands with history.

Chapter Three: Bourgeois Catalonia, Backward Spain

Barcelona, in the last dozen years of the 19th century, was a bourgeois paradise.

Robert Hughes[21]

Barcelona has seen more barricade fighting than any other city in the world.

Fredrich Engels[22]

THE SPANISH STATE which is now in crisis is a paper-thin modern edifice built round an authoritarian, medieval core. For the first half of the 20th century Spain was arguably the most backward part of Western Europe – economically and therefore socially. Spain entered the last century as a largely subsistence peasant economy dominated by a tiny, rich, arrogant feudal aristocracy and an over-large military caste with little to do but play politics. In other words, early 20th century Spain looked more like Latin America than Europe. The modernisation process of the English and French Revolutions and of the German and Italian unification process passed by Spain completely. There was no transformative bourgeois revolution to oust the landed aristocracy, military and crown from politics and control of the economy. To comprehend contemporary Spanish politics and Catalan and Basque nationalism, we need first to understand how Spain entered the 20th century as a medieval throwback. In Spain's radically uneven economic and political development lies the roots of the present-day Catalan and Basque demands for freedom.

Spain's failed bourgeois revolution

In many ways, the Spain of today looks very similar in its class and employment structure as it did at the end of the 18th century. The aristocratic, land-owning class still plays a key economic and political role in Spanish society.

For example, when she died in 2014, at her Dueñas Palace in Seville, Spain's premier aristocrat and landowner – the Duchess of Alba – left a massive fortune of £2.4 billion. Born Maria del Rosario Cayetana Fitz-James Stuart, the 18th Duchess of Alba was the most titled individual on the entire planet, with more than 40 noble titles and 150 hereditary ones. Still a massive landowner, it was said she could walk the length of Spain without ever leaving her properties. As her names imply, the Alba lineage goes back to the Stuart dynasty in Scotland and England. Indeed, Cayetana was a childhood friend of Queen Elizabeth, whom she got to know in London when her father was Franco's ambassador before and after the Civil War. In 1953, Cayetana married in Seville Cathedral in a celebration that cost the equivalent of £1.4 million. Her wedding was said to outclass that of Elizabeth the following month – at a time when post-war Spain was still living in abject poverty. On her death aged 88, Cayetana divided her fortune between six children and eight grandchildren – giving them each a palace and estates.

At the other end of the scale, until well into the 20th century, the largest part of the Spanish workforce was tied to the land. As late as 1960, 40 per cent of the workforce still worked in agriculture. Here is what makes Spain exceptional in contemporary West European history. While industrial capitalism in Spain undoubtedly came to dominate the economy, it did so very late on. And in the process, the tiny industrial bourgeoisie were not able to effect the sort of thoroughgoing transformation of political structures that would give outright control. Instead, Spain became trapped during the 19th and much of the 20th centuries in semi-permanent political crisis, with alternating bouts of dictatorship and institutional stasis. Again, Catalonia trod a different path economically. Catalonia would undergo a significant industrial revolution, creating both a prosperous, politically-active bourgeoisie and a rebellious working class. Together they would find themselves at constant odds with backward Spain from the end of the 19th century onwards, re-igniting Catalonia's quest for self-determination in radically new conditions.

As Spain underwent its relentless decline throughout the 18th century, Catalonia's economic fortunes improved, despite the loss of political autonomy. Barcelona grew from 30,000 inhabitants in 1717 to 100,000 by 1800. The reason: textiles. The volume and value of Catalan trade quadrupled between 1760 and 1792. By the 1790s there were almost 100 textile manufacturing enterprises in Catalonia employing 80,000 people.[23] After 1715, Catalan manufacturers had access to a Spanish market of seven and a half million people. Then the opening up of direct access to trade with the Americas in 1778 enlarged the market to 30 million.

The disparity between Spain and Catalonia in agriculture was all too obvious. Two-thirds of the land in Spain was held by the Church or the great nobles, who showed little enthusiasm for investment or innovation. In 1815 less than 25 per cent of Spain's arable land was under cultivation. In contrast, Catalonia's peasants either owned their land or had secure tenancies. As a result, they could respond to opportunities. As the 18th century progressed, Catalan agriculture shifted from subsistence to production for the market and became successfully integrated into international trade. With the opening up of the American market, Catalan wine producers made a hefty profit exporting the local firewater, *aiguardent*, which took up less cargo space than wine. The rising urban population in those areas of Catalonia devoted to grapevines increased the number of potential consumers for other goods like grain and manufactures. These developments – primitive capital accumulation, free labour, a foreign trade infrastructure, rising internal demand, and the beginnings of a local banking system – in turn helped stimulate a native cotton textile industry in Barcelona, and with it an embryo Catalan bourgeoisie. As early as 1770 Catalonia had been christened 'a little England in the heart of Spain'.[24]

Meanwhile sleepy, feudal Castilian Spain was about to be woken by the trumpet blast of modernity in the shape of the French Revolution. In self-defence, the Spanish Bourbons and landed aristocracy joined with the other European monarchies in trying to crush the revolution in 1794. But within months the Spanish forces were driven back across the Pyrenees into Catalonia and then soundly defeated, forcing Spain to sign a peace treaty. With the rise of Napoleon, the Spanish king judiciously allied himself with the new French emperor, but that did not stymie Bonaparte's ambitions. In March 1808, he ordered 50,000 soldiers to take Madrid. As French troops entered the capital they faced a popular insurrection, which they ruthlessly suppressed. Napoleon summoned both Charles IV and his son Ferdinand to tell them they were both redundant and handed the crown to his brother, Joseph Bonaparte.

The uprising in Madrid was followed by the creation across Spain of local councils of resistance (*juntas*) to the French occupation. Most of these were led by liberals who supported a constitutional monarchy under Ferdinand. In 1810, *junta* delegates met in Cadiz to constitute a national assembly (*Cortes*). After two years deliberation, the *Cortes* agreed on a constitution.

The so-called Cadiz Constitution of 1812 established the principles of universal male suffrage, constitutional monarchy and freedom of the press, and supported land reform. Presiding over the Cadiz assembly was Antonio de Capmany, one of Catalonia's leading intellectuals, whose vision for Spain was as a 'nation of nations'.[25]

When Ferdinand recovered the Spanish throne in 1814 (with the help of Wellington's army) there were hopes that he would bring about a liberalisation of Bourbon rule. Instead he revoked the Constitution of 1812 and set out to restore the hegemony of the absolutist monarchy, Castilian nobility and the Church. Ferdinand died in 1833 leaving the crown to his daughter, Isabella, rather than to his son. Catholic traditionalists and defenders of local and regional rights (especially so in the case of the Basque Country) rose in support of the claim of the son, Don Carlos. The army, liberals and both Britain and France backed Isabella. This first, so-called Carlist War lasted until 1839. The social basis of Carlism was made up of peasants, rural landowners, clergy and craftsman. Carlism took deepest root in the Basque Country and, to a lesser extent, rural Catalonia. The towns and cities of Catalonia's littoral were anti-Carlist.[26] It ended with Isabella secure on the throne. In retribution for the Carlist rebellion, her government abolished trade guilds, ended regional customs barriers, allowing for free trade, and seized Church lands.

This whole episode seems confusing to modern eyes. We see liberals backing Isabella in the hope of modernisation pitted against a peasant revolution in the Basque and Catalan countryside (supported by artisans in the towns) that seemingly backed absolutist reaction. Alas, real history is very messy. The popular uprising was in defence of the ancient rights and privileges being threatened by the centralism of the liberals and the intrusion of market forces. The Catalan and Basque peasants were defending control over their own lives. Carlism and the Carlist Wars rekindled the spirit of popular resistance in Catalonia and the Basque Country, laying the foundation for modern demands for autonomy. Karl Marx himself chided those who dismissed these peasant revolts as reactionary, calling them 'lying, well-paid liberal historians'.[27]

Had there been a larger urban working class to hand as an ally, this progressive streak in early Carlism might have succeeded. Instead, the Carlist leadership repeatedly sold out the peasantry, veering off towards a uniquely Spanish ideological melange that combined Catholicism, traditionalism and regionalism. This became embodied in a mass political party and even in Carlist trades unions (the better to counter the popularity of syndicalism).

By the early decades of the 20th century, Carlism defined itself as a bulwark against the left. Its muscular Christian democracy lapsed into a corporatism that allowed the Carlists to become bedfellows with the (genuinely) fascist Falange movement. After a shadowy existence during the Franco regime, Carlism evaporated in a puff of smoke following the Dictator's death.

Meanwhile, in retribution for the First Carlist War, the victorious Isabella continued the abolition of Catalan institutions, including its tribunals, tax assessment system and separate coinage. In 1825 and 1857, education laws were introduced which recognised no language except Spanish.

But if the monarchy was victorious at home, it faced certain defeat in the colonies.

The early 19th century saw Spain lose most of its massive overseas empire to liberal, nationalist revolutions in South America led by Simon Bolivar. Shorn of the tribute of empire, backward Spain had to fall back on its own resources for economic survival. The result was a long series of coup attempts by progressive forces, mostly in the army. These coups sought to overthrow the absolutist monarchy which served as the bastion of political support for the oligarchy of feudal landowners. The aim was to open the path to an English-style parliamentary democracy and industrialisation led by a new urban bourgeois class. There were no less than 12 such coups between 1814 and 1874. Far from unleashing modernisation and industrialisation, that would let Spain catch up with the rest of Western Europe, the outcome was chronic instability that allowed the ruling feudal oligarchy to retain its grip over Spain.

Through all this period the peasantry suffered, but not in silence. There were repeated, bloody peasant uprisings. The legendary Pep de l'Horta – often referred to as Valencia's Robin Hood – led a peasant uprising in 1801 in which some 40 villages rose against their feudal *seigneur*. Similar local revolts by the peasantry punctuated the 19th century. To counter unrest in the countryside, in 1844 the government in Madrid created a special militarised forced called the *Guardia Civil*, the most hated arm of the Spanish state. The massive degree of state repression used against the peasantry throughout the 19th century, co-joined with the traditional, historical inability of peasant movements to create stable political representation, ensued that rural unrest was unable to effect any revolutionary change in this period. Instead, much of the anger and resistance of the peasantry was channelled into banditry and a ferocious localised counter-violence against both the state and the Catholic Church, which was seen as an agent of the landlords.

Despite the failure of revolution in the countryside, persistent rural resistance to the landed oligarchy did have major repercussions. For one thing, the Spanish army became a key agent in protecting the oligarchy from an insurgent peasantry – especially after the loss of empire deprived the officer class of its traditional foreign role. As the 19th century waned, progressive elements in the officer corps disappeared and the Spanish army became transformed into a reactionary, Bonapartist clique that held the ring between the landed oligarchy, the monarch, the tiny urban bourgeoisie, the proletariat in Catalonia and the Basque Country, and – above all – the sullen peasant mass in the countryside. With none of the contending class forces able to resolve Spain's descent into poverty and economic backwardness, the officer class became a key political and social instrument in maintaining stability and order. Of course, in practice this meant the army ensured that Spain was frozen in time, economically, culturally and socially. It also resulted in the army becoming heavily politicised and seeing itself as 'saviour and guardian' of national unity.

None of this is to ignore the fact that there was significant change in the Spanish countryside throughout the 19th and early 20th century. To alleviate budgetary problems and fund military expenditure – Spain's numerous generals had to be funded – successive governments auctioned off Church and municipal land and property. Between 1766 and 1924, some 18.4 million hectares of state, church and municipal lands were sold – equivalent to 36 per cent of the country's area. Old feudal rights were also gradually eliminated, often – as in the case of the payment of tithes – because a truculent peasantry increasingly refused to pay. But noble titleholders remained exempt from tax until 1923. Big landlords used their power over tenants and employees to coerce rural electors and fix parliamentary elections. As a result, Spain even at the start of the 20th century looked uncannily like the feudal Spain of half a millennium before. But not Catalonia.

Birth of the Rose of Fire

The historical catalyst was the advance of Catalan industry at a time when most of Spain remained in the grip of a *latifundia*-based agricultural economy. 1833 saw the first steam-powered looms, imported from Britain, set up in a Barcelona textile plant. In the 1840s an English visitor noted of Barcelona: 'It is the Manchester of Catalonia, which is the Lancashire of the peninsula.'[28] Mechanisation meant that Catalan industrial production multiplied by 22.2 times between 1817 and 1877. In the 1840s, steam-pow-ered factories spread out onto the plain beyond the city walls.[29]

Rapid industrialisation would create not just a new, wealthy Catalan bourgeoisie and a rebirth of Catalan national self-confidence. A new his-torical actor was about to enter the stage of Catalan history: the urban working class. The factories of Barcelona sucked in landless peasants from the Catalan interior. Crammed into some of the worst slums in Europe, they worked for 12 hours every day. Unions were banned. Catalan employers might begrudge the Castilian-run state but they were quick to utilise it when the workforce rebelled. In 1835, only two years after it was opened, Barce-lona's first steam-powered plant was burnt down by militant workers. Four of them were executed.

The militancy of the Barcelona working class would now play a central role in the city's future, and Catalan politics in general. Strikes, rebellions, anarchism and anti-clericalism would be the hallmarks. The city was soon to have a new title: *Rosa del Foc*, the Rose of Fire, after Tragic Week in 1909 when the city was turned it into a sea of flames as religious buildings were burned to the ground. From the start, working class resistance in Barce-lona involved extreme anti-clericism and the burning of churches by popular crowds who resented the Church's wealth, social control and overt support for reaction. The Barcelona liberal bourgeoisie had little problem with this: they built their opera house on the site of a burned-down church and openly encouraged anti-clericalism as a safety valve for popular unrest (burning down a factory was a different matter!).

The emergence in Catalonia of a militant working class, alongside the resurgence of a vigorous cultural and political Catalan nationalism, was the predictable result of being an economically advanced region trapped inside underdeveloped Spain – indeed, a Spanish state suffering from rapid imperial decline. This is a classic case of combined and uneven development triggering sudden, new political responses. In 1843, Barcelona's workers and small businessmen joined in protest against a city-wide tax. Then a rumour spread that Madrid had signed a free trade deal with Britain, threatening Catalan industry's near-monopoly of the Spanish market. The protest turned into an uprising. Unable to control the streets, the army was forced back to the fortress of Montjuïc and to the Citadel, from where they began a bom-bardment of the city, damaging or destroying some 460 buildings before crushing the rebellion.

In 1854 there was another uprising. This time the city's workers set fire to half a dozen factories, threatening a general strike if their demands for collective bargaining, shorter hours and increased wages were not met. A new military Captain-General (his predecessor had fled) negotiated a deal between employers and their workers. But to divert the passions of the city's population he also agreed that the city's walls could be demolished, although not the citadel. The city could now expand beyond the limits set by the walls. In 1855 came Barcelona's first general strike, in protest against the importing of spinning machines from Britain. These threatened to replace domestic labour in the textile plants. Strikers also demanded a 10-hour day under the slogans 'Bread and Jobs' and 'Unions or Death.' The army answered by gunning down dozens of strikers. In a fresh development, the managing director of one enterprise was shot in retaliation. Writing in the 1880s, Frederick Engels noted that Barcelona was 'the city whose history records more struggle on the barricades than that of any other city in the world'.[30]

By then political anarchism – a decentralised form of communism – was gaining mass support in the city. Early Spanish anarchism was heavily influenced by the Catalan journalist and liberal, Francesc Pi i Margall, who first translated the works of Proudhon (the seminal French anarchist) into Spanish. Pi is historically significant because his anarchist views on decentralised decision-making plus his avowed Catalanism melded into a strong support for a federal Spanish state. But the sheer terror imposed on the Barcelona working class by the Catalan bourgeoisie drove the workers' movement in a different direction: 'propaganda of the deed'; in other words, carrying out assassinations and terrorist bomb attacks on the bourgeoisie, such as the one at the Liceu Opera House, in the Rambla, in 1893. But this only provoked more repression by the state. Fortunately, the dead end of terrorism soon gave way to an emphasis on creating combative trades unions that might overthrow capitalism through a revolutionary general strike.

The growth of anarcho-syndicalism was not unique to Barcelona. Anarchist currents were to be found in Glasgow and other major industrial cities where workers were concentrated in factories by the tens of thousands. But anarchism in Barcelona became hegemonic in the local working class to the detriment of parliamentary social democracy. The cause was the toxic mixture of extreme poverty, the regular use of the army and the obvious bankruptcy of seeking a parliamentary solution in Spain's rigged electoral system. As a result, the parliamentary sphere was ceded for a time to the rising Catalan bourgeoisie.

The First Spanish Republic and the Restoration system

In 1868, a military putsch by liberal officers led to the overthrow the monarchy, sending Queen Isabella into exile in France and seeming to end the reactionary Bourboun line in Spain. These officers favoured a new constitutional monarchy under under King Amadeo 1, the son of Italy's King Victor Emmanuel. Victor Emmanuel, aided by an armed uprising led by Garibaldi, had recently united Italy under a modern, bougeois constitution. But the new Spanish monarch lacked the political skills of his father while the various factions of the tiny Spanish middle class remained deeply divided on what sort of state they wanted to build. Meanwhile, the overthrow of the Bourbons had unleashed a wave of Carlist, peasant and workers' revolts, as pent-up social and economic frustrations were given vent across the Spanish state. The instability also spread to Cuba, Spain's remaining source of colonial wealth. All this was more than King Amadeo had bargained for and he soon abdicated. This ushered in the First Spanish Republic in 1873 and the promulgation of a radical, democratic constitution that included universal male suffrage (not granted in Britain till 1918).

This could have been the bourgeois political revolution Spainish liberals had long sought, ending the grip of the Castillian landed aristocracy on the state and opening the path for general capitalist modernisation. Possibly such a development could have reconciled the Catalan middle classes to the Spanish state. Indeed, the Catalan journalist and federalist Francesc Pi i Margall – he who inspired the early anarchist movement – was to become President of the First Republic. But history took a radically different direction. The failure of the First Republic after less than two years would cast a shadow across Spanish and Catalan politics thereafter.

The ignominious collapse of the First Republic had many causes. The military, faced with open revolt in Cuba and chaos at home, recanted their earlier support for reform, in favour of repression and a return to Bourbon stability. The various liberal political factions proved incompetent, disunited and prey to personal opportunism. As in Germany in 1848, the nascent Spanish bourgeoisie proved too pusillanimous to force through democracy for their class, even one hidden behind a constitutional monarchy. And there was no Spanish equivalent of a Garibaldi to force a successful confrontation with the landed oligarchs. As a result, conservative forces in the military, supported by the big landowners, restored Queen Isabella and the absolutist Bourbon monarchy in December 1874.

With this *Restauracion*, attempts at political reform in Spain all but petered out. Instead, the landed aristocracy, the bourgeoisie and the military caste agreed to share power behind a sham democracy in which governments in Madrid alternated by agreement between a Conservative bloc and a slightly more liberal one. These parliamentary blocs were not political parties in the modern sense but alliances of local interests who secured votes through their control of the peasantry and electoral fraud. This system was known as: *caciquismo*.[31] Hopes that Spain could be transformed into a modern Western European democracy, albeit dominated by the needs of the industrial bourgeoisie, were permanently thwarted.[32]

This elite accord ensured that Spain would remain one of the most under-developed corners of Europe with a famously reactionary ruling class. Low pay in the civil service meant that officials looked for bribes. In the army, senior officers pocketed money for barracks and equipment while junior officers traded in soap, food and building equipment. Deputies and ministers made money from government contracts or sold their votes in the *Cortes*. The deal also ensured that there was no federal solution which might have solved the Catalan and Basque issues. The mainstays of the new system were the landlords and relatively small bourgeoisie of Castile, the army, where the officer corps was virtually completely Castilian, and the Church. [33]

The political architect of the Restoration system was Antonio Cánovas, Spain's Prime Minister six times between 1874 and 1897, when he was shot dead by an anarchist. In 1997, the Popular Party organised a campaign featuring exhibitions, books, TV documentaries and seminars in which Cánovas was presented as the conservative leader who – by restoring the monarchy – had brought Spain stability after years of civil war and revolution. This historical resurrection ignored Cánovas' opposition to universal suffrage, the repression he meted out to the working class, and the system of organised corruption he presided over. Of course, the factor endearing Cánovas to the PP was his strongly centralist policies and his promotion of Spanish nationalism, centred on Castile's role in creating the nation and empire.[34]

In reality the Restoration system held Spain back – economically as well as politically. Desperate for money, Spanish politicians began selling off assets to foreign buyers. Spain became in effect a semi-colony for foreign capitalism. The buyers – particularly the British – were both arrogant and borderline racist even in their dealings with the traditional Castilian elite. The British racist epithet '*dago*', which emerged first in Menorca in the 1830s, was applied freely to Spanish citizens of all classes.

The story of the imperialist intervention in Spain begins with the Río Tinto River. The Río Tinto – named for the reddish mineral streaks that colour its waters – rises in the Sierra Morena Mountains of Andalusia, then flows southwest, reaching the Gulf of Cádiz at Huelva. Since ancient times the course of the Río Tinto has been mined for copper, iron, silver and gold. Desperate for cash, the Spanish government sold off the Río Tinto's mineral wealth in 1873 to a syndicate put together by Hugh Mackay Matheson, an enterprising Church of Scotland lay preacher and senior partner in Matheson and Company – which made its fortune from the opium trade. The bid specified that Spain permanently relinquish any right to future royalties on the mine's production. Today Rio Tinto is one of the largest and most profitable mining companies on the planet.

This was only the start of a massive fire-sale of Spanish assets and domestic markets to foreign capitalists. The Belgians owned the railways, while French concerns moved into mining and textiles. American companies controlled the phones. Germany controlled the power companies. But it was Rio Tinto who led the way in effectively raping the Spanish economy. The company created its own shops so that its workers were compelled to buy what Rio Tinto sold them. The firm's machinery and coal were imported from the UK. Processing pyrites by burning the mined ores in the open air despoiled vast tracts of local agricultural land. The aristocratic owners of the big *latifundia* in Andalusia were as much plagued by the burning of pyrites as ordinary peasants. Rio Tinto responded with a vast bribery operation which bought off Spanish politicians, adding to the endemic corruption of the reactionary Restoration era.

Renaixença and Lliga – the birth of Catalanism

The *Restauracion* reinforced a centralised Spanish state that offered nothing in the way of autonomy for the Catalans and Basques. On the contrary, following the abortive Third Carlist War (1872–1876), what remained of Basque home rule was abolished, with the abrogation of the feudal charters (*fueros*) that traditionally guaranted local self-determination. The Spanish state continued under the domination of landed, aristocratic interests whose narrow ideological references were Spain's mythic Golden Age, adherence to the Catholic Church and the continuing superiority of Castillian culture.[35] This Spanish national stasis was bound to provoke a radical response in Catalonia. It came in the form of a resugeance in Catalan cultural identity heavily infused with late 19th century modernism – the *Renaixença*, or Renaissance.

Already the first half of the 19th century in Europe had witnessed the birth of the Romantic Movement. This was a cultural assertion of aspiring national identity, especially in Germany and Italy. Such politicised Romanticism soon began to influence Catalonia. An early indication was the publication of Bonaventura Carles Aribau's patriotic poem 'Oda a la Patria', in 1833. Another milestone came in 1859 with the inauguration of the *Jocs Florals*, the Floral games, a celebration of medieval Catalonia (and thus a reference to earlier Catalan autonomy).

But domestic politics and economics – rather than external influences – contrived to create the full-blown *Renaixença* by the 1880s. The transformation of Barcelona into a great industrial metropolis brought into being (and supported) an intelligentsia who would provide the writing, painting, architecture and journalism to shape a new sense of national identity. At the same time, the extraordinary affluence of the new Catalan bourgeois created a ready market for works of art and domestic architecture. Gaudi's iconic Parc Güell is named after his benefactor Eusebi Güell, one of Barcelona's biggest businessmen. Denied a political outlet, a modern Catalan identity emerged robust and innovative through the nation's writers, poets, artists, musicians and architects. The contrast with decadent Castillian Spain could not have been starker.

The cultural confidence generated by the *Renaixença* soon stimulated renewed interest in Catalan self-determination. Initially, this movement remained within strict federalist boundaries. In 1880, a *Centre Catala* (Catalan Centre) was formed, championing a federal Spain. Five years later, King Alfonso XII was presented with the *Memorial de Greuges* (Report of Grievances), arguing for autonomy and tariffs to protect Catalan industry from foreign competition. But even this tepid assertion of Catalan identity provoked a sharp reaction in Madrid which grasped that Catalan identity was now taking a political form. The reaction was particularly sharp in the Spanish army, which saw itself as the embodiment of Spain and therefore threatened by federalism.[36]

The next transformative moment in the emergence of modern Catalanism was the loss of Cuba. Sixty per cent of Catalan exports went to Cuba. But in 1895 another rebellion against Spanish colonial rule broke out on the island. Madrid sent 200,000 troops but their generals were incompetent, and the colonial administration corrupt. 2,000 men were lost to the rebels and an astonishing 53,000 to tropical diseases. The Americans, who coveted the island themselves, then intervened opportunistically, destroying Spain's Atlantic fleet off the island and its Pacific fleet at anchor in the Philippines. Humiliated, Madrid had to accept the loss of not only Cuba, but Puerto Rica and the Philippines. The Spanish Empire had come to an abrupt end at the hands of a new Yankee imperialism.

One lesson was very clear: the corrupt, incompetent Restoration regime had shown itself unable to defend the economic interests of the Catalan bourgeoisie. As a result, the *Lliga Regionalista* came into being in 1901, backing autonomy for Catalonia but not independence. It also wanted to reform the Spanish state and take more control of running central affairs. The Lliga's key figure, the businessman Francesc Cambó (1876–1947), seemed more concerned about defending order and saving the monarchy than in risking itself for autonomous and reformist experiments that might destabilise the political system and society itself.[37] This was a point driven home by Cambó himself:

> The market of Catalonia is the rest of Spain... to such a point that if they separate, both will be ruined... Every Catalan, there-fore, who leans towards separatism is attacking the interests of his country and is a bad Catalan.[38]

The Lliga would dominate Catalan politics until the Civil War

But the Cuban disaster also led to a rise in Spanish nationalism. In 1908, a law was passed to ensure that public buildings had to fly the national flag. Numerous monuments to monarchs and national heroes, real or imag-ined, were erected across Spain. In 1919 the Day of the Race was made a national holiday. A Law of Jurisdictions, passed in 1906, restricted free speech with the justification that Catalan nationalists were acting 'against the Fatherland'.[39]

The loss of Cuba left one symbol behind in Catalonia. Inspired by the Cuban example, radical Catalan nationalists added a white star on a blue triangle to the Catalan flag, creating the *Estelada*, the pro-independence flag.[40]

Meanwhile, Catalonia was changing socially. The balance between town and country had altered forever. Between 1850 and 1900, Barcelona expanded, taking in previously independent villages such as Gràcia, Sants and Sant Martí. The population increased by over 300 per cent, only to double again between 1900 and 1930. By 1930, Barcelona was the biggest city in the Spanish state. In 1900, 73 per cent of the city's population of 533,000 had been born in Catalonia. Most of the rest came from the neighbouring areas of Aragon and Valencia. By 1910 the number of Catalans had fallen to 66 per cent of the population, and that would fall further as the economic boom during the First World War sucked in labour from further afield.[41]

Skilled work was largely monopolised by Catalan workers, so the new arrivals were restricted to unskilled work. Often, they would resent owners and foremen who spoke Catalan. Yet the working-class communities in which they settled were Catalan-speaking, and migrants from Valencia spoke a Catalan dialect. The formation of the CNT in 1911 created a union federation representing 26,571 workers organised into 140 unions. It quickly won a clear majority of Catalan workers. But it also set out consciously to organise the unskilled and migrants, playing an important role in breaking down barriers between different groups of workers.

Tensions were soon apparent between the new Lliga and the labour movement. In 1902 the anarchists organised a general strike in support of the eight-hour day and the right to strike. It was met with repression, with 300 workers arrested and 14 killed. The strike was defeated. The Lliga supported its suppression.

Another fork in the road occurred with the Lliga's response to the *Setmana Tragica* (Tragic Week) of 1909. Spain was faced with a popular revolt in its Moroccan colony, and decided to conscript men from Catalonia to suppress it. The response was predictable. After women clashed with troops trying to take young men away, the left called a general strike and Barcelona rose in revolt. Madrid declared martial law. Crowds turned on obvious symbols of authority, burning down 12 churches and 40 religious establishments across the city. Three clergy were killed. In return, hundreds of workers were killed by artillery fire. The Interior Minister in Madrid issued these instructions:

> The beast is in its lair. We have cornered it. Now we have to whip
> it until it jumps and then finish it off.[42]

Five executions followed, including that of the anarchist educationalist Francisco Ferrer. The charges against him were fabricated.[43] But Tragic Week was tragic for more than just this reason. The workers' protests had been diverted into a display of mindless anti-clericism, by the petty bourgeois Republicans. The Spanish state and the Catalan bourgeoisie emerged unscathed. In due course, Sagrat Cor church was built on Tibidabo to atone for the sins committed in the *Setmana Tragica*, just as the church of the same name, Sacré Cœur, was built on Montmartre to atone for the sins of the 1871 Paris Commune.[44]

Once again, the bourgeois leaders of the Lliga preferred to denounce anarchist destruction of private property and cheer on the Spanish army. Catalanism faced a political crossroads: to side with the regime or side with the Catalan working class. However, at least one current in Catalanist politics was decisively opposed to the regime – the editors and cartoonists at the Barcelona satirical magazine *¡Cu-cut!* (Cuckoo). On 23 November 1905, the magazine published a cartoon ridiculing the military. The actual wording of the cartoon translates:

> Officer: What's being celebrated here? Man: A victory banquet.
> Officer: Victory? They must be civilians then. [45]

The victory referred to was of the *Lliga Regionalista* in recent elections, but the butt of this rather feeble joke was the military, who hadn't won. In retaliation, 300 thin-skinned army officers stormed the *¡Cu-Cut!* offices and burned them to the ground. The Spanish government declared martial law in Barcelona and passed a law which made satirising 'Spain and its symbols' (i.e. the army) a criminal offence. *¡Cu-Cut!* was soon back on the streets but when it dared to poke fun at the leaders of the *Lliga Regionalista*, they had it shut down permanently.

Slide towards dictatorship

By 1917, tensions in Catalonia were coming to a head. Spain remained neutral in the First World War, but only because political sentiment was split regarding who to support. The aristocracy, Church and Spanish army leaned towards the Central Powers. Pro-Allied sentiment, especially for France, was more common amongst liberals and in Catalonia. But the war boosted Catalan exports and employment. This emboldened the working-class movement, resulting in yet another general strike in Barcelona, in August 1917, which led to 70 dead, hundreds wounded and thousands arrested.[46]

The conservative Lliga now found itself trapped between, on the one side, the workers' movement and a growing radicalism among young Catalans;

and on the other, the intransigence and incompetence of the Madrid regime. Fearing a loss of influence, the Lliga tried to pressure Madrid into making political concessions, gambling that the economic power of the Catalan bourgeoisie would tip the scales in favour of reform. Francesc Cambó traveled to Madrid to demand that the Spanish *Cortes* was convened. Otherwise, the Lliga would call a constituent assembly in Catalonia to draw up a constitution for an autonomous government. When this call was ignored, Catalan deputies were summoned to meet in Barcelona. The Madrid government declared this congress a 'truly seditious act' (shades of 2017) and placed Barcelona under martial law once more. When the Deputies met in secret the Civil Governor arrived to order them to disperse.

But the August general strike had frightened the Lliga and Madrid knew precisely how to play on those fears. Cambó was invited to join the Cabinet in Madrid. He accepted, and the Lliga duly retreated on pressing its demand for autonomy. The Lliga 'seemed more concerned about defending order and saving the monarchy than in risking itself for autonomous and reformist experiments that might destabilise the political system and society itself.'[47]

In contrast, evidence of a radicalisation among Catalanists came in late 1918 and early 1919:

> Barcelona experienced a real street war of flags and anthems. On one side the Catalanist anthem, *Els Segadors,* accompanied the four-striped Catalan flag, the Senyera, while beside it the Marseillaise was also heard, an indication of the strength of Catalan republicanism. Their opponents vigorously brandished the Spanish flag... Violent clashes occurred between Catalan separatists who held up the *Estelada* flag with the added white-on-blue star and Spanish nationalists of the extreme right.[48]

The end of the war had brought a sudden end to the short boom and exacerbated social tension. The 1917 October Revolution in Russia had been welcomed by the CNT, which liked the soviets if not the Bolshevik Party, and, as elsewhere radicalised the working class. Between 1917 and 1919 the number of strikes doubled over the previous two years to 835, involving 359,000 workers; then doubled, and grew again in 1920 and 1922 to 1,086 strikes, involving 447,000 workers.[49] With Barcelona teetering on the verge of insurrection, Madrid conceded the 8-hour working day and set up arbitration commissions with the CNT, giving some 70,000 strikers back their jobs.

These concessions staved off revolution, but they were deeply resented by Catalan industrialists and the Lliga. Lockouts continued for years and the employers organised death squads of armed company thugs to assassinate hundreds of CNT activists. Cambó later explained that the leadership of the Lliga 'understood that the question of liberty had to be put off for a time when faced with the question of life itself'.[50]

The Lliga now entered into an alliance with both the military and the Spanish right – an alliance with a clear authoritarian, if not fascist, agenda. The main Catalan bosses' organisation called for an 'iron surgeon' to crush Bolshevism.[51] The 'iron surgeon' to whom the Catalan bourgeoisie, the king and the Spanish army now looked was none other than the Captain-General of Catalonia responsible for crushing the Barcelona proletariat – Miguel Primo de Rivera.

In September 1923, a year after Mussolini's March on Rome, de Rivera launched his agreed 'coup' from Barcelona. He did so with the backing of much of the Catalan elite. This aristocrat, landowner, notorious womaniser and now aspiring dictator was urged on by prominent Catalan businessmen including the president of the *Foment del Treball Nacional*, Catalonia's main employer's organisation. The latter even convened a meeting of its members to vote support for the coup.[52]

In 2017, with no hint of irony, the very same *Foment del Treball* issued a statement condemning the Catalan Parliament's vote to hold the 1-0 referendum as 'a legal coup d'état contrary to domestic and international law'.

Primo de Rivera's military dictatorship brought to an end the Restoration era. But by backing Primo, the Lliga destroyed its own support, not least because the dictator soon adopted anti-Catalan policies. The Catalan authority created by the coming together of the councils of Barcelona, Tarragona, Girona and Lleida was abolished, and FC Barcelona football club was closed, as was the *Orfeo Catala* (the Catalan choral society). The public use of the Catalan language was banned in church and in education. Irony of ironies, the Lliga itself was outlawed, as well as the CNT.

Conclusion

The history of the *Lliga Regionalista* proves, if proof were needed, that independence has never been the project of the majority of the Catalan bourgeoisie. On the contrary, when the economic chips were down, the Catalan big bourgeois turned their backs on their own country and its working people in favour of a military dictatorship that would protect their property and class interests. Catalanism would now pass into the hands of the radical middle class and working class. Civil war loomed on the horizon.

Chapter Four: Civil War and Revolution

It was the first time that I had ever been in a town where the working class was in the saddle. Practically every building of any size had been seized by the workers and was draped with red flags or with the red and black flag of the Anarchists; every wall was scrawled with the hammer and sickle and with the initials of the revolutionary parties; almost every church had been gutted and its images burnt.

George Orwell, *Homage to Catalonia*

AS THE 1920S ENDED few could have guessed that Catalonia would be entering the rapids of revolution. The Primo de Rivera dictatorship had organised in 1929 the Hispanico-American exhibition in Seville and the Universal Expo in Barcelona, both designed, 'to project an image of Spain characterised by efficiency and economic progress... emphasising Spain's unity.'[53]

In fact, the repression inflicted on Catalonia had radicalised Catalanism with the rise of Esquerra Republicana de Catalunya (Catalan Republican Left, ERC). Two personalities were key to the new party. One was a former Spanish army engineer, Francesc Macià, who had been forced to quit the military after publicly condemning the assault on the Catalan satirical magazine *¡Cu-Cut!* in 1905. The other was a labour lawyer named Lluís Companys. The new party's programme centred on independence and unification of all the Catalan speaking-areas (though in some form of association with Spain), the democratisation of the Spanish state including an end to the monarchy; and social reform. The ERC resulted from the merger of a number of Catalan parties, and in the period before the outbreak of the Civil War would number over 100,000 militants – an extraordinary size for a political party in the Spanish state. Its political influence remains, of course, down to the present day and the events of October 2017.

The nucleus of the new party came from splinters from the socialist PSOE; from militant Catalan nationalist groups radicalised by opposition to the de Rivera dictatorship; and from anti-monarchist republicans influenced by the insurrectionary Carlist tradition. One component, the Catalan Republican Party led by Lluís Companys, had actually adhered briefly to the Communist International. The ERC's early popular base was in the peasantry, radicalised by the collapse in food prices following the Great War. It had close links with the peasant trade union, the Catalan Union of *Rabassaires* (vine growers). Companys himself was for a long time the lawyer for the anarchist CNT union. Certainly, the party's programme was far from socialist, and its electoral support came more from petty-bourgeois intellectuals and the peasantry rather than the working class. But the ERC was the antithesis of the old Lliga of the big bourgeoisie, which it now replaced as the leadership of Catalan self-determination.

The creation of Esquerra at this time was not simply due to political developments inside Catalonian or the Spanish state – international forces were at work. The two decades following the carnage of the Great War saw the high tide of Modernism in culture and politics, across Europe and North America – signalling a profound ideological break with the liberal, monarchist past. Lenin's new Soviet State had announced self-determination for its national minorities. The Versailles Peace Conference created a host of new, small nations in Europe and the Middle East, as a result of the break-up of the Austro-Hungarian, Ottoman and Czarist Empires. In the UK, the Irish were fighting a bloody war of independence to free themselves, successfully, from the United Kingdom. New nationalist and secessionist parties were springing up, of similar ideological parentage to the ERC. For instance, the Scottish National Party was created three years after Esquerra, inspired by left-wing poets such as Hugh MacDiarmid and socialists such as Robert Cunninghame Graham. New Scottish independentist currents had also appeared out of the revolutionary workers movement, including John Maclean's Scottish Workers Republican Party. This was an era internationally of revolution and rupture with the old 19th century order. In Catalonia, the ERC crystallised that profound mood shift.

These winds of change were about to sweep away the dictatorship of Primo de Rivera. The 1929 Universal Expo in Barcelona left behind a rich architectural legacy and a beloved fairground, but little else. Both opened just as Wall Street crashed, leading to a global recession which undermined de Rivera's rule. His inability to deal with the growing economic crisis lost him the support of the army, forcing him to resign and go into exile. On 12 April 1931, the various republican parties won a landslide victory in municipal elections. On 14 April, King Alfonso fled Spain as well, accompanied by his Scottish-born wife Queen Victoria Eugenie – she only ever returned to Spain once, in 1968, for the baptism of the current King Felipe VI.

The first Catalan Republic

The new Esquerra – founded officially only three weeks before the elections – won double the votes for the Lliga. From the balcony of the *Generalitat*, ERC leader Francesc Macià proclaimed an independent Catalan Republic. As a teenager the Catalan artist, Carles Fonserè, was in the crowd listening to Macià and recalls chants of 'Long Live Macià, Death to Cambó [the Lliga head].'[54]

Macià had expected that the other nationalities of Spain would also constitute themselves as republics, and establish an Iberian Confederation. But the grip of centralism and Spanish-Castilian nationalism proved too strong. So as not to de-stabilise the infant Spanish Republic, three days later Macià accepted a compromise in the form of a Statute of Autonomy for Catalonia. This was agreed in a popular referendum across Catalonia held on 2 August 1931. It was approved by a majority of 99 per cent. Unfortunately, the *Cortes* in Madrid immediately began rolling back the provisions of the Statute. After an abortive army coup in September 1932, the *Cortes* finally approved the Statute defining Catalonia as autonomous within the Spanish State.

Elections were held for the newly revived Catalan Parliament in November 1932, with the ERC winning 55 out of 86 seats. Macià became President (Prime Minister) but died within a year, replaced by Lluís Companys. The new Statute of Autonomy quickly proved problematic. The new Catalan Parliament had unlimited powers over agriculture, transport, public health, municipal government and Catalan Civil Law. In addition, the *Generalitat* government was allowed to administer education, public works, labour services, police and law courts but Madrid retained a veto in these areas. As a result, the *Generalitat* existed in constant tension with Madrid.

In particular, it now found itself having to deal with growing labour unrest (led by the CNT) but lacking the authority to resolve disputes effectively. The end of the de Rivera dictatorship and the birth of the Republic had released all the suppressed grievances of Barcelona's working class. August 1931 saw 41 strikes in Barcelona, with 40,000 metalworkers staying out for a month before winning their demands.[55] Mass picketing was key to the success of the strikes. Striking barbers repeatedly blockaded hairdresser shops until they eventually won pay rises and recognition of the *bolsa de trabajo*, the CNT labour exchange. The CNT's ranks swelled by hundreds of thousands.

The Catalan government responded by sending in the Guardia Civil to evict workers occupying factories in Poblenou and Sants. The crucial battle came during a telephone strike, when the Spanish authorities announced that any pickets engaged in sabotage would be shot on sight. CNT posters, a key means of transmitting information, were declared illegal. Those distributing them were liable to arrest. Strikers were detained for threatening behaviour, including a group of children in Raval for taunting a telephonist with chants of 'Maria the scab'. The Assault Guards – a heavily armed police reserve created by the Republic – were deployed to guard those turning up to work and impose 'lightning bans' on union assemblies. This prompted violent clashes with pickets.[56]

One of those who abhorred the new Republic was the leader of the bourgeois Lliga, Francesc Cambó. He said it gave him 'veritable terror'. Consequently, Cambó fled into exile in Paris.[57] Carles Fonserè recalls that 'elegant high-class people, many of whom boasted the most ancient Catalan lineages' now joined organisations opposed to the Republic and made a show of speaking Spanish, not Catalan.[58]

A rent strike involving the unemployed and employed had begun in Barcelona even before the Second Spanish Republic was installed. It was initiated by street committees and neighbourhood groups who demanded a 40 per cent rent reduction and nothing from the unemployed. Soon over 100,000 people were withholding rents in Barcelona and the protest began spreading to surrounding towns.[59]

The Republican government in Madrid grew anxious and banned a rally called in support of the rent strike. Spain was edging towards social revolution. Trapped, on the one hand, between the working class and peasantry demanding an end to exploitation, and on the other, between an officer class, big bourgeois and landed aristocracy desperate to preserve their privileges, the Republican government temporised. To placate the right, it began to crack down on the left.

A new Law for the Defence of the Republic was used against the Barcelona rent strike. But the level of solidarity in the neighbourhoods was so powerful that this failed. Crowds clashed with the Guardia Civil, who had been drafted into the city, as they tried to enforce evictions for rent arrears. Eventually, mass arrests helped undermine the rent strike. However, in response to the crisis, the Esquerra-led Catalan Government passed a law allowing tenants to claim redress for 'unfair rents'. For many younger CNT activists, the rent strike represented a formative experience of state repression and of street fights with police.[60]

The CNT was given more reason to dislike the new Catalan government in January 1932, after miners in the town of Figols took control of the town and declared libertarian communism. The rising spread along the Llobregat valley among textile workers. In solidarity, CNT militants set up barricades in Clot and Sant Andreu in north Barcelona and became embroiled in gun battles with the Assault Guards. By that first day, over 200 workers had been arrested as the Assault Guards occupied the working class *barris*. Meanwhile, the army had taken control of Figols, where the rebels surrendered. As a consequence, 104 CNT members were deported without trial to Spanish Morocco, among them Buenaventura Durruti and Francisco Ascaso, neither of whom had been involved in the rising. Both would make history in 1936.

The conflict between the ERC government and the CNT hardly helped the left or the cause of Catalan self-determination. The problem as regards the CNT, and especially its hardline FAI current, was that it rejected any parliamentary initiative, and treated the autonomist and left social-democratic parties as traitors rather than potential allies. Paradoxically, the CNT itself was unwilling to seize power. Instead it trailed behind episodic and isolated local peasant and worker uprisings which – by their limited nature – were bound to end in failure. Esquerra was also in a political bind. Its petty bourgeois and republican heritage meant that it was not ready to break completely with capitalism or constitutional order. Yet it now faced what was becoming a mass, anti-system peasant uprising in the countryside.

Companys declares an anti-fascist Catalan State

The unrest was being mirrored across Spain. In November 1933, fresh Spanish-wide elections were held, the first-ever where women had a vote. The largest party to emerge was a new Catholic, conservative alliance – the Spanish Autonomous Right Confederation, or CEDA. Many saw CEDA as a bridge towards an outright fascist regime like Hitler's Germany and Mussolini's Italy. A complicated topping-up process gave CEDA a plurality of seats in the *Cortes* but not an outright majority. Eventually, after much dithering, a government was formed between CEDA and the moderate bourgeois Republicans. The Spanish left had entered the elections divided, with the anarchist CNT predictably abstaining. The left now paid the price as the right moved to reassert control over the new Spanish Republic.

Once again, in Catalonia, matters were different. Locally, the election was won by an alliance of the ERC and the left. It was now clear that staying part of Spain risked Catalans losing the social and democratic gains achieved under the Republic. A Spain-wide general strike broke out against the CEDA government, led by the PSOE – a strike from which the anti-parliamentary CNT remained aloof in a bizarre act of sectarianism. In rural Catalonia, peasants began seizing land, in many cases led by the pro-independence Workers and Peasant Bloc. Under the leadership of Joaquín Maurín, the Bloc had originated as a split from the official Communists. But unlike the Moscow-leaning Stalinists, the *bloquistes* were prepared to forestall the fascists by seizing power and declaring a Catalan Republic.

On 5 October 1934, the Bloc declared a general strike in Barcelona and across Catalonia. Despite initial opposition from the ERC government and the CNT, the strike succeeded. By that evening, spontaneous workers' militias were patrolling the streets of Lleida, Tarragona and Girona. Arms were being appropriated and distributed in Barcelona. At 6pm on the Saturday evening, a crowd demonstrated in front of the *Generalitat* shouting: '*Visca la Republica Catalana!*' – just as they would in October 2017. Though on this earlier occasion they added: '*Armes! Armes!*' At 8.00pm Companys bowed to the general will. He appeared on the balcony of the *Generalitat* and declared 'a Catalan State of the Spanish Federal Republic'. The phraseology was significant. With the political balance of forces still precarious, Companys was unwilling to leave the rest of Spain in the lurch, and at the mercy of fascism. Denouncing the 'monarchical and fascist forces' that had 'betrayed the Republic', he declared a Catalan provisional government free of the CEDA government in Madrid, and clearly intended to act as a bulwark against an impending fascist coup.

Having made this public gesture, Companys immediately surrendered the *Generalitat* when it was attacked by military units bent on restoring constitutional order. He could have escaped to the countryside, which was under the control of the armed peasantry. Instead he and his entire Cabinet allowed themselves to be arrested. There was scattered resistance by *bloquistes* but they were poorly armed and isolated by the failure of Companys to turn the declaration of a Catalan Republic into reality. Meanwhile, the CNT leadership called on workers to return to work. The revolt had collapsed, with inevitable results. The 'Statute of Autonomy' was suspended, municipal councils run by the left were suspended, and yet again (the default of any Madrid administration, it seems) the use of Catalan in public offices was prohibited. Political power was handed to Catalonia's military governor.[61] Companys and the whole of the *Generalitat* were sentenced to 35 years in jail.

A similar popular uprising against the new CEDA-dominated government also took place in Asturias, led by the PSOE and its union affiliates. Here armed miners actually took power but were brutally crushed by troops under the command of a certain Francisco Franco. Some 30,000 rebels were interned. Again, the CNT-FAI leadership failed to become involved directly (though local anarchists undoubtedly were sympathetic). Divisions on the left were proving costly. It is possible to argue that, given the scale of repression in Asturias, Companys was right in Catalonia not to push confrontation with the Madrid government to the point of armed conflict. On the other hand, the events of October 1934 suggest that confrontation between the popular left and fascist right was only a matter of time. A genuine Catalan Republic might have proved a firm base to prepare for the inevitable.

The frustrations of October 1934 had one major repercussion: the Spanish left and bourgeois republicans finally united in a Spain-wide Popular Front to oppose the authoritarian right and the generals. In Catalonia it was called the *Front d'Esquerres* (Left Front). To this was counterposed the *Front d'Ordre*, formed by the *Lliga,* which included all the parties of the right. In a dramatic change of policy, the CNT urged its members to vote for the *Front d'Esquerres* in order to secure the release of working class prisoners. At a Spanish level, the Popular Front won narrowly, with 4,654,226 votes to the right's 4,503,524. It was enough to form a government. In Catalonia, however, the *Front d'Esquerres* won a decisive 58.9 per cent, taking all four Catalan provinces.[62] Coming together in the Left Front were the ERC, a clutch of smaller Catalan nationalist groups, the Socialists, the Communists and the POUM – the latter being a merger of the *bloquistes* who had instigated the October 1934 rising, with Andreu Nin's small Left Communists group.

The political seesaw now tipped in the other direction. Companys and the entire Catalan cabinet were released from jail. On Sunday 1 March, they were greeted by jubilant crowds in Barcelona. The Catalan Statute of Autonomy was restored. In the remaining months of parliamentary rule, the *Generalitat* enacted new land reforms for wine-growing smallholders, the *Rabassaires,* so they could take ownership of any vineyards they had worked for 15 years or more. And again, the Madrid government appealed to the Tribunal of Constitutional Guarantees, which found that the *Generalitat* had no power to do this. Companys ignored their ruling. The Lliga walked out of parliament in protest at his action.[63]

Spanish generals had, meanwhile, chosen the dates 18, 19 and 20 July 1936 for an armed uprising against the democratically-elected government. It would begin in Morocco and culminate in uprisings across Spain. But things were to go badly wrong for them in Catalonia.

Franco, El Cadillo

The Spanish Civil War was a decisive moment in the history of the 20th century. It is safe to say that the victory achieved by Franco and the right – and the feeble response to this by Britain and France, the key Western democracies – was key to Hitler believing that force would ultimately get him everything he wanted. But the dynamic of the Civil War and its outcome are central to the story of Catalonia for the next 90 years. The vortex of the conflict redrew the boundaries of Catalan politics, ended Catalan autonomy, generated national mythologies, and ultimately turned Catalonia into an oppressed, semi-colony for over 40 years. The emotions stirred in Catalonia on the 1-0 referendum day, when baton-wielding Guardia Civil attacked polling stations, were conditioned by memories of the Civil War and the long Franco years that came after. One cannot understand Catalan politics without understanding the Civil War.

And one cannot understand the Civil War and its aftermath without understanding Francisco Franco Bahamonde. He was born in 1892 in Ferrol, Galicia, on Spain's north-west Atlantic coast – about as far from the Andalusian *latifundia* heartlands as you can get. The young Franco was slated to follow his father into the navy but after the disaster of the Spanish-American War, and the loss of the remaining Spanish colonies, he opted to join the army. Franco earned a reputation for exceptional personal courage and leadership in Spain's bloody colonial war of conquest in Morocco, between 1913 and 1926. It is easy to see his motivation was in part a provincial's romantic attachment to the lost dream of empire, and in part a need to justify himself to the preceding six generations of his family who had served at sea. Driven by a ferocious ambition, by 1926 and aged only 33, he was the youngest peacetime general in any European army. On the psychological side, Franco was devoted to his mother Pilar, who was deserted by his dissolute, womanising father. But the obverse of this sentimental side was an extreme cruelty towards his enemies.

Franco was far from the stiff person he appeared towards the end of his life (when he suffered from Parkinson's). On the contrary he was extremely amiable and talkative. This led Adolf Hitler – hardly taciturn himself – to remark he would rather have three or four teeth pulled than sit through another conversation with Franco. Hitler also called him a 'Latin charlatan' with the 'manners of a sergeant major'. That perhaps suggests the Spanish dictator had an earthier disposition than the inflated ego of the Austria-born ex-corporal. Franco clearly possessed at least as much guile as the Fuhrer.

Politically, Francisco Franco is more complex. He was not the classic political general made common by a century of army meddling in domestic Spanish affairs. His fighting experience in North Africa set him apart and, indeed, kept him out of politics till he became army chief of staff in May 1935. Indeed, those genuine fighting qualities were probably what helped him outmanoeuvre the other rebellious generals, to seize overall power. Ideologically, Franco was a devout Catholic and a lifelong monarchist. But above all, the Francisco Franco was a Spanish nationalist – and it was this vision of Spanish nationalism he would bequeath to posterity.

Until Franco, there were competing visions of Spanish nationalism but they were lost in the cacophony of ideologies that competed for the attention of early modern Spain: Carlism, monarchism, anarchism, Catholicism, Catalanism, Modernism, and regional nationalisms. Spain's economic backwardness and failed bourgeois revolution precluded the development of a modern, unified state. In doing so, it also blocked the emergence of a unifying bourgeois nationalism. Spain was not (and still isn't) a Castilian formation with antagonistic and ill-digested national formations in Catalonia and the Basque lands. Rather all of the Spanish state remains fragmentary and with it any hope of a Spanish identity. Hence the repeated tendency in the 20th century towards Bonapartism (eg de Rivera and Franco) as a unifying force. Where the Catalans and Basques are unique is that they were (and are) capable of forming their own states, as a result of their internal economic and social development. That was not the case in most of the other ill-digested parts of the Spanish state.

Franco's self-confessed historic role was to impose order on this unstable melange of competing class and national interests, for long enough to let a modern middle class capitalism emerge. And he did so by inventing (or extrapolating) an extreme Spanish nationalism, imposed from the top down. Ideologically, he plundered ideas from the Carlists, the fascist Falange, Catholicism and his own colonial experience in North Africa. The so-called

Golden Age of Isabella and Ferdinand was disinterred and refreshed, hence the drive to make Castilian the dominant language it never was before. Franco even talked of a new Spanish Empire extending deep into Equatorial Africa. His conditional revival of the monarchy was designed to add legitimacy to this muscular new Spanish nationalism – not to subordinate the new state to the crown, as in the 19th century.

Franco's version of Spanish nationalism has warped Spanish political life ever since. Like him, it is authoritarian; lacking in any appreciation of Spain's regional and national cultures, except as exotic elements tolerated as part of the imperial zoo; fearful of embracing any language or community on equal terms with the supposed Castilian norm; unrepentantly colonial, as witnessed by the retention till this day of the enclaves of Ceuta and Melilla, in North Africa; and routinely subordinates modern democratic values to the needs of the state. It is no accident that the ideology of the Popular Party of Mariano Rajoy – the direct linear descendent of the Francoist apparatus – is based on this narrow version of Spanish nationalism inherited from El Cadillo himself, hence its militant opposition to Catalan self-determination.

Civil War gives birth to social revolution

The response in Catalonia to Franco's military uprising was markedly different than anywhere else in Spain. In Barcelona the coup was met head on by the city's working class, led by the CNT. The city was soon in their hands. Those events are captured in George Orwell's *Homage to Catalonia* and in Ken Loach's film, *Land and Freedom*. With the outbreak of the Civil War and revolution in Catalonia, 'the upper bourgeoisie of the country, most of them *Lliga* supporters, fled to the "fascist" camp and ceased forever to harbour any more "regionalist" daydreams'.[64]

Without exaggeration, it is possible to describe Catalonia between mid-1936 and the start of 1939 as the first and (to date) only fully socialist state ever to emerge in Western Europe. On 24 October 1936, all companies with 100 workers or more were officially collectivised and put under local workers' control, subject to central co-ordination by a Catalan Economic Advisory Council. Banks remained under the direct control of the *Generalitat*, though they were not nationalised. Peasants were given their land, except in those parts of Aragon liberated by Catalan forces, where it was collectivised. All housing was municipalised. This makes it hard to understand those on the left today who dismiss Catalan demands for independence as a right-wing deviation – no other nation in Western Europe has ever gone as far as actually abolishing capitalism.

But there were deep political repercussions. The social revolution unleashed by the military coup of July 1936 would lead to a clash between, on the one hand, the revolutionary workers and peasants led by the CNT, backed by dissident communists of the mainly Catalan POUM; and on the other, the leadership of the parliamentary republicans in Esquerra, who were running the *Generalitat*. In that split, the ERC was supported – rather as a rope supports a hanged man – by the rising force of the Spanish Communist Party and its Catalan affiliate, the *Partit Socialista Unificat de Catalunya*, or United Socialist Party of Catalonia (PSUC).

There was also a power struggle between the Catalan autonomist government and the centralising Republican one in Madrid. The Republicans in Madrid were of a different order than the ERC: they were bourgeois liberals in the same vein as all those 19th century Spanish liberals who had opposed the monarchy, the landed oligarchy and the military, only to turn tail at the last minute. They were also, in the last resort, devout centralists, as was the pro-Moscow Community Party. The Prime Minister of the Spanish Republic, Juan Negrín, stated in 1938 that 'I am not making a war against Franco... so that its offspring is a provincial and stupid separatism in Barcelona'. In this fight the Communists backed the latter. [65]

After the Barcelona working class had taken effective control of the city in July 1936, a delegation of CNT leaders went to see Lluís Companys at the *Generalitat*. He told them:

> If you do not need me or do not wish me to remain as President of Catalonia, tell me now, and I shall become one more soldier in the fight against Fascism. If, on the other hand, you believe that, in this position which, only as a dead man, would I have abandoned had the Fascists triumphed, if you believe that I, my party, my name, my prestige, can be of use, then you can count on me and my loyalty as a man who is convinced that a whole past of shame is dead and who desires passionately that Catalonia should henceforth stand amongst the most progressive countries in the world. [66]

Companys had – literally – no troops. He was also acutely aware that power lay in the streets. But he was also gambling that the CNT would not take power because they did not believe in creating their own state and had no plan to organise new, revolutionary political structures. Reassuring themselves that Companys and the republican order were impotent, the CNT did not destroy the old state apparatus.[67] Instead, the CNT decided to allow Companys and the *Generalitat* to continue while they created a parallel Anti-Fascist Militias Committee of Catalonia, to run military affairs. This was made up of delegates from the unions, the left and republican parties, and the peasant *Rabassaires*. In reality, the new Committee remained just that – a committee made up of delegates from the various leaderships. It did not develop into a directing body representing direct democracy. The CNT committed itself to 'democratic collaboration' with the republicans for the sake of unity in the war against fascism. Yet, increasingly, that would translate into accepting the need to centralise the war effort around the Republican state, which was first based in Madrid but later in Barcelona itself.[68]

What did emerge in the *barris* were district committees (as on 1-0) based on neighbourhood solidarity, as one POUM activist recalled:

> It was not the leadership of the CNT, POUM or PSUC, who told the workers in the towns and neighbourhoods to form committees and occupy the town halls. The committees were formed on the night of July 19-20 on the initiative of local militants... Even if the unions quickly succeeded in taking over the factory committees, they never succeeded in completely controlling the town and neighbourhood committees. Each organism acted on its own. There was an element of anarchist distrust of authority... and a rank and file suspicion about the leaders, a fear that in Barcelona the leadership would allow itself to be pacified by the republican politicians.[69]

These neighbourhood committees were the driving force in the social revolution. Church property, business offices, hotels and the villas of the rich were occupied. A network of communal restaurants was set up, food distribution was organised in the *barris,* and essential foodstuffs and clothes were expropriated from shops and warehouses. Working-class patrols provided security. Yet this was going on just as the CNT leaders were agreeing to collaborate with Republican forces opposed to revolutionary change.[70]

Counter-revolution and the May Days in Barcelona

The tensions between the various wings of the popular movement now began to show. In late September there was a general agreement to reorganise the

Generalitat government to represent all the main pro-Republican parties, though still under the presidency of Lluís Companys. A new Catalan administration was formed which included ministers from the ERC, POUM, the peasant union, and the PSUC (the now unified Catalan Communists and PSOE). Crucially, for the first time in its long history, the CNT decided to join the government, being allocated three ministries, the same as the ERC.

There was no difference of opinion over the need to create a unified political command to lead the war effort. But to whom should this new government be responsible? For the POUM and CNT, the government had to be linked directly to the popular committees in the factories and neighbourhoods, in order to push forward the social revolution. For the Stalinists, the focus was on centralising the entire Spanish war effort, professionalising the Republican army, and not frightening the middle classes or foreign governments with talk of revolution – or Catalan independence.

In the middle sat Companys and Esquerra. There was no doubt of their commitment to the anti-fascist struggle: Josep Suñol, a prominent ERC member and popular president of the FC Barcelona football club, was captured by fascist troops early in the war and summarily executed. But Companys and the ERC were conflicted. They remained suspicious of the ingrained ultra-leftism, sectarianism and adventurism that often characterised elements of the CNT leadership. Also, for liberal Catalanists like Companys, the autonomous parliamentary institutions they had long fought for seemed to embody Catalan national aspirations better than the unruly neighbourhood committees in the Barcelona slums. For Companys, the struggle was defined in terms of republican, Catalan democracy against fascism, not class against class or anti-capitalist revolution. Yet by turning his back on the popular movement, Companys risked losing its support.

The inevitable result was that the new *Generalitat* began to usurp the power and initiative of the popular movement, particularly under pressure from the Communists. Russia was the only country willing to supply military aid to the Spanish Republic, though Stalin was careful to demand that the country's gold reserves were shipped to Moscow in return. The Republic's gold reserves were the fourth or fifth largest in the world, at the time. Stalin's aim was self-interested – he wanted to buy time for Russia to recover from the internal crises caused by a botched collectivisation of agriculture, and the chaos of the Purges. And by stomping on the idea of social revolution in Spain, he could prove to the democratic Western powers that Russia wasn't a threat. Along with Russian guns and aircraft, Republican Spain was soon swarming with Soviet secret police, the notorious NKVD. These would soon become the shock troops to crush dissident leftists in the CNT and POUM.

A month after the CNT entered the Catalan government, the *Generalitat* issued a decree disbanding the local revolutionary district committees, which were replaced by conventional municipal councils. In areas where the CNT and POUM were strong, local activists ignored this call but elsewhere popular power began to be rolled back. A single police force was now created, while the neighbourhood patrols established at the time of the July military uprising were disarmed, then dissolved. Trade union membership was not allowed in this new body.[71]

In November 1936, when Andreu Nin was expelled from the Catalan Cabinet at the behest of Stalin's representative in Barcelona on the spurious grounds that the POUM was 'Trotskyite' and therefore 'counter-revolutionary', the CNT failed to respond. With the prestige afforded by Stalin's military aid to the Republic, the Catalan PSUC had grown to over 40,000 members, though it was overwhelmingly middle class. At the same time, the ERC lost much of its membership to the more radical parties. The Communists now preached one state, one authority and one army. POUM militia units, which included international volunteers such as George Orwell, now found they were no longer being supplied with weapons.

Matters came to a head in May 1937 when Communist-led units tried to take control of the central Barcelona telephone exchange from the CNT, who resisted. Local committees, CNT militants and the POUM responded by seizing control of their neighbourhoods and building barricades. Gunfire was exchanged with the Stalinists and 'official' security forces. The local committees were in effective control of Barcelona when CNT ministers arrived from Madrid and demanded their members cease fire. Regular army units flooded the city. Workers control was ended, the POUM was outlawed and its main leader, Andreu Nin, arrested, tortured and murdered by the Russian NKVD. By November 1937, there were 15,000 anti-fascist prisoners in the Republic's jails, about 1,000 from the POUM.

Nin's political evolution is fascinating, as Angel Smith explains:

After an odyssey which took him from Catalanism to social democracy and syndicalism, his final home became Leninist

Bolshevism, and from 1923, with a group of colleagues within the CNT, he laid the basis for a movement which could combine Communism with support for the Catalan 'national liberation struggle' against the central state.[72]

But for now the revolution was over, and with it Catalan autonomy. Companys and the *Generalitat* were sidelined by Madrid. Almost immediately the Communist-controlled press, which had hailed Companys and the *Generalitat* during the May fighting, turned on both. It particularly set out to discredit the administration of Josep Tarradellas, head of the *Generalitat's* War Industries Commission, so that Catalan public opinion would accept as necessary the central government's appropriation of these industries, the last vestige of Catalan autonomy:

> Thus the Communist triumph of May 1937 marked the end of the political power secured by Catalonia on 19 July 1936.[73]

The POUM and CNT militias were now forcibly disbanded and re-enlisted in the regular Republican army under Russian control. This included the remnants of the 35,000 International Brigade volunteers who had flocked from all round the world to fight for the Spanish Republic. Britain supplied something over 2,700 volunteers, roughly a quarter of whom came from Scotland. Many Scottish International Brigaders were members of the Independent Labour Party (ILP), which had split from the official UK Labour Party in 1931. The ILP was affiliated with the POUM and maintained strong support for Scottish Home Rule. The revolutionary ILP members soon proved a thorn in the side of the increasingly Stalinised Republican army and most were sent home.

Franco gets help… from the British

The emphasis now was on creating a centralised Republican army to defeat the right in a conventional war. But the Republic could not hope to match Franco in such a struggle. He had the officer corps and trained Moroccan troops, plus ample arm supplies from Mussolini and Hitler. Italy sent 75,000 troops at one time or another, and both regimes provided elite air force units. The infant Nazi Luftwaffe used Barcelona to test its new Stuka dive bombers.

But Franco also had aid from another source – Tory Britain. The British Secret Service had been quick to provide covert aid to the Nationalist insurgency in 1936. It was on a biplane provided by MI6 agent Major Hugh

Pollard that Franco flew from the Canaries to Spanish Morocco to initiate the coup. But the Nationalists also needed foreign currency and war materials. Considering that the bulk of Spanish industry was based in Catalonia and the Basque country, that could have been a problem. Fortunately, there was the Rio Tinto company at hand.

Rio Tinto's chairman from 1924 until 1947 was another tough-minded Scot, Auckland Campbell Geddes. Originally an Edinburgh-trained medic, his organising skills led to his appointment as a minister in Lloyd George's wartime government. Rio Tinto's Spanish iron ore operations fell inside the Nationalist zone but production never faltered – indeed it increased. To keep Franco sweet, Rio Tinto supplied the Nationalists with goods and all-important sterling currency with which to import materials for the insurgency. However, Franco requisitioned significant amounts of Rio Tinto pyrite output for Germany. Indeed – just as Stalin cynically demanded the gold reserves of the Republican government as *quid pro quo* for supplying aid and war materials – Hitler insisted on access to pyrite and iron ore from Nationalist Spain in return for Nazi support.

As boss of Rio Tinto, Auckland Geddes was happy to support Franco. But as a card-carrying member of the British Establishment, he was not willing to supply Nazi Germany with a stockpile of raw materials that could (and would) be used against Britain in a European war. Geddes first plan was to persuade Neville Chamberlain's Tory government to bribe Franco and his generals a ploy later used successfully by the British during World War II. However, in the middle of the Civil War, Franco could not afford to fall out with the Germans. Tempers flared and there were hints that Rio Tinto's assets in Spain would be nationalised. Enter Don Jacobo Fitz-James Stuart, 17th Duke of Alba, and the father of Cayetana Fitz-James Stuart, the 18th Duchess whose demise in 2014 we recorded in Chapter Two.

The 17th Duke was a typical Spanish landed aristocrat and an Anglophile, like many of his class. Don Jacobo had been educated at Eton and was also, in his own right, the hereditary Duke of Berwick-on-Tweed in England. Always close to power – the better to protect his vast properties – Don Jacobo had been briefly Spanish Foreign Minister after the fall of Primo de Rivera. With the insurgency, he became the Nationalists' private representative in London. Franco could not have found an intermediary with greater access to the heart of the British Establishment. In 1938 Don Jacobo brokered a deal with Neville Chamberlain's cabinet to recognise the Nationalist regime

– making the 17th Duke of Alba Spain's official ambassador to the Court of St James even before Barcelona fell to the fascists. Chamberlain's haste to come out in favour of the Nationalists required and received a secret *quid pro quo* from Franco: the threat to nationalise Rio Tinto disappeared. Nazi Germany, of course, still got its iron ore. But Rio Tinto's shareholders made fat profits supporting Nazi rearmament and supplying the wherewithal to build the Condor Legion bombers that were pounding parts of Barcelona to rubble. And the Dukes of Alba kept their lands till this day.

By the autumn of 1937, with German and Italian aid, Franco's forces had taken both the Asturias and the Basque country. Now he could concentrate his troops, but against which target? Against symbolic Madrid, or industrial Barcelona, or Valencia, where the Republican government was located? Meanwhile, the Republicans, though outnumbered and outgunned, chose to launch a surprise offensive against Teruel in Aragon, in December 1937. They succeeded in taking the town, but Franco was able to deploy ample reinforcements and heavy weapons to counter-attack, driving the Republicans back. Flush with this success, in March 1938, Franco chose to press on to the sea, cutting off Catalonia from the rest of Republican Spain. The Spanish Republic would now live or die by what happened in Catalonia.

Catalonia defeated

The Republicans decided to strike first. In July 1938, they launched yet another offensive from Catalonia, across the River Ebro. Strategically, it was well planned and executed, and at the beginning very successful. But, as before, Franco could bring up reinforcements and heavy weapons, and he turned the tide. Catalonia now lay within his sights, with too few troops left to defend itself.

Meanwhile the civilian population was suffering hunger because of food shortages. It was being bombed mercilessly by Francoist and Italian planes. When the Nationalist forces took Gernika, a member of General Mola's staff was asked if bombing the town had been necessary. The officer answered: 'This is what has to be done in all of Vizcaya and Catalonia.'[74]

The President of the Spanish Republic, Manuel Azaña, was based in Barcelona throughout 1938. Observing the daily bombing of the city by Nationalist and Italian planes he said, tongue in cheek:

> An acquaintance assures me that the need to bomb Barcelona
> every 50 years is a law of Spanish history. Philip V's system was

harsh and unjust but solid and comfortable. It has worked for centuries.[75]

Between 16 and 18 March 1938, Barcelona was bombed heavily by aircraft of the Italian air force, in Spanish markings, operating from Mallorca. It was the first major city in Europe to be subject to indiscriminate area bombing – a tactic that would become common during World War II. Fortunately, Barcelona had taken pains to protect its citizens by creating bomb shelters deep underground, some of which can still be visited. These were engineered by Ramón Perera, who fled to the UK after Barcelona fell to Franco's troops. Once there, Perera failed to persuade the British government to invest in similar shelters for London. Instead, there were cheap and virtually useless Anderson shelters, made of thin corrugated iron, situated in the open.

Franco would leave the bombed-out ruins of Barcelona's working-class districts to fester for decades, as a punishment for Catalan opposition to Madrid. The city remained stoic under the bombing but slowly, inexorably, the hopes that had inspired the population of Barcelona to rise against fascism in July 1936 were crushed. Morale – that ephemeral but all important ingredient in any war – collapsed overnight. Catalonia's workers and peasants had struggled and died fighting for social justice since 1917. Two decades of sacrifice had ended in disaster. As for the Catalan leadership, the ERC, CNT and the POUM had been decapitated. Now the super-centralist Communist Party and the Stalinist gunmen of the NKVD secret police rooted out any hint of Catalan exceptionalism. As a result, proud Barcelona fell without a fight as the remnants of the Republican army and hundreds of thousands of civilians fled towards France and supposed safety.

But they were not welcomed by democratic France. Republican military personnel and refugees were interned in 15 camps which lacked basic amenities. In the first six months of their internment, 14,672 died of hunger and dysentery. Some 70,000 managed to claim asylum, mostly in Latin America. Britain took in only a few hundred. But over 150,000 remained in the French camps. When France fell in June 1940 the Nazis deported some 15,000 to concentration camps. Of those that got away, 10,000 joined the French resistance, providing vital military experience which has rarely been acknowledged since.[76] Throughout World War II this Catalan Republican *maquis* would play a central role in helping Allied airmen escape from France to neutral Spain. In 2017, many Catalans would feel aggrieved when the UK government sided with Madrid in the independence struggle, feeling that their contribution to the Allied cause during the war had been unjustly ignored.

The Butcher's bill

The Spanish Civil War was a truly horrific conflict, resulting in the deaths of an estimated 500,000 soldiers and civilians, and possibly as many as 700,000. Death or injury was inflicted on at least one in ten of the entire population. Air raids killed 10,000 to 15,000 people. Estimates of revenge or extra-judicial killings range from 110,000 to 235,000 – appalling at either figure. Another 500,000 people, many Catalan, fled into exile in France and beyond, after Franco's victory. The casualty numbers remain a bone of contention in post-Franco Spain. There has always been an official reticence to examine the Civil war which was, after all, an unconstitutional military putsch against elected democratic governments in both Spain and Catalonia.

Could the Spanish Civil War have had any other outcome, especially for Catalonia? It is possible to imagine that a more robust response to the right in 1934, especially if the ERC had been more organised and the CNT more flexible, might have stymied a military coup. It is also completely feasible that the Spanish Republican government might have taken more effective steps to control the army, following the Popular Front election victory in 1936. On the other hand, given the political differences in Spain at the time – the result of a century and more of economic and social stasis – it is unlikely that civil conflict on some scale could have been avoided. But it certainly could have occurred with a better balance of forces towards the progressives and the mass of the ordinary people.

Again, the Civil War could have been conducted on a different basis. The Republicans could have fought a different war, offering, as the Bolsheviks did in Russian in 1917, to break up the *latifundia* estates and distribute land immediately to the peasants. That could have transformed a conventional, positional war into a guerrilla conflict behind Nationalist lines that would have favoured the Republican side. Accepting the autonomy of Catalonia under a popular administration that directly represented the mass of workers and peasants would have mobilised Catalan sympathies to an even greater extent, and maintained morale in Barcelona. But, of course, such developments would have run counter to the line taken by the bourgeois Republicans and Stalinists in Madrid.

It is also hard to see how a militantly left-wing Spanish Federation would have survived internationally unless it had been able to find foreign allies. That opens an even wider counterfactual discussion. The Spanish Republicans were virtually doomed after the French Popular Front government of Leon Blum – fearful of civil war in France – imposed an arms embargo in 1936, and left Spain to its fate. Yet an alliance of the two left-wing regimes might have transformed the anti-fascist struggle in Europe. A Catalonia receiving arms, aircraft and supplies across the border from France would have been much more difficult for Franco's armies to defeat.

But there we must leave historical conjecture. In the world as it happened, Catalans would now find themselves under the heel of Franco. Independence had never been so far away.

Chapter Five: Under the Iron Heel

We carried the Civil War defeat on our backs like a dead body.
Manuel Vázquez Montalbán[77]

IN JANUARY 1939 General Alvarez Arenas entered Barcelona at the head of a conquering army. General Francisco Franco, with the help of Fascist Italy and Nazi Germany, had occupied Catalonia, a decisive step to victory in the Spanish Civil War. Nearly half a million Catalans had fled across the border into France. Arenas bluntly told his propaganda chief: 'This is a city that has sinned greatly, and it must be sanctified. Altars should be set up in every street of the city to say masses continually.' A Francoist poster put up around the city declared, *Ha llegado Espána* (Spain has arrived)! In effect, Catalonia had been recolonised. It would stay that way for the next four decades: a nation under siege.[78]

Even before the Ebro offensive, Lleida had been captured in April 1938 – the first Catalan city to fall. A proclamation was issued, signed by the new governor, claiming the city was free of the 'separatist yoke' and 'the crime of separatism'. It finished with 'Long live Spanish Lérida!' According to the Catalan historian Conxita Mir:

> ...repression in the Lleida region was indiscriminate and resolute, and was carried out by the military authorities in co-operation with the Falangists and local right-wingers. Dozens of non-combatants were executed merely on the grounds that they were perceived as sympathetic towards the Republican cause. Certain extremely violent acts were perpetrated against women from the Pallarès region.

She puts the number executed in Lleida after trial by Military Courts as 558 with another 148 Republicans executed without trial, while 169 political prisoners were simply murdered.[79]

Franco had abolished the Statute granting Catalan autonomy in April 1938. After entering Barcelona, with immediate effect, Alvarez Arenas banned the public use of the Catalan language and enforced strict censorship. Banned too was the *Sardana*, the traditional circle dance, and Catalan

Christian names. Catalan newspapers were taken over and replaced by pro-regime, Castilian publications. Catalan books were withdrawn from sale, from libraries and from use in schools and universities. All Catalan cultural institutions, theatres and literary societies were disbanded. This was cultural as well as political repression. In one degree or another, it would continue till Franco's death.

This cultural and national oppression was more than Franco's spite. It became a systematic policy designed to eradicate Catalan identity and its separate history. Posters appeared across Catalonia declaring, 'Speak Castilian, the language of Empire'. Between April and August 1939, 700 teachers from Castile and Estremadura were drafted into Catalonia to teach solely in Castilian. Meanwhile half of Barcelona's teaching staff were sacked. Catalan books were pulped and burnt in public. Even the dead were not spared. In Barcelona's Montjuic cemetery the tombs of anarchist heroes like Durutti, Ascaso and Ferrer were destroyed and their human remains scattered.

All of this followed Franco's own narrow conservative ideology. He happily described Catalan as *la lengua de perros* (the language of dogs). Robert Hughes argues that the *Caudillo* never forgave Barcelona for being 'a bastion of resistance' to himself and that he viewed the great port city with particular distaste because it was open to 'strange and non-native ideas'. Barcelona soon came under intense repression. Military tribunals began rooting through the prison camps and the *barrios* of the city for left wingers, republicans, separatists, freemasons and all those deemed enemies of the New Order. In Barcelona, over 1,600 executions took place in the open air at the Camp de la Bota in the Poblenou district. Count Ciano, Mussolini's Minister of Foreign Affairs, claimed that 150 executions a day were taking place in Barcelona in July 1939. Even now, official Spain refuses to follow international law and investigate these crimes.[80]

But this was only the beginning of Barcelona's travails under Franco. The writer Manuel Vázquez Montalbán was born in the defeated city in June 1939. His father, a communist labourer, was imprisoned for five years after the city fell, while his mother (a seamstress and CNT supporter) struggled to keep the family alive. Montalbán vividly recalled 'the post-war deprivation which fell upon the city':

> Cripples, beggars, stub-end tobacco sellers, charlatans, street singers, organ grinders, rag-and-bone men, uniformed Falangists marching to their epic songs: Snowy mountains... flags in the

wind...: Fascist commandos who shaved their heads to the scalp and forced people to drink castor oil to disseminate an emasculating, repressive fear, *estraperlo* (black market), white bread and blonde tobacco sellers and misnamed 'Ideal' cigarettes. Military priests who led punitive processions and urged the mob on to chants like: 'What shall we do with the Protestants? Throw them into the sea.'[81]

The Franco dictatorship's creed was an ideology they called *nacional catolicismo*, Catholic and national, meaning Castilian. Central to it was the army as the symbol and backbone of the Spanish nation, the Catholic Church as its essence, and a centralised and authoritarian state as the instrument to achieve national regeneration. The Falangists, keen as they were on currying favour with Nazi Germany, even took to describing the population as *Judeos-Catalanes*.[82]

Economic change and the eclipse of the Catalan bourgeoisie

Yet none of this prevented the Catalan elite from trying to cosy up to Franco, as Salvador Giner points out:

the upper Catalan bourgeoisie escaped to France... When they came back to Catalonia, they often obtained enormous benefits: they were given sinecures, governorships, important trade licences. Many of them were very active members of the *Lliga*, from whose ranks a great part of the Catalan Francoist establishment arose. Much local government and industrial corruption, in many years to come, had ex-*Lliga* men at its centre.[83]

Meanwhile, attempts to maintain a Catalan leadership in exile in France were struck a blow in 1940, when the Gestapo handed over Lluís Companys to Franco. He was executed at Montjuic, the only European head of state to suffer that fate during World War II. The story goes that his last request was that his shoes be removed so that his feet could feel his land. The loss of Companys created a crisis of leadership in the exiled *Generalitat* and faction fights followed. As well as an ever-present threat of discovery and arrest by the Gestapo, the *Generalitat* also faced a severe shortage of funds. If anything, the divisions between the Catalan parties that had been all too apparent during the Civil War now got worse. As a result, the *Generalitat* ceased to function in anything other than name. The ERC, the real leadership of the independence movement throughout the 1930s, now shrivelled in exile. Effectively it would be re-founded in 1976, after the fall of the dictatorship. External resistance to the regime now passed from Catalan parties to the exiled Spanish Communist Party in Moscow, led by the arch-Stalinists Dolores Ibárruri (known as 'La Pasionaria') and Santiago Carrillo. This had significant political repercussions because the official PCE line remained virulently antagonistic to Catalan separatism. That included hostility to any signs of independent thinking inside the Catalan Communist Party itself. For example, in 1949, Joan Comorera, exiled head of the party's PSUC wing in Catalonia, was expelled for 'bourgeois nationalism' and 'Titoism'. In practice, Comorera's sin was refusing to follow Ibárruri's orders blindly. Comorera was famous for the phrase 'we are Catalan by nature, Spanish by coercion'. Unsurprisingly, he responded to his expulsion by clandestinely re-entering Catalonia and distributing his own opposition newspaper. Carrillo then ordered his execution as a waring to others to toe the Moscow line. However, the Francoists arrested Comorera before that could happen. It is possible he was betrayed by his former comrades with a view to letting the regime take the blame. In 1954, Comorera was sentenced to 30 years imprisonment and entombed in Burgos prison. He died there four years later.

Inside Catalonia, survival was the first order of the day. The Catalan bourgeoisie now made its own accommodation with the regime. Despite the onslaught on all things Catalan the words of the former head of the *Lliga*, Francesc Cambó, speaking in 1943, summed up the feelings of much of the Catalan bourgeoisie:

> I repudiate the regime and wish to see it transformed... but the important thing is the maintenance of internal order and the prevention of the outbreak of a further Civil War and right now the only person that can guarantee this is Franco.[84]

In other words, you could at least count on Franco to keep the workers in order. Catalan big business interests soon benefited from a massive reduction in wages and the absence of restrictive labour laws, courtesy of the regime. However, under Franco the centre of industrial and financial capital continued its drift towards Madrid, and to a lesser extent the Basque Country, a shift continued by the PP government today.

Isolated economically during World War II, then a pariah state before the Cold War changed its political fortunes, the Franco regime was forced to pursue an autarkic economic policy, trying to keep out foreign imports and expand native industry. Rio Tinto's Spanish mining operations were effectively nationalised – typically, the Brits extracted a hefty premium on the price – but the centre of industry still lay in Catalonia. During the 1940s and early 1950s, Catalan industrialists were in the fortunate position of having at their disposal an entirely domesticated work-force. Wage rates were kept low both by force and by virtue of the constant inflow of raw labour from the countryside. Violent accumulation of capital had some positive effects, reflected in the considerable number of new companies set up over the period in Catalonia. The capital invested, however, tended to be much smaller than that of the new companies formed in Madrid and elsewhere: large private enterprises, when constituted, tended to be outside Catalonia. Catalan entrepreneurs during the aftermath years encountered legal difficulties of all sorts, while they were given helpful facilities to transfer their businesses' central offices and set up new ones outside their 'region'.

Likewise, the fascist-inspired autarkic ideology soon prompted the regime to engage in development financed by the state holding company, the INI, modelled on Mussolini's IRI. The INI grew to be a giant, with interests all over Spain. However, the lack of an industrial infrastructure and skills base in the agricultural south made it difficult to ignore Catalonia completely in this process, as did Barcelona's unique location as a major port. As a result, the INI was forced to invest in the region, starting in 1950 with the creation of the SEAT car manufacturer, whose plant outside Barcelona would become the biggest in Spain. INI also invested in a Catalan-based hydroelectric company and in the old Hispano-Suiza automobile and heavy lorry factory (rebranded as Pegaso). Yet, though all these were, and still are, based in Catalonia, managerial control ceased to be Catalan in the traditional sense. We can see a similar process in Scotland, where the post-war era saw the great Scottish-owned engineering and shipbuilding firms nationalised, and their managerial control transferred to London.

As the economy revived through the 1950s and 1960s, local capitalist accumulation and expansion in Catalonia became focused on small and middling-sized enterprises. The commercial banking sector remained weak, in contrast with the powerful Catalan savings bank movement, based on the thrifty habits of the natives. As a result, credit had now to be sought from the large Basque or Madrid banks. The former had direct links with their own heavy industry while the latter (for political reasons) were more inclined to be helpful to companies associated with the regime. This is one reason why a substantial number of new Catalan enterprises in the 1940–53 period opened their head offices in Madrid. They included everything from aircraft and automobile firms to cement and chemicals concerns. Bizarrely, Catalan-owned shipping and forestry companies now had registered offices situated 600km from the Catalan ports and the forests they were managing. All this added to the erosion and political fragmentation of the Catalan big bourgeoisie.

With the onset of the Cold War, and Franco's rapprochement with the West, the Spanish economy was again opened to American and European investment. Competition from abroad became so fierce that many of the traditional Catalan family enterprises – and quite a few of the more advanced, joint-stock ones – opted for selling out to foreign firms. Likewise, incoming multinationals took the initiative in the takeovers and mergers that took place in the 1960s and 1970s, again diminishing the degree of autonomy in local economic decision-making once enjoyed by the local traditional entrepreneurial class.

The influx of foreign investment in Catalonia became a flood after the fall of the regime. This led to something of a revival in the domestic small business sector, with local companies acting as suppliers to the big multinational manufacturers. For these reasons, allied to Barcelona's strategic location as a transport and communications hub, manufacturing has remained important in Catalonia. But the Franco years effectively destroyed the political dominance of the Catalan big bourgeoisie. Resistance to the regime, and leadership of the Catalan national movement, would now increasingly come from below.

The 1951 Barcelona general strike

The guerrilla war campaign waged by isolated bands of militants since the fall of the Republic was mostly suppressed by 1949. Seemingly broken by years of deprivation, repression, and the failure of the armed struggle, working class and nationalist resistance in Catalonia was at a low ebb. That was about to change. One of the first challenges to Francoist repression came from an unlikely source – the Catholic Church; unlikely because its hierarchy and the bulk of the priesthood had fervently backed the Nationalists in the Civil War against the 'godless republic'. But the ban on the use of Catalan was a blow to the Church because in much of rural Catalonia it was the sole language. If the priest could not preach in Catalan he could not be understood.

The iconic Benedictine Abbey of Montserrat, perched high on a rocky outcrop within sight of Barcelona, has always been at the centre of Catalan culture. The annual ceremony in honour of the Black Virgin of Montserrat was and is a key event in the Catalan calendar. In 1947 the monastery held a festival to mark the success of a fund-raising campaign to provide a throne for the Virgin. Over 100,000 people attended, turning the event into a celebration of the Catalan language, culture and resistance to the regime. A sermon was read in Catalan, its first public utterance since the end of the Civil War. And the authorities were powerless to prevent the crowd from singing the Virolai, a Catalan patriotic song, all through a speech by Franco's Foreign Minister, Alberto Martín-Artajo. A giant Catalan *senyera* flag was flown from the mountain above the abbey and it took the Guardia Civil hours to remove it. The episode represented the enduring social strength of Catalan culture and the language – still crucial symbols of resistance to the dictatorship. It also indicated the start of a process of reconciliation between sections of the Catholic Church and the Catalan autonomy movement.

In January 1951, the US Sixth Fleet sailed into Barcelona. It stayed for the next 37 years. It was the first time the city had been open to the world since the end of the Civil War. Barcelona would have a love-hate relationship with the Americans. They brought with them new music, bubble gum, new ideas and (above all) pockets stuffed with dollars. But this was the Cold War and the arrival of the US military meant the West had made its peace with the Franco regime. The Yankee dollar provided the regime with the foreign currency it needed to survive. On the other hand, it condemned Spain and Catalonia to another 25 years of dictatorship.

The war-ravaged Barcelona first glimpsed by those American sailors was almost Third World. Bombed-out buildings were everywhere. As they disembarked, they would have headed for El Raval (the port's red light district) which was still in virtual ruins as a punishment for supporting the Republic. But in hungry Barcelona, American dollars instantly boosted local morale – not to mention the sex industry. Prostitutes quickly hiked their prices from 15 pesetas to five dollars (115 pesetas). Bars, tailors and souvenir shops also boomed. Francoism's straitlaced conservative culture was suddenly challenged by the revolutionary appeal of American consumerism: jeans, Coca

Cola, Lucky Strikes and nylons. Jazz and Rock 'n' Roll were soon emanating from little bars in Carrer Escudellers. Night life had returned to Barcelona and with it, hope. And with hope came defiance.

In 1951, Barcelona was the scene for the biggest act of popular resistance since the Republican defeat. Post-Civil War Spain was still gripped by poverty and Francoist repression. Over 150,000 people lived in caves or open fields around Barcelona, with many thousands more sleeping on the streets of the city. Areas bombed during the fighting had seen little repair work, and many people lived without plumbing or electricity. More than a decade after the conflict, the regime still held over 200,000 political prisoners in jail or labour camps.

The spark that finally ignited open defiance after years of submission came from the most innocuous source: a 40 per cent increase in Barcelona tram fares. Opposition forces called a boycott. For two weeks trams and buses ran with no passengers as the population refused to pay the increased price. On the first Saturday of the protest, FC Barcelona were playing Racing Santander at their Les Corts stadium on the edge of the city. Despite heavy rain fans made their way to and from the game on foot – a 40-minute journey. The local Governor General, Eduardo Baeza Alegría, explained to the exasperated regime in Madrid that, 'I can't shoot at citizens who simply don't use a means of transport.' Instead, he tried to encourage strikebreakers by using the tram himself. This ended in public humiliation for the regime when Baeza Alegría's tram took a wrong turn and crashed into a stone barricade.

In a bid to defuse the situation, the official Francoist 'trade union' in Barcelona convened a meeting of 2,000 workplace representatives from across the city. The plan was to allow the boycotters to let off steam. This too backfired. One participant recalled that union officials 'finished the meeting by signing *Cara al Sol*' [Face the Sun, the Falangist anthem] and then told them to go home.' But no-one moved. Instead, the rank and file Barcelona workers held their own impromptu meeting and declared a general strike. In the end they had to be removed by Guardia Civil. The next day the fare increase was annuled. [85]

Matters did not end there. On the following Monday, the general strike went ahead but now with the purpose of freeing those arrested during the tram boycott. Beginning in the textile mills of the Poblenou area, the strike quickly spread to involve workers in metallurgical and chemical plants, communications, construction, government workers, and taxi and tram drivers. Some 300,000 workers joined the general strike, including many in the nearby cities of Badalona, Sabadell, Tarrasa and Mataro. The regime mobilised thousands of troops and Guardia Civil, and four warships carrying hundreds of marines were docked in Barcelona harbour (shades of what happened in the 1-o referendum). Clashes took place across the city, and thousands of strikers were arrested and imprisoned for the duration of the strike. Order was eventually restored but the regime was badly scared. Terrified by the prospect of further unrest, the regime released the vast majority of those arrested, and ordered employers to pay full wages to those on strike. Governor Baeza Alegría, the mayor of Barcelona, the police chief and the head of the official trade union were all fired.

The Barcelona general strike of 1951 had repercussions. Several weeks later, disturbances flared up in the Basque lands, in Vizcaya and Guipúzcoa. In late April a general strike took place in Bilbao, involving some 250,000 workers from docks, arms plants, metal factories, and textile plants. The movement then spread beyond the traditional areas of resistance in Catalonia and the Basque country. A large strike broke out in Pamplona during which workers attacked the Falange party headquarters. Transport workers in Madrid also went on strike during May. The motivation for this unrest was primarily economic but in the absence of democracy any protest could quickly turn against the regime.

Language and culture as forms of resistance

The Barcelona tram boycott and strike represented a major victory but in a way it was the final act of defiance by a generation who had lost the Civil War. In future new forces would come to take centre stage in the opposition to the regime. One casualty was the anarcho-syndicalist CNT, which had dominated the Catalan working class up until Franco's victory. In the wake of the Civil War defeat, the CNT suffered the brunt of post-war repression. Between 1939 and 1952, 73 per cent of those executed belonged to the CNT. The result was that the CNT lost 80 per cent of its membership between 1945 and 1960. As a political force in Catalonia, anarchism was dead.

Meanwhile, political repression continued unabated. In 1952, despite the fact that an International Eucharistic Congress was being held in the city, five executions took place in Barcelona's Camp de la Bota. But as the 1950s progressed, a new generation was taking up the struggle against the regime. In 1956, students at Barcelona University used the suppression of the Hungarian Revolution by the Soviet Union as an opportunity to demonstrate in solidarity with another small nation being subjected by a far larger neighbour. Franco responded by shutting down the university temporarily. From then on, the universities remained a bastion of anti-Franco, pro-Catalan resistance.

The 1950s also saw an amazing revival of literary publishing in Catalonia – though in Castilian, to circumvent censorship rules. However, the contradictory result was to give Catalonia both an international voice and a major publishing industry. The prime mover in this was an unlikely source: José Manuel Lara, founder and owner of what would become one of Catalonia and Spain's biggest media empires, Grupo Planeta. Lara came to Barcelona with Franco's conquering armies and stayed, marrying a woman from the Catalan middle class, María Teresa Bosch. Their mutual love of literature led Lara to establish a small publishing house, Planeta, in 1949. The endeavour floundered for lack of a market until Maria Lara chanced on the manuscript of *The Cypresses Believe in God,* by the Catalan writer José María Gironella. This was one of the first novels to portray the Civil War. It was published by Planeta (in Castillian) in 1953 and became an instant success. This novel would become the foundation of modern Catalan literature.

Though anything but a Catalan nationalist, Lara's liberal inclinations led him to turn his publishing house into a lifeboat for opponents of the dictatorship. His protégés would include Manuel Vázquez Montalbán, who found employment with Planeta in the 1960s after being released from Franco's jails. Lara persuaded Montalbán to turn novelist, publishing his iconic (and gently subversive) Pepe Carvalho crime novels. Lara would act as a bridge between the Catalan business community and opponents of the regime, especially the PCE in exile. He boasted that Dolores Ibárruri had cooked him an unforgettable tortilla in Moscow. Ironically, Lara and Planeta would vehemently oppose Catalan independence, in later years.

In 1957, Barcelona got a new appointed mayor, Josep Maria de Porcioles. A lawyer and former member of the *Lliga*, Porcioles had left Spain at the start of the Civil War. He returned to make his peace with Franco and was eventually rewarded with a 16-year stint as city boss of Barcelona. His period in office saw an unregulated building boom, massive corruption, the neglect of the city's great architectural heritage, and the arrival in greater Barcelona of some 750,000 immigrants from the rest of Spain. The result was overcrowding and urban sprawl on a truly massive scale. True, Porcioles relaxed some of the anti-Catalan cultural repression – the *sardanas* and *castellers* could again be seen in public. The trams were replaced by a new metro system and Barcelona recovered some of its international commercial reputation. But Porcioles' main job was to keep Catalan resistance under strict control, party by creating jobs at any price, and partly by buying off what was left of the Catalan big bourgeoisie with construction contracts.

Yet the resistance continued to make a nuisance of itself at every opportunity. On 19 May 1960, the regime permitted a concert celebrating the centenary of the renowned Catalan poet (and arch-nationalist) Joan Maragall. Various Francoist ministers were set to attend. When the Civil Governor heard that Maragall's Catalanist anthem *Cant de la Senyera* was to be included in the programme, it was immediately prohibited by the censors. However, during the packed concert in the Palau de la Música Catalana, the audience began to sing the song. The police reacted violently, and arrests were made. A few days later a young Catholic Catalan nationalist, Jordi Pujol, was arrested and charged with organising the incident. Pujol was tortured before being hauled before a court martial and sentenced to seven years in prison. Famously, he would become President of the *Generalitat* in 1980.

A new Catalan leadership was emerging. In early 1966, more than a thousand students occupied the Economics Faculty of the University of Barcelona. Then in March 1966, 500 student delegates, together with staff and Catalan intellectuals, met to form a new independent student union – the *Sindicat Democràtic d'Estudiants de la Universitat de Barcelona*, or the Democratic Student Union of the University of Barcelona. The event became known as the *Caputxinada* after the Capuchin convent in the Barcelona suburb of Sarrià where it took place – another sign that the Church was making overtures to the Catalan resistance. The new union quickly won near-total support on campus, with 20 per cent of students actively involved. It organised a major concert with the famous Valencian Catalanist singer Raimon, whose working-class lyrics had broken away from traditional middle-class preoccupations. In response, the dictatorship expelled over 100 students and professors and suspended all student registrations to the University of Barcelona for a full academic year. Over the coming years student protests would be a thorn in Franco's side. As one frustrated police commander noted:

> If they get hurt, they show their battle wounds to their friends;
> if they get arrested, they become martyrs and their lecturers pass
> them even though they know nothing.[86]

Resistance was now spreading to popular culture. In 1961, the Catalan record label Edigsa was established, as was Òmnium Cultural. Most important was the emergence of Nova Cançó, a new wave of Catalan protest songs exemplified by the music of Raimon. Singing only in Catalan, Raimon was effectively barred from Spanish television. Nevertheless, he performed to packed houses. One of the poems he sang was by the 15th century poet, Ausiás March, from Valencia, the major Catalan poet of the time. It went:

> We have lived to guard words for you.
> To return the name of each thing.
> You lose names, you lose precision,
> You lose your place in the world if your
> Culture and language are crushed.[87]

Maria del Mar Bonet sang about the police who had 'persuaded' a student to 'jump' from a window thus:

> What do they want, these people
> Who knock in the early morning?[88]

In 1968, Joan Manel Serrat was chosen to sing for Spain in the Eurovision Song Contest – held that year in Madrid – but he refused unless he could sing in Catalan. He was immediately replaced. As it happened, Spain won with Serrat's song performed in Castilian by Massiel, beating the UK entry *Congratulations* sung by Cliff Richard by just one point. A 2008 documentary on Spanish television claimed that Franco had the results rigged.

Perhaps the biggest star of the Nova Cançó was Lluís Llach who turned down a mega recording contract because it required him to sing in Castilian. He wrote *L'estaca* (The Stake) which became the anthem of Catalonia's 1968 generation of rebels:

> If you pull it all the way, it'll fall
> And it can't last long.
> So push, push it down
> It must be rotted through by now
> If I pull it hard this way
> And you pull it hard that way,
> So push, push it down
> And we can all be free.[89]

Not only would Lluís Llach famously sing *L'estaca* at the first public concert following the end of the dictatorship, he would return to sing it in person at the final rally of 70,000 people in Barcelona before the 1-0 referendum.

Return of working class resistance

But no matter how widespread the student revolt, and no matter how impassioned the songs, confronting the dictatorship and restoring democracy required heavier social forces. The year 1962 saw the revival across Spain of popular working-class resistance when strikes in the Basque country spread to Barcelona, then to Madrid and Valencia, with the 40,000 Asturian miners then joining in. With one-eighth of the entire workforce on strike the regime was forced to grant major concessions for the first time.

The strikers had created a new form of organisation, the Workers' Commission. Because trade unions were illegal, the only way the workforce could voice its grievances was by electing a delegation to address management. These began to organise at regional level, then across the Spanish state, with activists using the 1966 elections for the lowest level of organisation to the state sanctioned 'union' – the *Organizacion Sindical*. Workers' Commission supporters were elected and used their new position to build their own, underground organisation. Armando Baró, a workers' leader in the SEAT car plant explained:

> It went against the grain to participate in these state controlled structures, but I think we were right. We had to wriggle into every crack that opened in the system... [they] gave you a certain legal gloss that allowed you to move.[90]

This argument is reinforced by historian Angel Smith:

> In some respects, *Comisiones* took up the heritage of the CNT (indeed they were largely dominant in the same areas as the CNT in the 1930s). They combined a weak central organisation with the power to mobilise whole factories or even regions. Yet the Communists were far better equipped to lead the movement in the context of Francoism than the anarchists could ever be; they were prepared to operate within the OSE (ideologically anathema to the anarchists), and had a hard core of clandestine militants hierarchically organised, thereby making it difficult for the regime to totally to dismember the movement.[91]

In 1967 the Workers' Commissions held a national congress. Initially, the regime seemed prepared to tolerate them because industrial unrest would adversely affect the growing economy. But at the end of that year it cracked down, declaring the Commissions illegal, imposing a wage freeze, and jailing a thousand activists. Many more were simply sacked. The Guardia Civil were now unleashed against strikers and protesters. In each year between 1969 and 1974 at least one striker was gunned down by police.

September 1967 also saw the Workers' Commissions take part for the first time in events to mark Catalan National Day – *La Diada*. In turn, this became the first National Day to involve significant numbers of the 1.5 million immigrants from the rest of Spain who had flocked to Catalonia in search of work. This migration had been deliberately fostered by the Franco regime in a bid to dilute Catalan nationalism. Now some of those immigrants, and certainly their Catalan-born children, were not only being assimilated into the local culture but adopting Catalanism as a badge of resistance to the regime.

True, in the vast, ugly working-class estates and satellite towns surrounding Barcelona (courtesy of Mayor Porcioles) Castilian Spanish still dominated and the local atmosphere was (and still is) more Andalusian than Catalan. But by the late 1960s, new neighbourhood organisations were emerging as part of the new spirit of popular resistance against the hated regime. These *Associacions de Veïns* (neighbourhood associations) began as self-help organisations dedicated to improving living and housing standards in the slum neighbourhoods that had resulted from Porcioles building boom. By 1970 they existed in every one of Barcelona's *barri*.

Carlos Prieto, a member of the Communist PSUC, led the neighbourhood association in Sants. He recalled:

> Before 1973–1974 it was an uphill battle. People were often reluctant to sign petitions. 'Of course we agree with you, but we can't sign,' they'd say. Fear in Franco's Spain was ubiquitous. The fall of [Mayor] Porcioles gave people in Barcelona confidence. In Sants we had meetings of up to 150, most of them overjoyed just to be able to speak and hear Catalan... And in 1974 we won the battle with our alternative Plaça de Sants. We defeated the idea for a flyover and we got the old tram depot, the Coxteres, converted into a Community Centre.[92]

The dying regime returns to violent repression

In Madrid, however, the Bunker – the hardliners in the regime – were in control. For many the opening up of the Spanish economy and the rise of the Commissions had seemed to point towards an early demise for Francoism. But as ever the Generalissimo's response was to reach for the gun and the *garrote.* 1969 was a dark year with a state of emergency declared, giving security forces a free hand to arrest, detain and torture opponents of Franco's rule. The political police in Barcelona produced a report detailing 448 oppositionists, listing 35 as socialists, 188 as Communists, 67 as Christian Democrats and 147 as 'Catalan separatists'.

In 1970, the regime staged a show trial in Burgos, Franco's HQ in the Civil War, of 12 supporters of ETA, the Basque separatist guerrilla group. They were tried before a military tribunal rather than a civilian court. Six were sentenced to death, with the rest being jailed for 30 years. But the trial backfired when a huge wave of protest swept across Spain. In Barcelona, there were street fights with police as 3,000 students and workers took to the streets. At the Abbey of Montserrat – scene of that great protest in 1947 – 300 Catalan writers, artists and intellectuals held an illegal assembly to protest against the ETA trials. Besieged in the building by the armed Guardia Civil, they only left after two days. Under international pressure, Franco commuted the ETA death sentences.

With the rising tide of Francoist repression, the various forms of Catalan opposition came together in November 1971 under a new umbrella organisation – *Assemblea de Catalunya.* The first formal meeting of the *Assemblea* was at the Church of Sant Augustí in the Raval neighbourhood of Barcelona but its platform had been thrashed out the previous summer in meetings held in the working-class neighbourhood of Sant Andreu. The initiative was taken by the Communist PSUC but it quickly broadened to include the majority of Catalan political parties, trades unions and civic organisations. Its slogan was *Llibertat! Amnistia! Estatut d'Autonomia!* – Liberty! Amnesty! Statute of Autonomy!

From then on, as the dictatorship entered its death throes, most popular resistance against the regime was organised by the *Assemblea.* It also led the demonstrations, such as the *Marxa de la Llibertat* in 1976, the year after the dictator's death, and was a constant force in keeping the broad front of opposition initiatives together. With its purpose served, the *Assemblea* dissolved itself once the post-Franco transition was under way in the late 1970s. However, the symbolic name and mission remained buried in the Catalan political subconscious and would be revived in the creation of the contemporary *Assemblea Nacional Catalana* (Catalan National Assembly) in 2012, with Carme Forcadell as its first president.

The unity of the resistance achieved in Catalonia – Communist, Socialist, nationalist, religious, civic – was not achieved in the Basque Country.

Not only was the PNV opposed to ETA, but the latter also had various break-aways. The unity achieved in Catalonia meant that there was little or no support for a strategy of armed struggle. Not so in the Basque lands.

The morning of 20 December 1973, at 9.36am, a huge bomb planted by ETA militants blasted the black Dodge Dart carrying Prime Minister Luis Car-rero Blanco, Franco's eminence grise and designated heir, 35 metres straight up into the air. The car sailed over a building and teetered on the eaves of the roof before crashing down into the inner courtyard. The regime reacted to the assassination like a wounded animal. In 1974 it took its revenge: two young men – neither a member of ETA – were strangled to death by the garrotte in Catalonia, the last to suffer this horrific form of execution. One was Salvador Puig Antich, an anarchist, who was sentenced to death for killing a member of the Guardia Civil. The other was an illegal refugee from East Germany called Georg Michael Welzel, who shot a policeman probably because he feared being returned home. Welzel took half an hour to die. There were protests in Catalonia, across Spain and worldwide. This time the regime ignored them. It was a reminder to the world that Franco's Spain was still a brutal tyranny.

But the Catalan working class were no longer cowed. In 1974, inflation was running at 25 per cent while wages were held down. Strikes spread like wildfire. In Barcelona, there was a huge strike by workers at the SEAT car plant, demanding higher pay and the reinstatement of those victimised ear-lier. One report described the scenes in the city: 'In those weeks there were demonstrations in Barcelona with people chanting "End the Dictatorship" and "SEAT will win"'. The strike did not end in a complete victory, but it did transform the atmosphere in the city, which was becoming the bulwark of the resistance to Franco. In the final days of Franco's regime supporters of the Commissions were actually declaring strikes from the headquarters of the official trade union in the Baix Llobregat area of Barcelona.[93]

Popular culture in Catalonia equals FC Barcelona and it was hardly a surprise that the rising tide of working class opposition to the dying regime would find itself reflected through football. This coincided with the arrival at FC Barcelona in 1974 of the great Dutch player (and later coach) Johan Cruyff. During Cruyff's first season, Barca played football not just with professional élan but also with particular zeal against the one opponent that mattered – Real Madrid, the football incarnation of Spanish-Castilian domination and Franco's favourite team. In 1974, Barca beat Real with a humiliating 5-0 on the latter's home ground at *Santiago Bernabéu* Stadium.

Real Madrid's club president, the eponymous Bernabéu, was a Franco loyalist, had been an officer in the Nationalist armies that invaded Catalonia, and was renowned for hating all things Catalan. Nicknamed *El Salvador*, Cruyff went out of his way to defy the regime publicly – ostentatiously he registered his son with the Catalan name Jordi, technically outlawed. At a time when flying the Catalan flag was still banned, the very similar FC Barca club symbol (no coincidence) served as a substitute for hundreds of thousands of Catalans.

Meanwhile the executions continued virtually to the end. Two months before Franco died in November 1975 five members of ETA and a left-wing guerrilla group were shot. By then neither of the strategies pursued by rival groups around Franco – technocratic reform or the straightforward repression favoured by the Bunker – were viable. Repression could not deal with a sea of industrial unrest in Catalonia, Asturias and the Basque Country. Equally, the international recession which followed the 1973 hike in oil prices had killed any technocratic hopes that increased prosperity would buy off political and economic discontent. The dictatorship would have to go. The only question at issue was: could it be dismantled in such a manner that the Francoist oligarchy could retain its wealth and privileges, and without the long-oppressed Catalans and Basques seizing their independence?

Franco ha muerto

On 20 November 1975, Prime Minister Carlos Arias Navarro announced to Spain that *Franco ha muerto*, Franco is dead. An old crony of the dictator, Navarro had been public prosecutor in the trials set up after the Nationalists took Málaga in early 1937. There he earned the nickname 'The Butcher of Málaga' (*Carnicero de Málaga*). Under the Butcher, 20,000 Republican prisoners were executed. Like his boss, he was never brought to justice.

The long nightmare was over in Catalonia. It was almost an anti-climax. Manuel Vázquez Montalbán describes Barcelona's muted reaction to Franco's demise:

> ...throughout 20 November 1975, the city filled with silent passers-by, walls reflected in their eyes, their throats dried by prudent silence. Up the Rambla and down. As ever. Security guards, police and paramilitaries observed the muted demonstrations while with their sixth sense they heard the 'Hymn of Joy', sung by the hidden soul of the 'Rose of the fire', by the cautious soul of the widowed

city, by the wise soul of the occupied city. Above the skyline of the Collserola mountains, champagne corks soared into the autumn twilight. But nobody heard a sound. Barcelona was, after all, a city which had been taught good manners. Silent in both its joy and its sadness.[94]

That legacy at least would take time to change. The Irish writer Colm Tóibín came to stay in Barcelona in 1975. He recalls:

People lived in a private realm. The parents had moved into that realm at the end of the Civil War, and they had remained in that realm... But what was also interesting was that Catalan, the language, was considered a way of being free... No one was talking about history. No one was talking about politics. But people were talking in Catalan. And they considered that a fundamental way of resisting, or being apart from official Spain, or the regime.[95]

Politics would soon return to Catalonia, though few in 1975 could have predicted that it would be another generation before independence was on the agenda. In the interregnum, Francoism would be replaced by a corrupt, strange, sham democracy – albeit one that retained all the same authoritarian instincts as the dictatorship itself.

Chapter Six: Flawed Democratic Transition

¡La calle es mía! (The streets are mine!)
Manuel Fraga, Franco's Interior Minister later founder of the PP
The transition is, basically, a process of historical and social amnesia...
achieving the unheard of situation in which the dictatorship's juridico-
political framework became the source of legitimacy for the new democratic
model

Salvador
Cardús i Ros[96]

IN THE THREE YEARS following Franco's death a new Spanish regime was constructed out of the old, culminating in 1978 in the promulgation of a new, so-called democratic constitution. The founding myth of this new '1978 regime' is that it represented a complete, democratic rupture with the old, fascist order. It is a comforting myth used by successive Spanish governments to oppose Catalan self-determination, jail elected representatives for daring even to debate Catalan self-determination, ban political opponents, exclude elected Deputies from the *Cortes*, employ indiscriminate police violence against peaceful demonstrators, and even justify a secret war of murder against Basque nationalists. At the same time the 1978 regime has claimed immunity from investigating any of the abuses of human rights perpetrated by the Franco regime between 1936 and 1975, in contravention of international law. And it has used the post-Franco settlement – with its politically biased judiciary – to protect the most financially corrupt oligarchy in Western Europe while it looted and pillaged the Spanish economy.

Far from being a democratic paragon, the '78 Regime was a flawed compromise foisted on opponents of the Franco era under duress and the ultimate threat of another military coup. Those who ran or benefited from the old regime were granted immunity and left with their economic power intact, by naïve democrats anxious to avoid further bloodshed or seduced by the lure of a fast access to power. Understandably, the long years of fascist repression in Catalonia had made its leaders unwilling to risk a new Civil War and prepared to accept limited autonomy as an initial goal. They failed to understand that the 1978 constitution, with its absolute refusal ever to countenance the division of Holy Spain, was a legal booby trap deliberately concocted to block any move toward self-determination. Above all, the genuine democrats who signed up to the '78 Regime and constitution failed to reform the security apparatus or change its rapid anti-secessionist, anti-left bias.

Ruptura pactada versus rupture democratica

Because the sham democracy that constitutes the post-Franco state has taken in so many, it is important to analyse the flawed transition from the Franco regime in greater detail. Throughout the winter of 1976 the old regime seemed still to be in existence, despite the Dictator's death. The new head of state was Prince Juan Carlos, son of the royalist claimant to the throne. He had been educated by fascist tutors and was surrounded now by Francoist ministers. In March 1976, the city of Vitoria, in the Basque province of Araba, saw a general strike across the city in solidarity with a number of ongoing strikes. Although situated in the Basque country, it had not opposed Franco in 1936 and had little history of militancy. The Guardia Civil were ordered to open fire if they could not disperse protesters, and did so, killing five. The strike spread across the Basque Country and 100,000 people came to the funerals. When the Interior Minister, Manuel Fraga, visited the wounded in Vitoria's hospital one of them looked up and exclaimed, 'Have you come to finish me off?'

In the old days, Fraga might well have ordered the 'disappearance' of the impudent protestor. Previously, as Franco's Minister of Information, Fraga had delighted in announcing (and justifying) the shooting of enemies of the state. But he was also a natural opportunist – after many twists and turns, he later became creator and first President of the *Partido Popular*. Back in Vitoria in 1976, Fraga realised that a revolution was brewing. His conclusion: 'We cannot afford a Vitoria soviet';[97] not because he was squeamish, but rather because the resulting chaos would wreck Spain's chances of joining the European Community.

Left-wing historians Emmanuel Rodríguez and Isidró Lopez explain Fraga's fears:

> His number two, the shadowy and chameleon-like Rodolfo Martin Villa, said he was 'more scared of Cornellá [a working-class district of Barcelona] than of ETA'.[98] The dictatorship's party recognised that its problems came from an uncontrollable labour

movement, not an armed group that, at the end of the day, could be managed through state power.

Fraga also grasped that, faced with such working class insurgency, he was too compromised to oversee the unavoidable transition to parliamentary democracy. Craftily he ceded that role to an ambitious and unqualified but photogenic young technocrat, Adolfo Suárez – unqualified except that he had a (relatively) cleaner pair of hands than Fraga. Mind you, Suárez had been Secretary General of the National Movement, Spain's sole legal political party. But a month before Franco's death, Suárez had told the ageing Caudillo that democracy was inevitable. Suárez was appointed Prime Minister by Juan Carlos on 3 July 1976. Fraga continued to pull strings in the background.

The way was now clear for the reformist wing of the Francoist regime to approach the main opposition groups with a deal that would introduce a form of parliamentary democracy as quickly as possible, to forestall industrial unrest turning into social revolution. This meant persuading the Socialists and Communists to drop their traditional commitment to a *ruptura democratica*, a complete democratic break with Francoism, the monarchy and – ultimately – capitalism itself. For big businesses and the ruling elite, any democratic rupture in those terms was to be avoided at all costs. The alternatives were either a Pinochet-style crackdown that would bring pariah-status within Europe, or a cautious shift towards a liberal-democratic framework that kept the economic ownership structure intact. But how to democratise without opening the door to the radical traditions of the masses – republicanism, socialism, communism, and, lurking in the wings, Catalan and Basque secession? The management of the transition would have to remain in elite hands and necessary deals done. Equally, obdurate elements in the old Francoist apparatus, the Army and the Guardia Civil would have to be persuaded of the necessity of reform if they were to keep their jobs and their heads.

On the streets, things were seen differently – Catalan nationalism had re-emerged. The *Assemblea de Catalunya* – under its slogan 'Liberty, Amnesty and Statute of Autonomy' – called for five separate marches, starting from different towns, to converge on 11 September 1976 (Catalan National Day) at the Monastery of Poblet, a Cistercian foundation located at the foot of the Prades Mountains. Police and the Guardia Civil attacked the marchers as they set out. One hundred and fifty people were arrested, and many received jail sentences. Despite everything, 300 people managed to meet at Poblet.

Meanwhile the main *Diada* demonstration was taking place in Sant Boi de Llobregat, near Barcelona, the burial place of the Catalan patriot Rafael Casanova. Some 80,000 people attended.

By now key sections of the Spanish elite and their counterparts in Western Europe and North America were becoming very nervous. If the dictatorship would not go, then it looked as if a general strike to force it out was on the cards. Across the border they had seen that the overthrow of a similar regime in Portugal in April 1974 had led to a revolutionary crisis. The solution now was to accelerate the *ruptura pactada* rather than a *rupture democratica* – a break by agreement rather than one involving popular forces.

In the summer of 1976 Suárez hurriedly unveiled a Law for Political Reform. This proposed setting up a two-chamber *Cortes*; the Congress of Deputies, elected by proportional representation, and a Senate by first past the post. That December it was put to a referendum, and 94 per cent of voters backed it. Suárez had entered into negotiations with the leader of the Socialist PSOE, Felipe González. The PSOE hardly existed on the ground after decades in exile, but it received a lot of support from the ruling German Social Democrats. Suárez and González agreed on elections by June 1977 and an amnesty for political prisoners. The Communist Party, a mainstay of the anti-fascist opposition, was still illegal. But González, with an eye to capturing the centre left, said he would contest the elections even if that remained the case. Suárez had split the opposition from day one.

In fact, the Communists were secretly negotiating their own *ruptura pactada* with the King and Suárez. The long-time leader of the Spanish Communist Party in exile was Santiago Carrillo, a hard-boiled Stalinist executioner. To everyone's great surprise he embraced the monarchy, calling Juan Carlos 'the hinge between the apparatus of the State and the authentic aspirations of civil society.'[99] The PCE urged its supporters to back a 'national reconciliation' and promised a social contract with employers and the state if it and the trade unions were legalised. Any notion of elections to a constituent assembly, to draw up a fair new constitution, was history. This reformist turn shocked many in the Party. Was it Stalinist cynicism designed to allow the PCE and PSUC (its Catalan branch) room to organise openly for the first time since the Civil War? In fact, Carrillo was quite prepared to embrace openly a reformist agenda, as he showed in early 1977 when, together with communist party leaders Georges Marchais of France and Enrico Berlinguer of Italy, he publicly launched the Eurocommunist movement at in a joint meeting held in Madrid.

In June 1977, the first post-Franco elections were held. Suárez's Union of the Democratic Centre won over a third of the votes across Spain. González's PSOE got 28.5 per cent, the Communists just 9.3 per cent and Fraga's Popular Alliance (seen as the party of Franco's Bunker) a mere 8.4 per cent. But in Catalonia things were different. The Communist PSUC came second with 18.31 per cent, with the Socialists taking 28.56 per cent. The still illegal ERC, standing under a pro-independence 'Left of Catalonia' banner, won a seat in Barcelona. Two groups supporting Catalan autonomy won 22.55 per cent. They later merged as Union and Convergence, led by Jordi Pujol. Progressive forces were alive and growing in Catalonia while the Spanish heartlands still rallied to the right. But in one footnote to history, the Civil War POUM – hugely weakened during the long years of dictatorship – polled a derisory vote in the 1977 elections and simply melted away.

How do we explain these results, which confirmed the old neo-Francoist politicians in power in Madrid, ending any hope of a clean break with the past? The media, representing the views of the oligarchy, had been overwhelmingly pro-Suárez. González had put himself forward as a left winger but one who would not antagonise the army and the Guardia Civil. The Communists had emerged from obscurity only a few weeks before the election and had little presence in much of Spain. The right had the money and the contacts. The left had the people on its side, but the whole point of these rushed elections was to demobilise the mass movement and restore normalcy in the factories. This plan succeeded admirably.

Of course, it is possible to argue that the *ruptura pactada* was the pragmatic best that could have been achieved without precipitating another Civil War. However, the example of neighbouring Portugal gives the lie to such a conservative view. The Salazar-Caetano regime was no less repressive than Franco's. Yet it was swept away completely after 1974. Initially, Caetano was removed from office in a putsh by conservative military officers, but only to forestall a popular revolution. The generals then sought to construct a new regime which would grant some democratic concessions – including ending Portugal's disastrous colonial war in Africa – yet allow the old elite to remain in real control. However, the popular movement (including younger officers and conscripts) refused to compromise. As a result, the left-wing parties, including the dominant Communists, remained committed to electing a constituent assembly to draft a new, democratic constitution. This was precisely the programme abandoned by the PCE and PSOE leadership in Spain.

We should also note that during the Portuguese democratic revolution the aging Franco regime contemplated military intervention to prevent the left gaining power next door. Despite that latent threat, the brave Portuguse people did not waver in their desire to dismantle their own dictatorship. Matters were different in Spain in 1976, because there was no neighbouring fascist regime on hand to offer Franco's heirs military support against the popular, democratic movement. On the contrary, had Fraga and elements of the military and Guardia Civil tried mass repression, the likelihood would have been an economic boycott by the European Community. Which, of course, is why Fraga himself opted for using the more presentable Suárez to negotiate a deal with the PSOE and PCE.

The first order of business in the newly elected *Cortes* was an amnesty for any crimes committed during the Franco era. In another set of backroom negotiations, the so-called *Pacto del Olvido* (Pact of Forgetting) was agreed between the parties. This aimed to draw a line under the Spanish Civil War, in effect burying discussion of it so as not to embarrass those who'd loyally served Franco but had now rebranded themselves as democrats. An amnesty was also declared for all those involved in acts of violence before 1977, shielding those involved in torture and human rights abuses during the dictatorship right up to the elections. In October 1977, this amnesty was given the force of law. It was the first major piece of legislation passed by the new parliament.

As we have seen subsequently, both in Northern Ireland and South Africa, it would have been perfectly possible to have combined an amnesty for ancient Civil War crimes and a truth commission that investigated the facts, dug up the unmarked mass graves, and afforded victims and their families a sense of closure. It would have been possible to investigate more recent incidents fairly, with a view to identifying police and Guardia Civil excesses. Any normal reconciliation process might have expected a decree of contrition from the Francoists. Instead there was a blanket amnesia and a legal bar on any victim of the old regime seeking justice or restitution. Forty years on, the PP and the Spanish right still defend this historic censorship, proving their unwillingness to criticise the Franco era.

Worse, this refusal to investigate past crimes against humanity is in contravention of international law. The UN General Assembly's 1992 declaration and convention on the protection of people against forced disappearance, which Spain ratified in 2009, expressly forbids the use of amnesty laws for such crimes. Over 114,000 men and women 'disappeared' during and after the Civil War, executed by the Francoists and dumped in unmarked graves; another 30,000 children were stolen from their Republican parents. There is no statute of limitations for such crimes. In 2013, the United Nations called on the Spanish government to overturn the 1977 amnesty law. It refused.

The transition, the Left and the economy

The transition from the Franco era was not conditioned solely by political questions. For Spain's ruling class, the economy loomed large. At a global level, the 1970s saw the first Oil Crisis, near hyper-inflation in many countries, and a halt to the long, post-war industrial boom. The modest, low-productivity Spanish economy was soon battered by these tidal economic forces. The regime now faced not only a rise in working-class militancy but the growing disenchantment of sections of the business community desperate to modernise the economy. Between 1973 and 1977, annual inflation never fell below 15 per cent while unemployment rose more than two and a half times. With social and economic unrest growing, employers demanded free market 'reforms'.

In October 1977, Suárez convened negotiations between employers, the government and nine major party leaders – including the PSOE and Communist Party – in Madrid's ornate Palace of Moncloa, the Prime Minister's new official residence. In what became known as the Moncloa Pacts, they agreed to wage restraint, tax rises and cuts in public spending to 'save' the economy. In return, the left parties were offered a miserly increase in unemployment benefit. No trade union representatives were involved in these negotiations. On the contrary, the leaderships of both the PSOE and PCE ordered their respective trade union federations to restrain workers from demonstrating against the new austerity measures.

The Moncola Pacts struck a serious blow to the morale of the 200,000 strong Spanish Communist Party, key organisers of the working class, who were now expected to prevent strikes and protests. In Manuel Vázquez Montálban's political thriller, *Southern Seas*, a woman Communist worker at the SEAT car plant in Barcelona explains:

> No-one swallowed this pact and we, with all the good faith we were capable of, had to go out and defend it... that in the long run it benefited the working class, in short, we said what they had told us to say. Afterwards, it became clear it was a swindle, like all the rest.[100]

It was a swindle in more ways than one. There was a political as well as an economic cost to the working class. Because Suárez was willing to negotiate directly with the PSOE and PCE on the transition to democracy and on the economy – seeming to incorporate them directly into the transition process – both Socialists and Communists felt able to drop their demands for an immediate dismantling of the Francoist state and for the formation of a provisional government. The old corporatism of the Franco regime was admirably suited to such private wheeling and dealing. While González and Carrillo believed they were honoured guests at the top table in the Moncloa Palace, their rank and file – the real power of the working class – had been demobilised. That left the institutional power base of the old regime still intact, though under a 'democratic' disguise. And with austerity measures agreed 'for the sake of safeguarding the transition to democracy', the Franco era elite could recover from the economic crisis with its property and profits preserved.

Political accommodation with the old Franco apparatus and economic elite was easier to make for the Socialist PSOE than for the Communists. The PCE had to drop its traditional militant republicanism and accept the continuance not only of the capitalist system but, with the Moncloa Pacts, an austerity package designed to restore the profitability of Spanish industry. As a result, the PCE lost its revolutionary image and purpose. Disillusioned militants left the party in droves. This was coupled with discontent over the authoritarian leadership of General Secretary Carrillo and the team he brought back with him from exile in Moscow. In 1981–82, the party split into three groups and ceased to be a major factor in Spanish politics. A humiliated Carrillo was forced to quit as PCE leader after the party's disastrous showing in the November 1982 elections, when its vote sank to 4 per cent. He was eventually expelled from the PCE in 1985.

Meanwhile negotiations over Spain's new written constitution were conducted in an even more intimate and seductive atmosphere. With the Communists neutralised, González's Socialists could be smoothly incorporated into the Spanish establishment. The political 'rancour' that one seasoned observer had deplored in the Second Republic was noticeably absent 40 years on. When discussions on the draft constitution threatened to get into difficulties in May 1978, a private meeting was arranged between four UCD representatives and four Socialist Deputies at Madrid's fashionable but intimate José Luis restaurant – one of the few photographs to show Franco smiling was taken at this tapas bar. Over good food and wine, the former

Francoists and the new PSOE politicians ironed out their difficulties regarding the Church (agreeing to disestablishment), divorce, abortion, education, labour relations, conscientious objection to military service and the role of the state in the economy. The Communists and the Catalan Deputies were not invited.

The official, cosy narrative is that Spain's transition to democracy was a civilised affair, orchestrated by reformist elements of the old regime and the opposition parties. But as the writer Michael Eaude points out: 'The way millions lived the transition... is radically different from this official version. The million people marching on the national day of Catalonia, 11 September 1977, the more than 20 per cent who voted for the PSUC (Catalan Communist Party) that year, the tens of thousands who supported far left parties, the millions who took part in strikes and protests – these too can claim to be the *main political actors* of the transition. It is because of their struggles that the more far-sighted representatives of the dictatorship, the King, Adolfo Suárez and Manuel Fraga, opted for changes in the political system. Their slogan was the Prince's famous paradox from Lampedusa's *The Leopard*: 'If you want everything to remain the same, everything has to change.'

The *ruptura pactada* allowed Spain to make the transition from dictatorship to parliamentary democracy; but it was a flawed democracy. Those who'd served Franco loyally remained as judges, officers and senior civil servants. In Barcelona, the notorious torturer Inspector Vicente Creix, continued in his position until his retirement. He carried out his torture acts at the national police headquarters in Via Laietana, which remains so today (and would be the Guardia Civil HQ for the attacks on polling stations during the October 2017 referendum). Corruption, endemic in the old regime remained endemic to successive governments, particularly under Mariano Rajoy. Above all the Spanish state would respond to ETA's continuing military campaign for independence with its own 'dirty war' of assassinations and torture in a fashion unreconstructed since the time when General Arenas entered Barcelona in 1939.

Spain is often held up as an example to countries facing the shift from dictatorship to democracy. But those in Catalonia who had lived through the Franco era know better. Manuel Vázquez Montálban, a member of the Communist PSUC during the 'transition' to democracy, had a more jaundiced view of the outcome:

> Once the modification of the superstructures was achieved to put them in tune with democratic standards, the democratising ambition anchored at the first port of arrival. It did not go further. Democracy came to Spain alongside the neo-liberal cultural offensive.[101]

Looking back, the *Nova Cançó* artist Lluís Llach said:

> We thought democracy was an end in itself... a big mistake. If you don't treat it as an instrument to be performed it becomes perverted.[102]

Transition in Catalonia and the Statute of Autonomy

The part of post-Franco Spain that posed the most difficult problem for a 'managed' transition was, of course, Catalonia. Franco's attempt to dilute Catalan nationalism using mass immigration had failed. Mutual opposition to the regime and the protests following the dictator's death had helped fuse the Catalan and non-Catalan sections of Barcelona's population. The PSUC and *Comisiones* activist López Bulla, who had immigrated to the city in 1965 from rural Andalusia, recalled a conversation with a friend at which he exclaimed:

> But have you realised? The number of *charnegos* [pejorative term for Andalusian immigrants] like you and me shouting Long Live Catalonia! Know what? Let's hold onto this country, because we haven't got any other.[103]

The *Diada* (Catalan National Day) on 11 September 1977 was the first to be celebrated openly in Barcelona since the fall of the Dictatorship. After 38 years of national and cultural oppression, as well as mass immigration, did anything still exist of the old Catalonia? Yes it did. More than one million people took to the streets and marched under the familiar slogan *Llibertat! Amnistia! Estatut d'autonomia!* The cry for Catalan autonomy was once again heard on the streets of Barcelona.

In Madrid, the new government of Adolfo Suárez was rattled by this fresh intervention from below. The carefully stage-managed transition from naked dictatorship to neo-liberal democracy was in danger from those pesky Catalans. As ever, Suárez offered an olive branch designed to buy time. On 29 September, he acceded to several of the demonstrators' demands. The exiled President of the *Generalitat*, 78-year-old Josep Tarradellas, could return home as head of a Provisional Catalan Government tasked with preparing elections, scheduled for 20 March 1980. This was a remarkable decision in that it both recognised the continuity of the *Generalitat* overthrown by Franco in 1939 and sanctioned a Catalan provisional government. This latter was the very thing the former Franco apparatchiks had fought tooth and nail to avoid for Spain itself, in case they lost control of events. Of course, in reality Tarradellas had no power. His role in supervising the Catalan elections was largely symbolic. But symbolism was an important ingredient in the Transition, as the veteran Tarradellas knew only too well. Before he agreed to the deal, he forced Suárez to grant him a military parade. Spanish Army commanders were unhappy but acquiesced. It was Tarradellas' canny way of ensuring the generals would accept the revival of Catalan autonomy.

On 23 October, from the balcony of the Palace of the *Generalitat* in the Plaça de Sant Jaume, Tarradellas addressed the crowds (this was precisely the 'balcony' moment that his successor, Carles Puigdemont would fail to provide 40 years later). Tarradellas used a phrase that would become famous: '*Ciutadans de Catalunya, ja sóc aquí!*' – Citizens of Catalonia, I am here!' The meaning was transparent to everyone listening. He had called them 'citizens of Catalonia', not Catalonians. In other words, he was invoking the Catalan Republic, not the restored Bourbon monarchy that stood guard over an 'indivisible' Spain. Also, the *Generalitat* – if only in name – had been restored in advance of the new Spanish constitution. Forty years later, Mariano Rajoy and Spanish Constitutional Court would insist on their right to depose the elected *Generalitat* government and imprison its members. But that October day in 1977, Josep Tarradellas was the living proof that the legitimacy of Catalan institutions pre-dates the 1978 constitution. More to the point, Catalan institutions emanate from the sovereignty of the Catalan people alone.

Meanwhile, in Madrid, Suárez was still left with the problem of passing a new constitution in a manner that would seem to satisfy Catalan demands for autonomy without creating a dynamic towards independence or federalism. The unity and centrality of the Spanish state was key to preserving the old elite and protecting it from recriminations. The new constitution was drawn up by a group of hand-picked lawyers from the main parties – again there was no popular participation. The seven-man commission (they were all male) consisted of three UDC representatives (including a Basque), one far-right AP (none other than Manuel Fraga), one PSOE, one Communist (actually Jorde Solé of the Catalan PSUC) and a Catalan autonomist, Miquel

Roca. While this line-up had three representatives of the constituent nations, it was heavily stacked against the left.

The Communist, Jordi Solé, is particularly interesting. He joined the PSUC in 1956 but soon went into exile behind the Iron Curtain. In 1964 Solé quit the party after the expulsions of Fernando Claudín and Jorge Semprún, who had challenged General Secretary Carrillo's slavish devotion to Moscow. Solé then became a Maoist but suddenly re-joined the PSUC in 1973, as the Franco regime entered its death throes. He made his peace with Carrillo and was soon a leading Eurocommunist. He was elected to the *Cortes* as a Barcelona Deputy in the 1977 Spanish elections. In 1985 he joined the PSOE, ending up as Minister of Culture in the neo-liberal government of Felipe González. This frantic opportunism may explain Solé's willingness during the negotiations over the constitution to abandon the Communist Party's longstanding demand for an explicitly federal Spain and recognition of the right to self-determination for Catalonia and the Basque Country.

The official Catalan representative on the drafting commission, Miquel Roca, was the grandson of the prominent Carlist and Lliga supporter, Miquel Junyent. Roca's political trajectory mirrors many of the Catalan middle class. While studying at Barcelona University in the mid-1950s, he was caught up in the anti-regime student protests. But in the 1960s, during the speculative building boom promoted by Mayor Josep Maria de Porcioles, Roca's Barcelona law practice specialised in helping developers push through urban clearances opposed by local residents. From then on, Roca represented those elements in the comfortable Catalan middle class who wanted rid of the Franco yoke, to be sure, but whose idea of reform was a devolved bourgeois parliament that would look after their interests without giving Madrid cause to interfere or unleashing social revolution. Skipping through various parties, Roca ended up in the autonomist Democratic Convergence led by Jordi Pujol, an old school friend. He was elected to the *Cortes* in 1977. So useful was Roca in this world of backroom deals that Adolfo Suárez later offered him a ministerial post.

The Spanish constitution that emerged from this cabal was an artwork in legal sophistry. Solé, Roca and the PSOE representative, Gregorio Peces-Barba (a defence lawyer at the 1970 Burgos ETA trials) meekly accepted not only the legal 'indivisibility' of the Spanish nation, but also a unitary state that 'granted' certain devolved powers to designated regions. At the time, this compromise looked much the same as federalism, given the extensive 'menu' of devolved powers on offer. But it was storing up trouble for the future because, in the words of the English politician Enoch Powell, 'power devolved is power retained'.

The fudge over the national question went much further. The 1978 constitution refers to 'nationalities' existing within the Spanish state but not to 'nations'. The latter, once officially regonised, could demand independence. Even these 'nationalities' are not specified – everyone merely assumed this term referred to Catalonia, the Basque Country and Galicia. Not actually identifying the constituent nations was seen as a reasonable verbal compromise in a document that had to be acceptable to Fraga's Francoist Bunker and the army. But, of course, this was a binding legal document. In 2017, it would be the political bludgeon used against the Catalan independence movement , sending elected Catalan politicians to prison for sedition and rebellion.

Back in 1978, from a Catalan point of view, the new constitution certainly laid down the basis for a decentralised system of Autonomous Communities, each with their own governing statute. This sounded like the return of the Statutes of Autonomy that Catalonia, the Basque Country and Galicia had enjoyed before the Civil War. But the devil was in the detail. The obvious trick was to extend the decentralisation process to other regions (invented or otherwise) thus diluting the political impact of Catalan and Basque autonomy. This became known as *café para todos* – coffee for all. Each new Statute of Autonomy would have to be negotiated separately with the Spanish government and approved by the Spanish parliament. Madrid was therefore in a position to play favourites and divide and rule, which is precisely what would happen when Catalonia came to negotiate its Statute of Autonomy in 1979. But by then the mass, anti-Franco movement had dissipated, and Suárez was in a position to start rolling back concessions made to the Catalans.

Far from being a model of decentralisation, any close reading of the text of the 1978 Spanish Constitution reveals a high degree of political and cultural centralisation by the central state.

Article 2 stresses the pre-eminence of the Spanish state:

> The Constitution is based on the indissoluble unity of the Spanish Nation, common and indivisible fatherland (patria) of all Spaniards.[104]

That could be read as a pious phrase included to keep the old Francoists happy. No reasonable person would assume that formulation was a barrier to peaceful democratic debate regarding the future self-determination of

Catalonia or other parts of the state. International law enshrines the right to self-determination – though not to unilateral succession – which implies that constituent parts of existing nation states have the right to discuss, hold referendums and lobby for constitutional change. But Article 2 has been consistently interpreted by the Constitutional Court in the narrowest possible way to preclude – indeed outlaw – any debate in the so-called Autonomous Communities that promotes independence, on the grounds that Spanish unity is legally 'indissoluble'.

This is backed up by Article 8, which states that the role of the Spanish Army is to guarantee Spain's sovereignty and 'territorial integrity'. You could read that as referring to defence against foreign invasion, though France has not attacked Spain for nearly two centuries. The Army read this clause as giving it a constitutional right to keep Catalonia and the Basque Country inside the Spanish state by force.

The drafters of the 1978 constitution were even far-sighted enough to block any attempt by the Autonomous Communities to group together, either as a counterweight to central rule from Madrid, or as a way of maximising their chances of gaining independence. In particular, the old Francoists were worried about the Catalan-speaking provinces of Catalonia, Valencia and the Balearic Islands federating, or the Basque Country linking with Navarre. So Article 145 states that 'no federation between Autonomous Communities will be permitted under any circumstances'. Note the political injunction: 'under any circumstances'.

Then there is cultural centralisation. Article 3 read:

> Castilian is the official language of the State. All Spaniards have the duty to know it and the right to use it. The other Spanish languages will also be official in their respective Autonomous Communities according to their own Statutes. The richness of the distinct linguistic modalities of Spain represents a patrimony which will be the object of special respect and protection.

The weakness in this formulation is that only Castilian is privileged and language rights in individual Autonomous Communities (not 'nations'!) are only recognised subject to the Statute of Autonomy agreed by Madrid. As a result, attempts by later Catalan administrations to protect the Catalan language have been systematically struck down by the Constitutional Court.

The entire Spanish electorate voted in a referendum on the new constitution in December 1978. In Catalonia the turnout was 67.9 per cent, with 95.2 per cent saying Yes – a larger majority than the Spanish average of 91.8 per cent. For the majority of people in Catalonia the new constitution formally recognised democracy and (to a degree they had not seen in 40 years) granted local autonomy. The actual question ('Do you approve of the Constitution Bill?') was a take it or leave it proposition. The Catalans took it. The dark days of Francoism were over. To its credit, only the ERC – then a tiny force – opposed a vote for the new constitution, on the grounds that it endorsed the monarchy rather than a republic, and because it made no provision for Catalan (and Basque) self-determination. Indeed, the one part of Spain that turned its back on the 1978 constitution was the Basque Country, where only 44.65 per cent of the electorate turned out at the referendum.

The next order of business was passing the Statute of Autonomy. Because there was as yet no elected Catalan legislature, a drafting commission was set up, consisting of Catalan members of the upper and lower houses of the Madrid Parliament. This gave the PSOE, the PSUC and the supporters of Suárez a huge majority. In the end, the real work was done by three men: none other than Jordi Solé and Miquel Roca, who had been central to the writing of the Spanish state constitution, plus a member of the PSOE/PSC, Eduardo Martín Toval. Another graduate of the anti-Franco student protests of the 1960s, Toval migrated through various Marxist and 'self-management' grouplets before adhering to the new PSOE-affiliate in Catalonia, the PSC, in 1978. This triumvirate would agree a badly flawed Statute of Autonomy. Solé and Roca had form and were hardly going to challenge the framework they had agreed for the Spanish constitution. They forced through a draft with only one vote against. It contained a major weakness – tax raising powers.

The minority of pro-Catalan delegates (from the ERC and Pujol's Democratic Convergence) wanted the *Generalitat* to be responsible for collecting all tax revenues in Catalonia and paying a proportion over to Madrid for central services, and into an inter-territorial compensation fund to support other regions. In effect, this would give Catalonia control over its cash resources, and make Madrid beholden. This was voted down by the drafting group at the urging of the Socialist Eduardo Martín Toval. The PSOE was looking forward to being the Spanish government some day and wanted to keep its hands on the purse strings. When it came to a vote, only the three

Convergence members and the ERC Deputy supported Catalan control over taxes. The significant point here is that in the negotiations over the Basque and Navarre Statutes of Autonomy, full tax-raising powers were granted to their parliaments. This was justified politically on the grounds that the Basques possess ancient charters granting them fiscal autonomy. The more prosaic reality was that the main Spanish parties were desperate to make concessions to the Basques to fend off the rising tide of Basque nationalism. This was the first use of the 1978 Spanish constitution to attempt to divide and rule the so-called Autonomous Communities. Genuine autonomy this was not.

Even then Madrid still had to approve the draft Statute for Catalonia. This was submitted to the *Cortes* following the March 1979 General Election, mandated to follow the introduction of the new Spanish constitution. The results left Suárez in power but with the PSOE breathing down his neck. The Suárez government insisted on 59 amendments to the draft Statute designed to limit its scope. Jurisdiction in matters of culture, environment, communications, transportation, commerce, public safety and local government was ceded to the *Generalitat*. But in education, health and justice, jurisdiction was to be shared between the *Generalitat* and Madrid. This was conditional autonomy, at best. In October 2017, Madrid would show just how conditional.

The Catalan Statute of Autonomy was passed by referendum in June 1979, although the turnout of 59.6 per cent was significantly lower than that for the Spanish constitution a year earlier. This 40 per cent abstention rate is indicative. It shows that a large segment of the Catalan population was dissatisfied with the content of the Statute of Autonomy but prepared to acquiesce because there was nothing more on offer. Here began the long march to October 2017.

The new Catalan Government came into being in 1980 after elections won by Jordi Pujol. For this election, Pujol's Democratic Convergence formed an alliance with the Christian Democrat *Unió Democràtica de Catalunya*, which was to become permanent in the form of *Convergència i Unió* (CIU). Pujol and the centre-right CIU would dominate Catalan politics for decades to come. Pujol's moderate, Christian Democratic coalition was in many ways a throwback to the days of the *Lliga*. It espoused Catalanism without threatening the '78 Regime. It sought to advance Catalan middle class interests through bargaining for concessions with the Madrid parties, often trading votes in the Spanish Parliament in return. Pujol himself – avuncular, well-connected, and pragmatic – proved a master at manipulating the system. From a banking family, medically-trained and a businessman in his own right, Pujol sat at the centre of new web of influence in Catalonia – which would later prove his downfall and disgrace. He also ensured that Catalonia had a direct diplomatic face in Europe. A rugby fan, Pujol could be seen downing a pint in Edinburgh pubs after enjoying a game at Murryfield stadium.

After the horror and travails of the Franco era, it is understandable that ordinary Catalans of the older generation might prefer the security and rising prosperity provided by Pujol's conservative Godfather regime. The dream of independence seemed very far away indeed. But the Transition would have one more act to play.

The coup of 23 February 1981 – 'democracy under vigilance'

In the early evening of 23 February 1981, Leopoldo Calvo Sotelo was being installed as Prime Minister in the *Cortes* in Madrid. Suddenly a group of heavily armed Guardia Civil stormed the building. Shots were fired and the Deputies took cover on the floor. A certain Lieutenant Colonel Antonio Tejero came to the front of the hall wearing the old leather Guardia Civil cap, associated in many minds with Francoist repression. He demanded silence, ordered the Deputies to lie down, and told them that they were to wait for an announcement from the King. Meanwhile, in Valencia, the Captain General of the Third Military Region, Jaime Milans del Bosch, had declared a state of emergency and sent tanks on to the streets of the city. In Barcelona, the head of the tank division in Sant Boi de Llobregat on the outskirts of the city, and the Francoist chief of the local police, *Mossos d'Esquadra*, were primed to arrest Jordi Pujol. A nationwide coup was in motion. Afterwards it would be referred to as 'El Tejarazo', after its putative leader.

Tejero had begun his career in the Guardia Civil in Catalonia in 1951. Later he was promoted Chief of the Guardia's Planning Staff, after successes against ETA in the Basque lands. The 1981 coup was not his first attempt at overthrowing the state. In 1978, Tejero and an Army General Staff colonel, whose name has still not been made public, attempted another coup, code-named *Operation Galaxia*. Tajero was charged with mutiny and received the minimum sentence of seven months. Bizarrely, he returned to duty afterwards – proof that the post-Franco state apparatus was still imbued with right-wing sympathies.

Tejero's second coup attempt was also a failure thanks to the man he expected to back it – King Juan Carlos. At 1.14am Juan Carlos went on national TV dressed in his full uniform as the Captain General of the Armed Forces. He announced: 'The crown, symbol of the permanence and unity of the nation, cannot tolerate, in any form, actions or attitudes attempting to interrupt the democratic process.' [105] With the Spanish left reconciled to the monarchy, Juan Carlos had clearly decided that the future of the Bourbon line was in safer hands if he stuck by the 1978 constitutional set-up. To prove the point, after the broadcast, Santiago Carrillo, the Communist Party General Secretary, issued an emotional statement, announcing: 'Today, we are all monarchists.'[106]

However, though Juan Carlos was hailed far and wide as the saviour of Spain's democracy, it took him seven hours before he appeared on TV. One of the coup's main supporters was General Alfonso Armada, the second in command of the Spanish Army and a former secretary-general to the King. In 2012 it emerged that Juan Carlos had admitted to the West German ambassador to Spain, Lothar Lahn, shortly after the coup, that he was broadly sympathetic to its aims, if not its methods.[107] According to a report sent by Lahn to Bonn, the King 'showed no indication of either antipathy or outrage vis-à-vis the actors [in the plot] but, rather, displayed much more understanding, if not sympathy'. The ambassador reported that Juan Carlos had stated 'almost apologetically' that the plotters had 'only wanted what we are all striving for, namely, the re-establishment of discipline, order, security and calm'. Juan Carlos went on to lay the blame for the coup at the feet of democratically elected former Prime Minister Adolfo Suárez because he had 'failed to establish a relationship with the military' and refused to take their 'justified wishes seriously.'

With the King's TV broadcast, the coup promptly collapsed. In Valencia, General Milans del Bosch cancelled his attempted takeover of the city at 5.00am. In Barcelona, Pujol escaped arrest when the military Captain General of Catalonia refused to join the conspiracy. Tejero himself held out until the following midday when he was arrested outside the *Cortes*. This time he was not so lucky and served a full 15 years in prison. Subsequently, in much of the Western media, Tejero's coup has been portrayed in comic book terms. But what the failed coup did do was put down a clear marker from the military that there was a limit to democratisation. One of the crucial issues motivating the military plotters was their belief that the process of autonomy had gone too far, threatening the unity of Spain. The impact of *El Tejerazo* was to ensure that process would not just be put on hold, but efforts would be made to reverse it by both the centre right and centre left. Spain's democracy entered a period known as the *democracia vigilada* or democracy under surveillance.

It also meant that Spain's rulers were even more careful to operate within the limits imposed during the transition process. Any thoughts of loosening central control from Madrid were kicked into the political long grass. In Catalonia, Pujol was confirmed in his belief that seeking concessions from Madrid was a more reliable strategy than seeking independence. The Socialist government of Felipe González, elected a year after the coup, abided by the Pact of Forgetting. In 1986, the 50th anniversary of Franco's rebellion, González pointedly refused to use the occasion to bring justice for the tens of thousands murdered by the old regime. 'A civil war is not an event to commemorate,' he noted. 'The Spanish Civil War is definitely history.'[108]

But not for everyone. From retirement in Malaga in 2006, Antonio Tejero had the last say. He penned a letter to a local newspaper denouncing the Socialist government for agreeing to a new Statute of Autonomy for Catalonia. Ironically, he demanded that the same Juan Carlos who spoke out against 'rebellion' in 1981 should speak out now against those 'trying to break the Crown of Spain'. In the letter, Tejero asked rhetorically, 'what is it all about, Catalonia being a nation?'.[109]

Chapter Seven: Kleptomaniac State

Speaking on Sunday, Rajoy sought to depict the issue as a case of a few bad apples... Less than 24 hours later, 51 people – including top members of Rajoy's ruling People's party (PP) – were arrested as part of an investigation into 'a network of corruption'...

Assifa Kassam, *The Guardian*[110]

THE INTEREGNUM between Franco's death and the rise of the modern Catalan independence movement are the years the locust ate. The Spanish state had the veneer of a legitimate democracy, any radical threat to the economic elite had been seen off, and the danger of a revival of separatism defused by granting toothless 'autonomy' to Catalonia and the Basque lands. The post-Franco elite were free to make money and make money they did, using corrupt links with the political establishment. What emerged can only be described as a kleptomaniac state. But a corrupt state with new reasons to maintain its grip over Catalonia.

The scale of financial corruption in Spain surpasses anything in Western Europe. Spain's General Council of Economists issued a report in June 2017 which estimated that tax fraud is costing the Spanish economy €25.6 billion a year – a staggering 16 per cent of GDP.[111] Some 1,500 people in Spain faced trial for corruption between July 2015 and the end of 2016, according to official figures. Around 70 per cent of them were found guilty. Since the fall of the Dictatorship, those who found themselves in the dock have included top business executives, ministers, regional presidents, mayors and even Princess Cristina, the king's sister. In late July 2017, Mariano Rajoy became the first serving Spanish prime minister to testify in a criminal case – he was subpoenaed to give evidence in the Gürtel case in which PP leaders stand accused of involvement in kickbacks. Note: at this very point in time Rajoy was berating the Catalan Government for pursuing an 'illegal' referendum. In another case, Rodrigo Rato – a former PP Deputy Prime Minister and latterly managing director of the IMF – received a (risible) four-year sentence for embezzlement.

On the *Corruption Perceptions Index* prepared by Transparency International (the global NGO concerned with monitoring corruption) Spain dropped seven points between 2012 and 2016, and now scores worse than most Western European democracies. According to José Ugaz, the Chair of Transparency International:

> Corruption in Spain distorts policy making and hurts people's basic rights for the benefit of a few. Just looking at recent scandals like the Pujol case in Catalonia, the linkages between the ruling People's Party and the construction group OHL, the Gürtel case, the Bankia fraud and Rodrigo Rato, gives a sense of the scale of the problem.[112]

Franco's legacy of corruption

British historian Paul Heywood reminds us that 'Spain's entire political history since the monarchical restoration of 1875 has been marked by corruption in one form or another.' He goes on to add: 'Yet the most corrupt of all regimes in Modern Spain was undoubtedly the Franco Dictatorship.'[113]

Corruption was there from the very start. The Francoist state was unable to boost agricultural production after the Civil War ended, or to distribute effectively what was produced. The result was the *años de hambre*, 'the hungry years'. Rationing was introduced, but food shortages led inevitably to a burgeoning black market and, in turn, corruption. Franco himself set the tone. It was commonly complained that Franco simply refused to listen to any charges of personal corruption levied against associates. He seems to have regarded corruption as a necessary lubrication for the system which provided the handy advantage of compromising many within the regime and binding them to it. In 1942, the Ministry of Justice complained to the *Caudillo* – to no effect – about the lenient sentences handed out to major black marketeers in Barcelona. Of 188 charged only 69 were found guilty, with just ten of those being awarded short jail sentences while the rest were put under house arrest. In contrast, petty offenders were harshly dealt with. In the same year, the anti-black market court (*Fiscala de Tasa*) sentenced close to 5000 people for modest infringement of the rules. As the head of the Francoist unions recognised in an internal memo written in mid-1942, 'the big sharks always get away with very lenient punishment'.[114]

One of these 'big sharks' was none other than Franco's aristocratic son-in-law, Cristóbal Martinez-Bordiú, the 10th Marqués of Villaverde. Using his connections to the regime, he made a fortune from banking, controlling import-export licences (at a time when Spain was a closed market with little foreign currency available) and property speculation. Martinez-Bordiú made a lot of this money through his association with none other than José Maria Porcioles, Franco's appointee as Mayor of Barcelona. Franco himself detested Barcelona and rarely went there. His son-in-law had a different relationship with the Catalan capital through his links to Porcioles and the *Banco de Madrid*. Despite its name, Banco de Madrid was based in the Catalan capital and had its registered business address at Porcioles' Barcelona law office. One of its main shareholders was Cristóbal Martinez-Bordiú. As well as enriching himself through building speculation in Barcelona (courtesy of the mayor) the 10th Marques built a stake in dozens of companies through his relationship to the dictator – having Franco's son-in-law on your board was a proven way of cutting corners in a corrupt regime.

Corruption at the highest echelons became endemic as Spain's economy recovered in the 1960s. In 1969 a scandal broke around the collapse of the *Mantesa* textile company, owned by *Opus Dei* member Juan Vila Reyes, who had misappropriated 10,000 million *pesetas* of state funding to line his pockets and to fund *Opus Dei* ventures. He was a close friend of the Minister in charge of Planning, Gregorio López Bravo y Castro, a key moderniser in the Franco government. Lopez Bravo and two other ministers were soon caught up in the affair. The *New York Times* reported on the findings of a secret *Cortes* session on this scandal:

> The report concerned the granting of a total of official export credits worth $140 million to a textile machinery company that exported no more than half of the 20,000 looms the credits were meant to cover... The *Matesa* case is the biggest, and by far the most public scandal that has hit the Franco Government. With three ministries involved in charges of favouritism and negligence, the prestige of the whole Government is affected.[115]

Juan Vila Reyes went to jail but the Supreme Court dropped any action against the government ministers – a trend that would be continued after the Transition.

During the 1970s, as the dictatorship moved to its inevitable biolog-ical end, economic power was concentrated increasingly in the so-called 'two hundred big families'. This oligarchy was composed of some 1,000 individuals who constituted the elite of Spain's financiers and industrialists. They were largely non-Catalan, linked to banks based in Madrid and, to a lesser extent, the Basque Country. They were also closely tied to the *Insti-tuto Nacional de Industria* (INI). After Franco's death these state monopolies would be privatised in name, but in essence they were transferred to the private ownership of the same elite which remained intimately tied to the neo-Francoist Spanish state.

But Franco did more than just turn a blind eye to the misdeeds of his cronies – he feathered his own financial nest. As the historian Paul Preston observes, Franco left a legacy of corruption that was passed down to dem-ocratic Spain:

> It is true that the *Caudillo* used corruption both to reward and control his collaborators. Recent research has uncovered proof of how he used his power to enrich himself and his family. In gener-al, the idea that public service exists for private benefit is one of the principal legacies of his regime.[116]

After the fall of the Dictatorship, journalist Mariano Sánchez Soler uncovered a mass of detail about the family's wealth, in a well-documented book *Los Franco* SA (*Franco Inc*).[117] Much was in a property portfolio amassed during the Dictatorship. Sanchez Soler uncovered a trail of properties from the Phil-ippines to Miami, and including 22 rural and urban holdings in Spain itself. While Franco himself pretended to austerity, his wife bought up properties in the choicest areas of Madrid, with the goal of giving one to each of her grandchildren as presents. Grateful Spaniards (or those just currying favour) flooded El Caudillo with gifts, from a herd of sheep to a palace in Torrelo-dones. The 2,000-square-metre El Canto del Pico palace, built early in the last century in Torrelodones, Madrid, was given to Franco by the Count of Las Almenas in 1941 as a weekend retreat. It was sold by his daughter in 1988 for 320 million *pesetas* (US$2.7 million). Then there is the 18th century Pala-cio de Cornide in A Coruña, which is still owned by the family. This was orig-inally purchased by the Ministry for Education in 1962 but strangely enough only three years later it was acquired by the Count of Fenosa, who registered it in the name of Franco's wife, Carmen Polo de Franco. The true extent of Franco's wealth is not known since accounts were never made public. But at the time of his death, one estimate puts it at 60-100 billion *pesetas* (US$500-US$800 million) in holding companies and real estate. According to Sánchez Soler's book, the family developed interests in more than 150 companies during the Franco years and salted much of the profits away abroad.

The fall of the Dictatorship did little to impinge on the wealth or status of the Franco family. Until the day she died, Franco's widow Carmen Polo received a pension that was higher than the salaries of the Spanish Prime Ministers Adolfo Suárez and Felipe González. Her only daughter and her son-in-law continued to use their diplomatic passports. Juan Carlos ennobled the family with a new title: the Duchy of Franco. The Spanish tax agency never investigated their accounts nor was their dubiously-acquired family fortune seized, as it was in the case of the Dominican dictator Leónidas Trujillo. Not even the assets that Franco had received as a head of state and which should have reverted to the state, have ever been claimed by Spain's democratic rulers.

Mr Blesa's corrupt banking empire

On 19 July 2017, the Guardia Civil was called to the expensive private hunting lodge of 69-year-old Miguel Blesa, sometime chairman of one of Spain's largest banks, the Caja Madrid. There they discovered his dead body. Blesa had committed suicide after being convicted of fraud, and was about to go to prison for six years. In all, some 100 prominent Spanish bankers have been named in continuing court cases in connection with fraudulent lending, conflicts of interest, excessive compensation packages and abusing expense accounts – Blesa was among the first to be convicted. But there is much more to the Blesa case than greed, even if it produced malfeasance on a gargantuan scale. Blesa and his banking empire maintained intimate relations with the Popular Party, illegally funding the PP and providing sinecures for its leading members.

In the 1950s and afterwards, Spain evolved an economic model in which a clique of big banking houses – run by political appointees – created, invested in, owned and directed a dense network of industrial, energy and construction companies. This banking-industrial network, with its bewildering family trees of interlocking and over-lapping share ownerships and corrosive personal rivalries, had more in common with the *keiretsu* system in South Korea than it had with the rest of Europe. Typically, in this model, industrial investment was funded by bank loans and debt rather than by share issues and equity, making it particularly vulnerable when lending sources failed, as happened in 2008. Equally, given the central role played by Spanish banks in funding and owning industrial companies, the system was prone to explosive growth, excessive risk-taking and (above all) political manipulation. It is this economic monster that underpins and influences the nature of the Spanish state in recent times. It is also the monster that brought Spain to the brink of economic collapse after 2008.

Miguel Blesa was a typical beneficiary of this corrupt system. At the height of his power, he headed Spain's fourth-largest bank (by lending), with more than seven million customers and annual earnings of over €2 billion during the real estate boom. Born in Linares in Andalusia (long a centre of British mining interests) Blesa began professional life as a lowly tax inspector during the dying days of the Franco regime, before gently working his way up the civil service ladder in the Ministry of Finance. There he might have languished in well-deserved obscurity but for his close friendship with José Aznar, later to become leader of the Popular Party and Spain's Prime Minister from 1996 to 2004. Aznar also started out as a tax inspector – which is how he and Blesa first met. But Aznar had political ambitions. As a student, he was a leader of the FES, a dissident Falangist youth group committed to the ideas of Primo de Rivera – ideas that supposedly had been corrupted under Franco. At the end of the dictatorship, Aznar shifted to the new Popular Alliance (AP), the political front for sanitised Francoist technocrats that would evolve into the PP.

Aznar's political ascent had begun but his friend Miguel Blesa was not forgotten. With the Socialists in power (from 1982 to 1996), Blesa quit the civil service for the more lucrative field of advising Spain's burgeoning private sector on how to minimise their tax payments. From here he was plucked by Aznar – when the latter eventually kicked out the Socialists at the 1996 election – to chair the board of Caja Madrid, Spain's oldest savings bank. Blesa had no banking experience to speak of. This was a political appointment pure and simple. The new PP government was engaged in a transparent political manoeuvre. The previous Socialist government under Felipe González had begun privatising the big state companies and conglomerates created under the Franco regime as the spearhead for industrialisation – a free market move designed to assuage the other members of the European Union such as Germany and the UK. Many of these public concerns were grouped under INI, the National Institute of Industry, a state-owned holding company modelled on Mussolini's IRI.

In these early privatisations, Felipe González had himself appointed Socialist Party supporters to board positions. Indeed, the Socialists were soon drawn into the net of financial corruption that is modern, post-Franco Spain. In retaliation, Aznar and the PP were determined to put in their own placemen (there were few place-women), hence Blesa's appointment to run Caja Madrid. But the placing of PP and Anzar supporters to run state-influenced companies did not stop with Blesa and Caja Madrid: there was Alberto Cortina at Repsol, the power utility; Juan Villalonga at Telefónica, Spain's main telecoms company; and Francisco González at another bank, Argentaria (now BBVA). Like Blesa, none of these men had any experience of managing large corporations. Their main qualification was loyalty to Aznar and the PP.

Blesa's lack of banking experience mattered little in these circumstances. Besides, Spain was about to join the new Eurozone and replace the traditional *peseta* with the euro, starting in 1999. The result of the new currency was a pan-European fall in interest rates and the start of the Spanish property bubble based on profligate lending. In this, Blesa's Caja Madrid would soon lead the way. The percentage of total Spanish bank loans allocated to mortgages, to real estate developers and to construction firms shot up from 40 per cent to 60 per cent between 1999 and 2007, the peak of the boom.

During these boom years, Miguel Blesa enjoyed the high life. But what really made Blesa stand out was the arrogant way he displayed his power and wealth. Remember, Caja Madrid had started out under his chairmanship as a public service savings bank dedicated to its depositors and local small companies. Leaked pictures published in the Spanish media showed Blesa on exotic hunting trips, posing with a rifle next to the corpses of recently-shot animals, including a bear, a lion, an oryx, a hippopotamus and the heads of two water buffalo. He paid himself a salary of 3 million euros a year plus unlimited expenses on the company credit card. Other board members followed suit. Blesa's name also popped up in the infamous Panama Papers, which showed that he controlled an off-shore company created by the lawyers Mossack Fonseca, which made large (but opaque) investments in Spain. Under Blesa, Caja Madrid also became a conduit for loans to cronies and friends on a truly massive scale. Between 2003 and 2010, Blesa approved major loans to for Gerardo Díaz Ferrán, owner of the Marsans Group and sometime president of the CEOE (Spain's leading employers' representative). Curiously, these loans – totalling 131 million euros – went not just to companies owned by Ferrán but to members of his family. Even more curious or maybe not so – Ferrán was also a board member of Caja Madrid. He is also doing time for fraud.

The issue here is not the misdeeds of Miguel Blesa, but rather the corruption that was and is endemic throughout the entire Spanish elite, and the intricate web of contacts between the elite and the Madrid political class, especially the PP. It is the threat of exposure of this corruption that is, in part, driving the elite to protect its political dominance by doing everything in its power to thwart Catalonia's desire for self-determination.

The extent of the links between Caja Madrid and the ruling PP emerged during the judicial investigations of Blesa's period as chairman. For instance, internal emails were recovered for the period 2007 to 2009 (when the property bubble was collapsing) recording communications between Blesa and leaders of the PP, including his old friend José María Aznar. These emails – more than 8,000 personal and professional messages – were leaked subsequently to the newspaper El País. They reveal how Aznar made suggestions about bank investments, including in works of art. On a more mundane level, they expose how PP leaders asked for cheap mortgages for acquaintances; and how the regional government ordered the bank to place party apparatchiks on its board (with lucrative fees). Under Blesa, over a period of nearly 20 years, Spain's flagship savings bank became a refuge for dozens of politicians who were granted a seat on its board as a reward for their loyalty to the PP.[118]

But the political link between the bank and the PP went even further. The main Madrid parties lack a mass membership base and so require more imaginative sources of funding than members' subscriptions. The solution is a scam whereby they 'borrow' large sums of money from major banks – debt which the banks eventually write off unpaid. Documents show that both the PP and the Socialist Party borrowed heavily from Caja Madrid but subsequently had most of the debts written off – 72 per cent in the case of the PP. There is also evidence that significant amounts of cash from the Fundación Caja Madrid, the bank's charitable giving arm, found its way to PP front organisations, to fund election campaigns and undertake propaganda work such as 'defending' Spanish unity.

The corruption of the PSOE

Paradoxically, the biggest corruption scandals in the early transition period centred on a party which had stood in opposition to Franco – the Socialists.

The PSOE could claim the historic mantle of champion of the poor, but in reality the post-Franco organisation had been recreated under a charismatic leader, Felipe González. A lawyer from Seville, Gonzales had risen in the PSOE ranks despite clandestine conditions, becoming its leader at the age of 32. In 1977, with the first free elections in over four decades, none of the political parties had much time to prepare. The result was that campaigning focused on the performance of the leaders on TV, something at which González excelled. This deflected focus from the cancer of corruption that instantly afflicted the PSOE.

The PSOE's success in coming second to the UDC in the first post-Franco elections - eclipsing the Communists who had been central to the opposition to the dictatorship - meant that the party quickly became a magnet for those looking to build a political career, or, in the poverty-ridden South, to secure a job. In the 1979 local elections, many of those elected on the Socialist ticket had only just joined or did so after being elected. Vetting of their backgrounds was almost non-existent. This was compounded by the fact that fact that there is little tradition of mass membership of political parties in Spain. The PSOE took 48.4 per cent of the vote in 1982 with just 116,514 members. Lack of members meant that the established parties had to find other ways to provide funding. One way to achieve such funding was through the old established system of creating clientist networks. The PSOE soon fell prey to this temptation.[119]

When first elected in 1982, the Socialist government of Felipe González used the slogan *Cien años de honradez:* A Hundred Years of Honesty. In fact, its first years of rule were what one author described as 'bureaucratic clientelism' – the systematic handing out of favours and sinecures to party favourites. For most people this was normal behaviour for Spanish politicians. But following González's re-election in 1989, corruption scandals became endemic. First the Deputy Prime Minister had to resign in early 1990 after it emerged that his brother had been using PSOE offices for his private business operations. Then in 1993 auditors revealed that a PSOE Deputy and a Senator were running a group of front companies which paid off party expenses from 1 billion *peseta*s raised by charging banks and business for fictitious consultancy work.

That year saw two other high-profile cases. In one a Portuguese company, with no experience in the field, won a contract to build prefabricated structures for the Expo92 site in Seville. Having secured the contract, it then sold it on. It then transpired that they had paid 150 million *pesetas* to the

PSOE as a 'grant'. Then it was revealed that Siemens, which won the contract to build the high-speed Madrid-Seville rail link, paid large sums to former PSOE officials for 'technical and commercial advice'. That railway had a troubled past. Two years before, the Health Minister, previously in charge of Transport, had to go when it was revealed that the state railway company had tipped off property speculators about land on the proposed line due for compulsory purchase.

By the time of the PSOE's annual Congress in 1994, an amazing 72 per cent of the delegates held elected positions, reinforcing the public view that feathering their own nest took first place. This was especially true at a municipal level. Spanish municipalities are funded through selling licences and building permits, lending themselves to corrupt clientelistic relationships. Looking back at the years of González's rule, the Spanish left-wing writer Carlos Prieto del Campo, noted:

> Corruption has pervaded every pore, flourishing most blatantly in the interface between the construction industry and the multi-tiered administration, but most profitably in the corporate deals, sell-offs and loans bartered between sections of the elite. Structural imbalances nurture a huge informal economy floating on credit, uninsured against recession.[120]

PP corruption

In 1996 the PSOE was thrown out of government, due to public revulsion at the party's descent into a quagmire of corruption. José María Aznar was elected as head of the new Popular Party administration, with the promise of 'clean government'. He did not deliver.

In 2001 the *Gescartera* brokerage house collapsed, and its head, Antonio Rafael Camacho, was jailed after $100m (£68m) of clients' money disappeared. The BBC reported:

> Camacho's aggressive marketing garnered *Gescartera* a high-profile roster of clients, including senior church officials, the naval pension fund, and some big charities, including a police orphans' fund, and *Once*, Spain's main charity for the blind.

Camacho had appointed the sister of the former General Director of Taxes turned junior finance minister, Enrique Gimenez-Reyna, as managing director. The family connection proved useful as Enrique was able to broker all sorts of meetings for Camacho. Also, members of the Gimenez-Reyna family – their father was a Guardia Civil general – ran the finances of charities and agencies that were clients of *Gescartera*. The minister claimed that he was innocent, but he had to resign. He now runs a tax consultancy.[121]

Next to be fingered was Aznar's Foreign Minister, Josep Piqué, a PP deputy representing Barcelona and head of the party in Catalonia. Piqué was from old Francoist stock. His father had been the last Francoist mayor of Villanueva y Geltrú. But Piqué had a curious (if not suspicious) political history, having been a member in his youth of the Communist PSUC and the Maoist Red Flag group in Barcelona, where he knew Jordi Solé, who would draft both the 1978 Constitution and the Catalan Statute of Autonomy. Whatever blinding conversion – or sudden bout of opportunism – he had, Piqué became a member of the PP and Minister of Industry when Aznar became Prime Minister in 1995. He was later appointed Foreign Minister.

In 1999, Piqué came under investigation for alleged financial irregularities relating to the sale of a Spanish oil company, Ertoil, to Nadhmi Auchi, a businessman of Iraqi extraction, who just happened to own the Luxembourg bank that looked after the personal fortune of Saddam Hussein. During the Iraq-Iran War, Auchi's group of companies created a commercial empire throughout Africa, the Middle East and Asia – controlled from their Luxembourg tax haven. The implication was that they were part of Saddam's arms trafficking and money laundering operation. Barely 24 hours after the transaction Ertoil was re-sold to the French state company Elf Aquitaine. Mr Auchi trousered a hefty commission. A few days after that, the West attacked and overthrew Saddam.

Ertoil was previously owned by a Barcelona chemical company called Ercros, whose Executive Director was none other than the ex-Maoist (and soon to be Spain's Foreign Minister) Josep Piqué. And it was Piqué who signed the authorisation selling Ertoil to Auchi, himself pocketing a commission on the deal. Along the way, payments to Ertoil that should have gone to Ercos seem to have disappeared. In August 1999, the Spanish Anticorruption Prosecutor filed a complaint against Pique for tax fraud and misappropriation. Pique denied any wrongdoing.

But the wheels of Spanish justice grind slowly and Pique became a PP minister. The State Attorney General, Jesús Cardenal, intervened to prevented prosecutors from the Supreme Court acting against Piqué. Eventually the case was dismissed for lack of evidence. However, the very first act of the PSOE Zapatero government in 2004 was to fire Cardenal for being politically 'partisan' in favour of the outgoing PP administration.

This was not the end of Josep Piqué. In February 2012, Mariano Rajoy appointed him the Spanish director on the board of EADS, which manufactures the European Airbus. Since January 2017 he has been a member of the board of SEAT, where he chairs its audit committee. Throughout the recent Catalan independence struggle, Piqué has been vocal in opposition. He frequently pops up in the international media (including in the UK) masquerading as a disinterested business man, denouncing the Catalan 'nationalists' for being divisive, and urging Madrid to intervene. The ex-Maoist now represents the Spanish big bourgeoisie and its opposition to the right of ordinary Catalans to control their own destiny. Along the way, he has made himself a multi-millionaire.[122]

In 2007 a whistle blower brought to light the Gürtel case, in which more than 37 PP members, including the premier of the Valencian Regional Council, the PP's national treasurer, five mayors and 12 national and regional deputies, were charged with taking kickbacks from major public construction contracts. These cases arose from Spain's housing bubble of 1997–2007. The investigation was given the codename 'Gürtel', a cryptic reference to Francisco Correa, the principal suspect. *Correa* means belt in Spanish, *Gürtel* the same in German. Correa just happens to be a close personal friend of Alejandro Agag, a son-in-law of José María Aznar, the former Prime Minister. Correa is charged with organising kickbacks in cash, prostitutes or gifts from real-estate developers, construction firms and other businesses in exchange for public contracts between 1999 and 2005. The bribes involved run to an estimated €120m. Another key defendant in the affair is Luis Bárcenas, former party treasurer of the PP, who is accused of stashing €48 million in Swiss bank accounts. It is alleged that this money was used to finance the PP illegally, funding election campaigns and providing undeclared wages for party leaders. The importance of the Gürtel affair is that it reveals that the organised nature of corruption inside the political process is on an industrial scale, and not simply restricted to a few rotten apples.[123]

Giving testimony in court, Correa recounted:

> In 1996, Luis Bárcenas told me: 'You have contact with businessmen and I have contact with politicians. We're going to try and make it so that when there are public tenders we favour businessmen who can later collaborate with the party.'

Correa went on:

> I spent day and night in Génova [the PP's headquarters in Madrid].
> I spent more time there than in my office. It felt like home.[124]

Bárcenas was put in pre-trial detention in June 2013 due to what judge Pablo Ruz of the National Court described as 'a high risk of flight and to prevent the destruction of evidence'. He gave an exclusive interview to the *El Mundo* newspaper while in prison, in which he admitted that the PP had been illegally funding itself since it was founded by Franco's henchman Manuel Fraga. Bárcenas would later tell the investigating judge that Fraga personally received backhanders from Spain's largest employers' group, the CEOE. When Fraga died in January 2012, his funeral was attended by Crown Prince Felipe.

Bárcenas also revealed that the PP received illicit cash from businessmen channelled via dummy companies. He, as party treasurer, redistributed the money among top party members and covertly funded election campaigns. The key question is how high did this conspiracy go? In July 2017, Prime Minister Rajoy testified in the National Court that he had no knowledge of any slush fund and that he personally had never received any secret bonuses. 'They're absolutely fake,' Rajoy told the magistrates when asked about documents on which his initials appeared next to amounts of money that allegedly constituted under-the-table bonuses. The Gürtel-Bárcenas corruption saga still drags on, partly because a lot of the potential evidence disappeared in 2013, when PP officials at the party HQ in Madrid destroyed the hard disks on computers belonging to Bárcenas himself.

The latest corruption scandal to hit the PP is perhaps the biggest of all – the so-called 'Lezo case'. This involves Ignacio González, the PP's senior figure in the Madrid region until 2015, who is accused of profiting from investments made in Latin America through a state-owned water utility. González's brother, and around a dozen former public officials and businessmen, were also indicted. The significance of the Lezo affair is that bugged conversations leaked to the press appear to show González using his political connections to try and evade justice. In one conversation, from 2016 (after he left office), González spoke to former PP minister Eduardo Zaplana about appointing a new and more pliable chief anti-corruption prosecutor. 'The state machinery and the media are key,' González was recorded saying. 'Either you have them under control or you're dead.'[125]

Not long afterwards, in February 2017, Rajoy's government appointed Manuel Moix – the very man González wanted – as the chief anti-corruption prosecutor! Moix lasted only a matter of months in office before resigning when it was discovered that he was using a secret off-shore company in Panama to hide his ownership of property in Spain. It was hardly a coincidence that Mariano Rajoy should be orchestrating a major campaign of state repression against Catalonia just as the major corruption trials and investigations involving the PP were reaching a crescendo: diverting public attention is an age-old political tactic.[126]

The Lezo Affair shows every sign of dragging in yet more senior PP figures. In April 2017, the veteran PP leader Esperanza Aguirre – a former head of the Madrid regional council and current leader of the PP group in the city – was forced to resign from public office because of her links to Ignacio González. Aguirre was appointed Honorary Dame Commander of the Order of the British Empire in 2004 and is the PP's 'public face' in the UK. Some 60 prominent political and business leaders are being investigated as part of the Lezo Affair. They include a former PP Labour Minister and the owner of the OHL construction group. The former chief executive of OHL is none other than Josef Piqué, who was implicated in the Ertoil scandal.

A politicised judiciary

On 15 November 2017 the PP itself was criminally charged for tampering with evidence in the Gürtel Affair. On 17 November 17 a trial opened against former PP economy minister and IMF director Rodrigo Rato, for cooking the books during his tenure at the helm of Bankia, a major Spanish bank. In any other Western European nation, the government would have fallen as a result of such revelations.[127]

The obvious question arises is how can this dense web of financial corruption continue to exist in a modern industrial state? The answer is twofold. First, far from being an aberration, corruption is an integral part of the 1978 regime. Post-Franco Spain is akin to post-Communist Russia and China, where the privatisation of former state assets led to the creation of a corrupt oligarchy with close relations to the ruling party. Second, as an integral part of the 1978 regime's bureaucratic architecture, the judiciary is heavily politicalised. As a result, this judiciary acts as a bulwark against effective prosecution of corruption cases.

In Spain, individual judges lead an investigation into corruption charges and public prosecutors are meant to back them up. In practice, this split can be used to delay or confuse proceedings. The prosecutor's office provides resources and manpower for a judge's investigations, which means that they are in a position to call into question the actions of judges and, with some exceptions, delay or reject bringing formal charges so that the case can go to court. This was precisely the interference of which Manuel Moix was accused during his time as anti-corruption prosecutor – activities which led to an office revolt by his own staff.

The chief prosecutor is appointed by the government of the day. The governing body of magistrates – the General Council of the Judiciary, or CGPJ – is selected by members of parliament. The CGPJ then chooses the judicial hierarchy, including the magistrates at the Supreme Court. As a result, the judicial hierarchy is appointed for its ideological or political closeness to politicians.

'The system is badly designed and generates some concerns, to say the least,' said Judge Jesús Villegas, who heads the legal association Plataforma Cívica por la Independencia Judicial (Civil Platform for Judicial Independence). Viada knows all about attempted influence from his days as an anti-corruption prosecutor in the *Audiencia Nacional*, the most important nationwide court investigating corruption. One chief prosecutor ordered him to stop investigating a politician. The problem was solved when Viada asked his boss to write the order down in a formal statement, which he refused to do. On another occasion, Viada said that a state secretary (ranked just below a minister in government hierarchy) had asked him to talk to a judge and convince him to stop an investigation against a banker. Viada refused.[128]

Under the 1978 constitution, ministers and elected politicians enjoy significant privileges when it comes to prosecution and trial. Any investigation into them must first be approved by the legislative chamber to which they've been elected. Even if this is granted, investigators lose the surprise factor – documents can disappear or, as in the Gürtel-Bárcenas case, computer disks can be destroyed. Also, investigating opaque financial transactions, as in the Lezo case, relies heavily on councils and government departments providing key documents. But transparency laws in Spain are very weak and many cases fall apart once the government or politicians under suspicion leave office.

In 2013, the Group of States Against Corruption – which was set up by the Council of Europe – said in a report about Spain:

> While the independence and impartiality of individual judges and prosecutors have been broadly undisputed to date, much controversy surrounds the issue of the structural independence of the governing bodies of the judiciary and the prosecutorial service – the primary concern being the appearance that partisan interests could penetrate judicial decision-making processes.

The organisation issued 11 recommendations to help Spain tackle corruption. Three years later, it concluded that none of the recommendations had been 'implemented satisfactorily'.[129]

Corruption in Catalonia

Catalonia has not been immune from the endemic corruption that pervades the kleptomaniac Spanish state. In July 2014, Jordi Pujol, the architect of Catalonia's post-Franco recovery of autonomy, issued a statement admitting that for 34 years – including 23 as the Prime Minister of Catalonia – he had kept secret foreign bank accounts. At the time, his sons Jordi and Oleguer were being investigated by the tax authorities. Another son, Oriol Pujol, had just resigned from the leadership of the CIU to face charges of public corruption. Pujol Sr. was stripped of his titles and remains under investigation. His eldest son Jordi was jailed in April 2017 for obstructing ongoing investigations into money laundering and a tax fraud allegedly carried out by the whole family.

The scandal soon engulfed the ruling CIU party and its successor, the PDeCAT. Both have been the target of a massive anti-corruption investigation by regional courts that alleges that party officials insisted on a mandatory three per cent kickback on all state contracts – the so-called Three Percent Affair. But as in the rest of Spain, securing indictments and convictions has proven difficult. The Three Percent saga has been going on since 2005. In March 2017, investigations were concluded in the so-called 'Palau case', which investigated allegations that Convergence had received €5.1 million from the construction company Ferrovial, channelled through donations made to Barcelona's iconic Palau de la Música concert hall. The accusation was that hundreds of thousands of euros from *Ferrovial* were passed to Convergence via Fèlix Millet, who ran the Palau de la Música. Millet was also accused of taking a commission for himself. The investigating judge also accused Daniel Osàcar, who was *Convergència's* treasurer between 2005 and 2010, of being involved. But the investigation was made difficult, according to the judge, because local banks would not reveal full details of the trail of the monies involved.

Of course, there is no reason why Catalan bourgeois politicians should be any more honest than Spanish ones. The real import of the Pujol affair is that it helped undermine the traditional Convergence/PDeCAT support for autonomy over independence. For many Catalans, the leaching of the '78 Regime corruption bacillus into Catalonia was yet another reason for a complete breakaway.

Conclusion

Spain is a kleptomaniac state. But the corruption of '78 Regime is not reducible to personal wrongdoing, even if it is on a heroic scale. The endemic fraud, theft, bribery and malfeasance served a political and economic purpose. When the old Dictatorship fell, Spanish capitalism was technologically backward, underfinanced and facing the full gale of European competition. The robber barons and oligarchs who seized control of the economy certainly enriched themselves to an obscene degree. But they were also forced by circumstances to accumulate investment capital in the fastest, crudest manner possible in order to modernise the Spanish economy, rather than rely on foreign inward investment. The tragedy is that having done so, they used this capital not for productive purposes but instead to finance an unsustainable property boom. At the same time, the Madrid regime waged war against Catalan economic interests in order to bolster its political security. As we shall see in chapter 10, the end result has been to hand over the most productive parts of the Spanish economy to foreign ownership. This serves as the background to Catalan demands for control over their own economy.

Chapter Eight: 'Dirty War' in the Basque Country

New cases of torture and other ill-treatment, including excessive use of force by law enforcement officers, were reported throughout the year.
Amnesty International report on Spain 2016–17

Incommunicado detention in Spain violates the European Convention on Human Rights, according to two recent rulings by the European Court of Human Rights
Civil Liberties Union for Europe, 2014

IN 2016, THE RESPECTED World Organisation Against Torture (OMCT) issued a strong warning regarding the case of Ms Nekane Txapartegi, a young woman accused by the Spanish authorities of membership of the banned ETA organisation. The Geneva-based OMCT is the leading NGO concerned with torture cases. It consulted officially by both the UN and the Council of Europe. Ms Txapartegi had been an elected municipal councillor in the Basque town of Asteasu but fled Spain in 2007 after being sentenced to six years and nine months in prison. Ms Txapartegi was arrested in Zurich on 6 April 2016 following an extradition request issued by the Spanish authorities. She had been living in exile in Switzerland for the previous seven years.

OMCT argued there was strong evidence to indicate that Ms Txapartegi was tortured to extract self-incriminating statements which led to her original conviction:

> Ms Txapartegi was apprehended by the Spanish Guardia Civil and held for five days in incommunicado detention. During the 120 hours in custody, she was subjected to brutal acts of torture including rape by multiple perpetrators, beatings, near-suffocation through plastic bags, threats of electric shocks, sleep deprivation, forced nudity and a mock execution.[130]

The case of Nekane Txapartegi is not unique. Spain has been condemned on frequent occasions in recent years by international human rights bodies, for detaining suspects incommunicado and for the lack of prompt, effective and independent investigations into allegations of torture by the

Guardia Civil and the security forces – particularly in the context of the campaign against ETA. The European Court on Human Rights has ruled against Spain on seven occasions for breaches of article 3 of the Convention governing the prohibition of torture and inhuman or degrading treatment, the last one being the case *Xabier Beortegi Martínez v. Spain* in May 2016.[131]

Ms Txapartegi was fortunate. In September 2017, the Spanish government withdrew the extradition warrant in the wake of an international campaign on her behalf. This was engineered first by retrospectively cutting her sentence, and then saying that this meant she no longer merited extradition. The real reason was because Mariano Rajoy's minority PP government was anxious to placate Basque sympathies while it dealt with the Catalan crisis. The UN special rapporteur on torture, Nils Melzer, was especially vocal in calling on Switzerland not to extradite Ms Txapartegi. Her case exemplifies the fact that the post-Franco regime in Spain is far from the normal European democracy it pretends to be – something that became universally apparent from the mass police raids, Guardia Civil baton charges on polling stations, and detention of elected politicians that have been used against the Catalan independence movement.

The brunt of the state violence used against opponents of the 'democratic' Spanish state has been in the Basque Country. This is not to justify the armed struggle methods of ETA or other paramilitary groups. But it is to say that the bastard post-Franco regime that emerged in 1978 – particularly its shadowy security apparatus – has never been weaned off the brutal, oppressive methods for handling political opponents of the regime that were commonplace during the Dictatorship. This culture of police immunity, of torture and brutality in handling peaceful demonstrations is a direct result of the failed 'transition' process from the old, Francoist regime. In June 2016, the Basque Government published an official report into Spanish state torture, using evidence collected and analysed by forensic experts at the Basque Institute of Criminology. Their preliminary findings showed that more than 4,000 individuals were tortured by Spanish state security forces in the Basque Country between 1960 and 2013. Most of that period is in supposedly 'democratic' times.[132]

In fact, the worst excesses took place between 1983 and 1987, under the POSE government led by Felipe González, when the Spanish security forces sanctioned the infamous *Grupos Antiterroristas de Liberación* ('Anti-terrorist Liberation Groups'), which were actually death squads which hunted down and murdered ETA militants primarily (but not exclusively) on the *French* side of the border. The GAL death squads, financed from the Ministry of the Interior, murdered at least 27 victims and maimed 30 others. Most were either members of ETA or Basque nationalist activists, but many had no links to political violence. This was the period known as the 'Dirty War'.

Spanish state repression in the Basque Country is hardly new. It concerns this history of the Catalan events because it gives the lie to the notion that the modern Spanish state is a normal West European democracy. For instance, the scale of the security apparatus in Spain remains unique in Europe. Today, even after significant cuts caused by recent austerity measures, Spain still has 506 police officers per 100,000 inhabitants compared with only 260 in England and Wales, 391 in France, and 300 in Germany. In fact Spain has the biggest police force per capita of any EU state, outstripping even Russia (546) and Turkey (484).

Spain also has a special political court, the *Audiencia Nacional* (National Court). The *Audiencia* tries crimes that are essentially political in nature, or a threat to the state itself in some way. Obviously, that includes alleged terrorist crimes but also genocide, international drug-trafficking, the execution of European arrest warrants, industrial disputes – and alleged rebellion in the autonomous communities. In 2017, the *Audiencia* would be responsible for remanding in custody elected Catalan ministers on charges of sedition and rebellion, as well jailing two prominent pro-independence activists, Jordi Sánchez and Jordi Cuixart. The origin of the *Audiencia Nacional* lies in the infamous *Tribunal Especial para la Represión de la Masonería y el Comunismo* (Tribunal for the Repression of Freemasonry and Communism) set up by Franco in 1940 as a latter-day Inquisition. Between 1940 and 1964, this body tried over 64,000 subversives.

In 1963, as the dictatorship sought respectability, the tribunal's exotic name was sanitised to the more prosaic *Tribunal de Orden Público* (Public Order Court). This followed the international outcry over the execution of Julián Grimau, the Communist PCE's leader inside Spain. While in custody, Grimau 'fell' from a second-storey window, suffering serious injuries to his skull. The Interior Minister, Manuel Fraga, claimed that Grimau threw himself out the window for an 'unexplainable' reason. Grimau was then sentenced to death not for his activities in the Communist underground but rather for his role in the Civil War (ironically, he led the repression against the POUM). Despite an appeal for clemency from Pope John XXIII, he was shot by a firing squad. In 2002, the PP majority in the *Cortes* rejected a proposal to exonerate Grimau lest it was taken as a criticism of Fraga.

The newly rebranded Public Order Tribunal was effectively the old Francoist political court in everything but name. Its primary purpose was still to guarantee public order as defined by the Francoist regime, by punishing 'those crimes whose characteristic was to subvert the basic principles of the state or to wreak havoc in the national conscience'. This version of the Tribunal operated until the first years of the transition. One of the high-profile cases handled by the *Tribunal de Orden Público* was the trial and imprisonment of the leaders of the Workers Commissions (CCOO) trade union, in 1973.

With Franco in his grave, the political court had yet another re-branding. Formally, the Public Order Tribunal ceased operations by Royal Decree in January 1977, two years after the Caudillo's death. In its place, on the same day and in the very same building, Juan Carlos created the current *Audiencia Nacional*. This was five months before the first democratic elections and almost two years before the approval of the Spanish Constitution. So the *Audiencia* is not a product of democracy. It remains what it always was: the judicial cloak for imposing political order – as defined by the regime.

Civil War and Dictatorship in the Basque Country

Catalan and Basque history, and their claims for self-determination, are heavily intertwined. For this reason, we need to examine in more detail events in the Basque Lands. The Civil War experience in the Basque Lands had a particular impact on future history. Unlike Catalonia, the Basques were reluctant to take sides in the military uprising against the Republican government. This was down to their Catholic conservatism and the right-wing, Christian democratic, bourgeois leadership of the Basque Nationalist Party, the PNV. The PNV rallied to the Republican side only after some hesitation. The PNV saw the CNT as almost as much the enemy as the Nationalists. Recalling the eventual decision of the PNV to rally to the Republic, one PNV member noted:

> Until the evening before, our real enemy had been the left. This was not because they were left wing but because they were Spanish…We vacillated for two weeks or more, hesitating to ally ourselves with our former enemies. Had it been possible, we would have remained neutral.[133]

The decision had been taken for them by the Nationalists, who advanced into the Basque province of Gipuzkoa crying *Death to Euzkadi!* and murdered any PNV members they captured. In fact, the fascist advance was fuelled by a viciousness bordering on outright racism towards the Basques. Yet relations between the PNV and the left parties remained strained. On 1 October 1936 the Republican *Cortes* in Madrid approved a Statute of Autonomy for the Basque Country, aware that the PNV were threatening to form a government regardless.

In April 1937, Franco ordered an offensive to crush Vizcaya. A few days after it began, the German Condor Legion carried out the infamous bombing of Gernika (Guernica), where the assembly of the Basque people had traditionally been held. The bombers were targeting a town of no military significance but of tremendous symbolic importance. The terror attack was designed to sap Basque morale. The destruction of the town was made famous by Pablo Picasso's painting.

The Basque forces retreated to a defence line around Bilbao, but the weight of Nationalist artillery and air attacks by the Germans and Italians broke their defences. The Basque Government ordered the abandonment of Bilbao. The night before they left, they released right-wing prisoners in the city's jails and passed them through the lines to the Nationalist forces. The Basque Government also ensured that the major steel plant was left intact, in working order – a tribute to its respect for private property. Within six months the Nationalists were exporting iron ore to Britain, earning much-needed hard currency and Bilbao's steel plants were producing material for Franco's forces. But the new Falangist mayor of Bilbao could still proclaim: 'The revolting, sinister, heinous nightmare known as Euzkadi has fallen forever.'[134]

Under Franco's rule Vizcaya and Gipuzkoa were treated as 'treacherous provinces'. The Basque language was banned from public use, children could not be christened with Basque Christian names and rights of assembly and free speech were abolished. Franco regarded the Basques as traitors and wished to eliminate their language and culture. It had the opposite effect. The father of a future ETA prisoner recalled: 'Franco made us nationalists by his persecution.'[135]

The Basque Government maintained itself in exile more successfully than its Catalan counterpart, but at the end of the Second World War its hopes rested on the victorious Allies moving on to topple Franco. With the onset of the Cold War and Washington's signing of agreements with Franco, such hopes were dashed. Younger nationalists began looking at a more radical strategy. Looking back, Txillardegi, a future leader of ETA recalled:

> From the Basque point of view, the situation was really sad. People had lost all hope. After 1953 no one believed the Americans would help restore democracy. Thus, we thought we needed to do something without relying on anyone else, and we went to work.[136]

Euskadi Ta Askatasuna (Basque Homeland and Liberty) was founded in 1959 by a group of young radical nationalists who had been active for several years in promoting cultural resistance to Franco. The PNV had tried to co-opt them but after a brief stay in its youth wing they left. They differed from the PNV in having a definition of Basque nationality which centred on use of the language rather than race and family. It was the events of 1968 – that year of international rebellion – which led ETA to a strategy of revolutionary war for a separate Basque state. Naïvely, they hoped the dictatorship would respond with a crackdown which would fuel popular resistance.

In August 1968, after an ETA member had been killed at a police check point, they assassinated the Chief of Political Police in San Sebastián. The Francoist response was fearsome and would culminate in the famous trial of ETA members at Burgos where six were sentenced to death. The defendants used the trial to bring to attention to the national and linguistic oppression of the Basques and ensured that ETA was seen as being in the forefront of the fight against the regime. But this propaganda success masked growing unease over the revolutionary warfare strategy. Francoist repression had not led to a mass rebellion (as in Vietnam). In 1974 the organisation split into a military wing, ETA *Militar*, the larger of the two, and ETA *Político-Militar*, which looked for political channels to pursue the struggle. The latter would split again over whether to pursue negotiations with the Spanish state. Opponents of this rejoined ETA *Militar* (henceforth just ETA).

After Franco: the Dirty War

In 1977 the first democratic elections took place in Spain and the Basque Country since the Civil War. A revived PNV came top of the poll in the Basque Country, unlike in Catalonia, where the Catalan autonomists and independence supporters were still a distinct political minority behind the left parties. In 1978, the PNV called for an abstention in the referendum on the new Spanish constitution, under pressure from the more radical nationalist groups. Less than 50 per cent of the electorate in Guipuzcoa and Vizcaya voted and approved it. Despite the boycott the result among those voting was overwhelmingly in favour. The subsequent negotiations over a new Basque Autonomy Statute saw the PNV accept that Navarre should be excluded, becoming a separate autonomous region. Their electorally opportunist argument was that while there was a strong Basque identity in the north, the rest of the region looked to Spain and voted for the right. In a public referendum in 1979, the new Statute of Autonomy was passed, although 41 per cent of the voters abstained.

Since its inception in 1980 the Basque government has been run almost continuously by the PNV, though sometimes in coalition with other separatist groups. The one exception was between 2009 and 2012, when a Spanish state ban on radical Basque parties allowed the PSOE and PP to form a brief, unlikely coalition government on the basis of this gerrymander. The return of a formal parliamentary democracy, and the strengthening of the PNV politically, led to a change in tactics by ETA. The group maintained an armed campaign in the hope this would force the Spanish government into negotiations, following which a mass non-military campaign for independence could be launched. But to prepare the ground, ETA used the democratic opening to launch its own, open political wing – *Herri Batasuna*, or Popular Unity.

Herri Batasuna first took part in the 1979 Spanish general election that followed the ratification of the national constitution. Standing on a left-wing programme, it won 15 per cent of the vote in the Basque Country and nine per cent in Navarre – suggesting that the armed struggle had a degree of support. It gained three seats in the *Cortes* but (like Sinn Fein in the UK Parliament) refused to participate. A year later, in the first Basque parliamentary election, *Herri Batasuna* came second to the PNV, taking 16.6 per cent and winning 11 seats. Though this was for the Basque Parliament, they again abstained from taking their seats, allowing the PNV to form a government. Being a member of *Herri Batasuna* was no sinecure: Santiago Brouard, a leading member, was gunned down by the GAL state death squad in 1984. The party would be eventually banned outright after a court ruling that it financed ETA.

The transition to democracy did produce a general amnesty which saw the release of Basque political prisoners. However, it also amnestied all those involved in human rights violations carried out under the Franco regime. This added to a sense of invulnerability inside the state security apparatus that would see the rise of the infamous GAL death squads a few years later. Even after Franco's death, during the last six months of 1977, the security forces attacked some 30 demonstrations in the Basque Country, killing three protesters and injuring 87.

That last point is important because, as the jails filled up again with ETA members and suspects, those prisoners won the support of many Basques who did not identify with the military campaign. By early 1981 there were 300 Basque political prisoners, by December 1982, 485. The use of torture by the Guardia Civil became routine – it always had been. And not just in the Basque Country itself. In February 1981 an accused ETA member, Joxe Arregi Izagirre, died under interrogation in the Madrid HQ of the Directorate for State Security, part of the Ministry of the Interior. In June 1981 Juan José Crespo died after 66 days on hunger strike in Madrid's Carabanchel Prison (his death followed soon after that of Bobby Sands in Northern Ireland). Amnesty International expressed its concerns over the provisions for arrest, detention and interrogation. As usual, the Spanish state ignored such representations.

The election of a Socialist PSOE government in 1982 under Felipe González might have seemed to offer hopes for a political solution in the Basque Country, and certainly of a stronger civilian control of the security apparatus. Quite the reverse happened. Anxious to pursue its neo-liberal reform of the economy, the González Government decided to take a short-cut to ending its problems with the Basques by actually intensifying state repression.

Enter the new Minister of the Interior, José Barrionuevo. His emergence as a PSOE minister is a tribute to just how bogus and rotten the 'transition' process from the Franco era had been. Under the Dictatorship, Barrionuevo had been the Chief of Staff to the Deputy General Secretary of the National Movement, the controlling bureaucracy of the Francoist corporate state. The National Movement ran the state trades unions, family and youth organisations, and cultural bodies across Spain – ensuring conformity to El Caudillo's conservative values. But the National Movement had an even more sinister aspect: it acted as a vast intelligence gathering network keeping tabs on millions of individual Spaniards and vetting their ideological suitability for public appointments.

How did so senior a member of the old Franco apparatus as Barrionuevo end up in the PSOE, and in charge of the Interior Ministry? With the ostensible end of the old regime, leading Francoists like Barrionuevo sought democratic camouflage by joining the many competing political parties and grouplets that were emerging. The ideology of these new parties was often deliberately vague or fluid, to say the least. Eventually, most of these groups would merge again into the PP. Barrionuevo ended up in the PSOE in 1977, when his tiny grouplet of former technocrats, called *Socialist Convergence of Madrid*, opted to merge with the genuine Socialists. Doubtless they were on the lookout for influence. They soon found it. After 40 years of dictatorship, the PSOE was short on people with experience of administration, so Barrioneuvo quickly found himself as 'security' advisor to the new PSOE mayor of Madrid, running the municipal police. From there it was a quick jump to Minister of the Interior when González became Prime Minister in 1982. Barrioneuvo was back with his old friends in the security apparatus and ready to turn up the heat on ETA.

The strategy of Barrionuevo and the new González government towards ETA involved a number of elements. There was a concerted campaign to shut down Basque publications seen as favourable to ETA. In April 1983, the Madrid magazine *Tiempo* highlighted 160 cases of torture by the security forces. In August 1984, the Pro-Amnesty Committees of the Basque Country presented a detailed study of 3,000 torture cases, while in November of that year, *Tiempo* reported that 20 police officers and Guardia Civil accused of torture had been decorated by the Barrionuevo himself. But the Interior Ministry was secretly planning to deploy another tactic in the fight against ETA: the use of clandestine death squads, just like any Latin American military dictatorship.

These *Grupos Antiterroristas de Liberación*, made up of both hired killers and members of the security services, were not the first of their kind in Spain. The use of vigilante death squads to murder opponents of the regime was endemic in the later Franco era, and during the early Transition years. They included groups such as Triple A, which bombed the editorial office of the magazine El Papus in Barcelona in September 1977, killing one and wounding 17; the Spanish Basque Battalion (BVE), the Anti-Marxist Commands, and Anti-terrorism ETA (ATE). Collectively, these groups were responsible for over 60 murders. The scale of this activity is important to note. It could not have happened without the authorities being aware or acquiescing – obtaining arms and explosives under the Franco regime was no mean feat. Only a limited number of these crimes were ever brought to trial or even investigated properly. Above all, the GAL atrocities during the 1980s did not spring from a vacuum. Some of those involved in the earlier death squads were also active in the GAL. All this points to a culture of state-sanctioned murder and repression. One obvious conclusion is that a strategy of armed struggles against the Spanish state by small groups of Basque nationalists was ultimately futile. The mass resistance of millions of Catalans marching on the streets for self-determination has proved more effective in confronting the Spanish state and winning popular support internationally.

The Dirty War against ETA was organised and financed directly from the Interior Ministry, according to evidence later given in court by Jose Amedo, a Bilbao police superintendent and one of the GAL organisers; and Ricardo Garcia Damborenea, the General Secretary of the PSOE in Vizcaya, and one of the leading architects in the party of a heavy policy of crushing ETA. More than a dozen police and Government officials and mercenaries were prosecuted (in France as well as Spain) in a series of trials lasting years. Throughout the judicial process, both PSOE and PP governments proved obstructive, denying access to documents and putting pressure on the courts. The Spanish authorities systematically refused to extradite suspected GAL terrorists to France, while publically berating their northern neighbour for harbouring ETA militants.

Court testimony revealed a secret strategy meeting involving Interior Minister Barrionuevo at which officials discussed an 'Israeli solution' to the Basque problem. This meant kidnapping or killing ETA militants or supporters in their safe haven across the French border. Barrionuevo maintained in court that the meeting discussed 'doing something in France', but nothing illegal. But what could Spain have done in France unilaterally that was not illegal? GAL attacks in France involved repeated indiscriminate attacks on bars and cafes using grenades and machine guns, carried out by underworld criminals recruited in Marseilles or Lisbon; or politically-motivated French right-wingers, some ex-paratroopers. This was almost a mini-war perpetrated by Spain. The cash came from a slush fund operated by the Interior Ministry.[137]

Fortunately or unfortunately, the GAL operations were often botched by their criminal perpetrators. In one notorious episode which eventually went to court, the two thugs involved – a Moroccan from Marseilles and a former French soldier – kidnapped the wrong man. Seeking an ETA activist, they abducted a French furniture dealer named Segundo Marey, who was held for ten days in a deserted farmhouse in Spain. The most notorious GAL atrocity took place on 15 October 1983 when two young Basques – Joxean Lasa and Joxi Zabala – were kidnapped in Bayonne, in France and taken to Spain. They were brutally tortured, then taken to a remote mountain spot, shot through the head and their naked bodies buried with 50 kilos of quick-lime. In the latter case, the murderers were the Guardia Civil themselves.

In 1991, José Amedo and Ricardo García Damborenea were each sentenced to 108 years in prison for their role in organising the GAL at an operational level. To buy their silence about the senior politicians and police officers involved, the Office of State Security in the Spanish Interior Ministry paid the wives of Amedo and García Damborenea $4,000 a month between 1988 and 1993, and each man received $800,000 of hush money paid into bank accounts in Switzerland. But in 1994 the two decided to tell the full story, angered when the hush money dried up. That triggered a fresh round of trials.[138]

Among those eventually jailed for these political crimes were the Spanish Interior Minister, José Barrionuevo, for the Marey kidnapping; the Guardia Civil head of anti-terrorist operations, General Rodriguez Galindo, for the murder of Lasa and Zabala; the PSOE governor of Gipuzkoa, Julen Elgorriaga, for the same murder; and Julián Sancristóbal Iguarán, the Director of State Security, also for the Marey case. That is equivalent to the British Home Secretary, head of the Metropolitan Police anti-terror unit, the Mayor of London, and the head of MI5 all being jailed for murder or kidnapping.

Prime Minister González was heavily implicated in the Dirty War but escaped prosecution. However, the scandal forced him to call an early election in 1996, which he lost to the new Partido Popular led by José María Aznar. Predictably, the heavily-politicised Spanish judicial system paroled both General Rodriguez Galindo and Elgorriaga on 'health grounds', after only a few years in prison. Barrionuevo was sentenced to ten years but given a partial pardon and instant parole by the incoming PP government. Some of the underworld characters involved simply disappeared or died mysteriously in prison.

A new Basque political initiative

The approach of González's government would be mirrored by the Popular Party when it succeeded him in government in 1997. In fact, the PP intensified repression in the Basque Country. In 2002, the Spanish Parliament voted to amend a law on political parties to ban Batasuna (the descendant of the original Herri Batasuna). Even Margaret Thatcher had not banned Sinn Fein, the political wing of the Provisional IRA, on the grounds that it would effectively close off a political solution to the Northern Ireland Troubles. The tough legal measures complemented police action against ETA and, by 2003, had clearly eroded ETA's operational capacity. That should have opened up the possibility of a political initiative. Would Madrid respond?

In October 2003 the Basque *lehendakari* (Prime Minister), the youthful PNV leader Juan José Ibarretxe, put forward a bold plan whereby the Basque Country would enjoy 'free association' and co-sovereignty with the Spanish state, with its own separate legal system and European EU membership. This was backed by the Basque Parliament and opened up the prospect not just of a permanent solution to the crisis in the Basque Lands, but the possibility of a thorough reform of the corrupt, repressive 1978 Spanish regime.

But once again Madrid was blind to the notion of dialogue. In March 2004, Spain elected a new PSOE Government. The PP, now led by Mariano Rajoy, lost much credibility only days before the election, when it errone-ously blamed the murderous terror bombing on the Madrid railway (which killed 192 people) on ETA. Shameless, Rajoy dismissed the Ibarretxe plan as the 'biggest challenge to national unity since 1978'. The new PSOE leader and Prime Minister, José Luis Rodríguez Zapatero, said it was 'secessionist, unconstitutional and incompatible with Europe.' On February 1, 2005, the Spanish Parliament formally rejected the Ibarretxe Plan by 313 votes against (PP, PSOE, IU, CC and CHA); only 29 in favour, mostly from the regionalist parties (PNV, ERC, CIU, EA, Na-Bai and BNG); and two abstentions. Inciden-tally, Juan José Ibarretxe would later come out in favour of the Catalan 1-0 referendum. He noted: 'It's not that Spain has a problem with Catalonia, it has one with democracy'.[139]

Having rejected the Ibarretxe Plan, the Zapatero Government went on a banning spree. After Batasuna had been outlawed by the previous Aznar administration, its members had regrouped as *Euskal Herrialdeetako Alderdi Komunista*, the Communist Party of the Basque Homelands. This party won 12.5 per cent of the vote in the 2005 Basque elections. It too was now banned. Supporters regrouped again in *Acción Nacionalista Vasca* – a historical, but inactive Basque party. The Supreme Court banned half its candidates because they had previously run for *Batasuna*, meaning that its lists were dismissed in Bilbao, San Sebastián and Vitoria. Finally, it too was banned. Despite this in 2006 ETA announced a ceasefire. For many the hope was for an end to political violence in the Basque Country. Matters were not quite so simple.

For ETA the post-ceasefire strategy was to proceed with two strands of negotiations. One led towards agreement on a permanent end to the conflict between ETA and the Spanish and French states – including the technical issues of demilitarisation, prisoners, refugees, and victims. The other was between Basque social and political forces on the future political arrangements for the Basque Country. The first strand went well. After initial secret talks with an envoy of Zapatero's, ETA announced its first permanent cease-fire in March 2006, on the basis of confidential commitments and 'guarantees'. A series of protests then erupted criticising the Spanish Government for engaging with ETA. These were led by the PP and some of the organisations representing ETA's victims. Rajoy refused to back the peace process saying that no 'political price' should be paid to defeat terrorism. It was a position he would maintain.

Under pressure, Zapatero offered to continue face-to-face negotiations, but only if there was a complete renunciation of violence. ETA representatives (from the still banned Batasuna) demanded the Spanish government make concessions such as bringing prisoners back to jails in the Basque Country. The result was a deadlock. On 30 December 2006 a massive bomb demolished part of the car park at Madrid airport, killing two Ecuadorians sleeping in their vehicle. ETA had ended its truce. Efforts continued to have the peace process restarted. One of those involved in the negotiations with ETA was Jonathan Powell, former chief-of-staff to Tony Blair and one of the architects of the Northern Ireland Peace Process. It became clear to him that ETA was under pressure from within its own ranks to resume its cease fire.

In February 2011, radical nationalists linked to the old *Batasuna* presented the statutes of a new party, *Sortu* (Create) which rejected violence - and ETA's violence explicitly. For Madrid, this was still not enough, and the new party was denied recognition by the Supreme Court. Consequently, in May of that year the radical nationalists announced the creation of a coalition, *Bildu* (Re-unite) to contest the municipal and local elections. Again, the Supreme Court refused recognition but at the last minute it was approved by the Constitutional Court. *Bildu* won 25 per cent of the vote in those elections. This was far greater than the radical Basque left had ever achieved and helped convince the ETA leadership that a political approach could work. A political opening was now possible – one that would be closed immediately by Mariano Rajoy.

In September 2011, ETA announced a definitive end to its armed struggle, though it continued to seek negotiations over the fate of more than 500 of its members who were still in Spanish prisons. Typically, the mainstream

Spanish press treated the event as if it were bad news: 'ETA neither dissolves nor disarms', 'ETA ceases their armed activity without disarming', 'ETA boasts of their murders and calls upon government to negotiate'. Two months before, Mariano Rajoy and the PP had returned to government in Madrid. Many in the Basque Country looked to the peace and conciliation processes in South Africa and Ireland. But the response of Rajoy to ETA's announcement that it was ending military operations was to insist that the group hand over its weapons and disband forthwith. He refused to make any concessions on the issue of ETA prisoners, even by allowing them to be relocated to prisons closer to Euskadi. The Rajoy administration also rejected any international involvement – unlike the approach in the UK to resolving the Northern Ireland crisis.

Mariano Rajoy wanted unconditional surrender, not negotiations. This political intransigence was in character. Rajoy had originally been a member of Manuel Fraga's ultra-right People's Alliance, which eventually transmuted into the PP. It would be wrong to call Rajoy a Francoist or fascist, but his pronounced authoritarian streak and deeply conservative Spanish nationalism were inherited from Fraga and the latter's ideological world view. Rajoy would maintain the same intransigence towards the Catalan demands for self-determination. Of course, this narrow political attitude is not the fault of one personality. It represents the fears of all of that group in the Spanish oligarchy that any retreat from the 1978 constitutional settlement will open the floodgates to reform and sweep away their economic privileges.

End of the armed struggle

In February 2014, ETA put part of its arsenal out of use, and published a video showing the hand-over of firearms and explosives to Ram Manikkalingam (a board member of the Sri Lankan President's Office for National Unity and Reconciliation) and Ronnie Kasrils (a leader of the ANC's military wing under Apartheid). Both were members of the International Verification Commission (IVC), founded in 2011 to verify ETA's end of violence. But the Spanish government refused to recognise the IVC. Interior Minister Jorge Fernández Díaz dismissed the handover as 'another step in a theatrical exercise'. The Spanish High Court then summoned Manikkalingam and Kasrils for questioning over their meeting with ETA members!

In fact, throughout 2014, the Rajoy's Government continued to arrest dozens of people suspected of being ETA sympathisers. This was partly in response to criticism from VOX, a right-wing party breakaway from the PP, led by José Antonio Ortega Lara, a former prison officer who was kidnapped and held captive by ETA for 532 days. VOX accused Rajoy of going soft on ETA by obeying a European Court of Human Rights order which had led to 50 of the group's most veteran prisoners being released on parole for good behaviour.

In April 2017, as the Catalan crisis was developing, the Verification Commission was informed of the location of ETA's weapons, ammunition and explosives dumps in France, which they conveyed to the French authorities. The French police collected 3.3 tonnes of weapons and explosives. The handing over of these arms was described by the French Minister of the Interior as a 'great step' towards peace and security in Europe. The Basque *Lehendakari*, Iñigo Urkullu, described it as a 'fundamental step in the process of an ordered end to violence'. Subsequently the International Verification Commission concluded that ETA has fulfilled its commitment to disarm and announced that its work was concluded. Yet the Rajoy Government still refused to make any concessions over prisoners or participate in direct peace talks.[140]

Between 1968 and 2011, ETA and related groups assassinated some 840 people, wounded 2,500 more, and kidnapped 80. This campaign included terrible deeds, including the bombing in June 1987 of a crowded Barcelona supermarket in which 15 people were killed and 35 injured. In its later stages, under increasing pressure from Spanish and French security services, ETA turned to killing Basque so-called 'collaborators,' meaning local councillors and journalists. The Basque Country has been systematically oppressed by Spain for long years and the modern Spanish 'democratic' state was more than willing to launch its own Dirty War to impose control. But all the ETA campaign succeeded in doing was demobilising and substituting for the mass democratic action of the Basque people themselves. ETA's activities also helped drive a wedge between the Catalan and Basque struggles for self-determination, to the political benefit of Madrid.

It should be noted that terrorism was not unknown in Catalonia during the early transition years, though it was on a more restricted basis than in the Basque Country. Catalonia's long struggle for autonomy and independence has created a political culture that was hostile to terrorism and the manner in which it substitutes the action of a military elite for mass, public activity. In 1978, there appeared a group called *Terra Lliure* (Free Land), from a merger of smaller, pro-independence organisations. *Terra Lliure*'s inspiration seems to have been ETA. Between its founding and voluntary dissolution, the organisation carried out more than 200 attacks, resulting in the death of five people, four of them *Terra Lliure* members.

At one time or another, over 300 people linked to the organisation were arrested, suggesting it was a reasonably-sized group – though not a very effective one. Its most notorious action was in May 1981, when it kidnapped the right-wing journalist Federico Jiménez Losantos. He was shot in the leg in protest against his signing a manifesto opposing the Catalan government's language policy. Later in the 1980s, inspired by the terrorist grouplets in Germany and Italy, *Terra Lliure* began attacking American interests, bombing a social club used by the US military. Increasingly ineffectual – not to say a political irrelevance – *Terra Lliure* disbanded in 1991. Some of its leaders and supporters subsequently joined the ERC, which demanded their explicit public renunciation of violence as a condition for entry.

Prime Minister Rajoy drew his own conclusions from ETA's demise. ETA had been seen off without any concessions. Emboldened, Rajoy became even more intransigent when dealing with the peaceful campaign of the Catalans for self-government. But that same Catalan approach of involving millions in political action is now influencing Basque attitudes. In the end, this threatens the 1978 Spanish regime more than ETA ever did.

Has Madrid learned anything from its repressive handling of the Basques – a repression which itself helped prolong ETA's existence? Hardly. On 5 February 2016, Alfonso Lázaro de la Fuente and Raúl García Pérez, professional puppeteers, were arrested and imprisoned for performing a play in which a puppet displayed a tiny banner bearing the sign 'Gora ALKA-ETA' ('Up with ALKA-ETA'). The puppeteers were charged with 'glorifying terrorism'. It is this kind of political overkill that results from the inflexibility of the 1978 Spanish regime. Fortunately, In September 2016, the National Court dismissed the charges against the puppeteers. The response of the Spanish authorities was to proceed with charges of incitement to hatred![141]

Chapter Nine: Battle for a New Statute of Autonomy

We are Catalan by nature, Spanish by coercion

Joan Comorera

Self-government in the regions of Spain, and especially in Catalonia, is being reduced because there's a very harsh campaign of recentralisation of power in Madrid... There are more independence supporters today than a few years ago because it's evident that this process is occurring. And accompanying this process is a great lack of respect for Catalan identity, language and culture.

Artur Mas

THE CORRUPT, AUTHORITARIAN '78 Regime did not go unchallenged. As the 21st century dawned, Catalonia demanded a new Statute of Autonomy. This was a chance to reform the entire post-Franco state as well as recognise Catalan sovereignty within some federal or quasi-federal system. Later demands for outright independence stem from the failure of this bold democratic initiative. The quashing of the project for a new Statute of Autonomy, after years of struggle, would expose the deep political bias of the Spanish judiciary. Many outside Catalonia remain bemused by the independence project and propose greater devolution or even federalism as an alternative. But this road was actively sabotaged by the PP, the Spanish right wing and a politically-motivated Constitutional Court, as we will now examine.

Undoubtedly, the period between the fall of the dictatorship in 1976 and the start of the new century was a time of economic and social renewal in Catalonia. But the hopes created in this period were soon dashed. A devolved government emerged that went some way towards returning political power to the Catalan people, yet those powers were rigidly circumscribed, with Madrid keeping a close control over taxation and spending. The pro-devolution but cautious and centre-right Convergence and Unity (CIU) came to dominate locally, but its apparatus was tightly controlled by Jordi Pujol and a small group of family dynasties for more than two decades. They operated a policy of propping up governments in Madrid in return for small concessions in Catalonia. Pujol and his cronies, while retaining popular support, soon succumbed to the endemic financial corruption of the period.

This corruption was magnified by the rampant property speculation and cowboy building that engulfed Barcelona. Even the 1992 Olympic Games, which gave the Catalan capital global publicity, had a darker side: the parkland of Montjuic, where the Olympic stadium was built, was turned over to urban construction and speculation on a mass scale. Much of the city's traditional character was lost in an orgy of cheap construction that helped underpin a mass inflow of people from the rural Catalan hinterlands, which were depopulated as a result, and the rest of Spain. Meanwhile many traditional industries, such as textiles, were swept away as the local economy was forced to adapt to global competition after Spain joined the EU in 1986.

Yet beneath the surface, a quiet revolution was taking place. First, the pro-independence ERC managed to stay aloof from the political compromises of the period and began to gather support. As its traditional base in the Catalan countryside was weakened by internal immigration to Barcelona, the party shifted its focus to the capital and surrounding areas, and towards workers in the public sector. As a result, the party moved to the left. The 2003 Catalan Parliament election was the first sign that the old political order was ripe for change. Jordi Pujol stepped down, having won the six previous elections. Handpicked to fill Pujol's place was his young protégé Artur Mas, the former economics minister. But Mas was only there by accident. The leadership was intended for Pujol's son, Oriol, but he was under indictment for corruption – a fate that would soon befall Pujol senior. As it was, Mas failed to deliver at the polls. CIU won the most seats (56) but on a sharply reduced share of the vote. The Catalan Socialists (PSC) – under the charismatic Pasqual Maragall, Barcelona's popular, former mayor, and chief architect of the city's Olympic Games success – were able to form a government with the support of the ERC, which had doubled its seats to 23.

The victorious ERC, which had remained solidly pro-independence through the Pujol years, backed Maragall on the condition that he sought to negotiate with Madrid a new Statute of Autonomy for Catalonia, effectively revising the post-Franco Constitution of 1978. Potentially, this would recognise Catalonia's national sovereignty, recognise Catalan as the first language, and give Catalonia the same control over local taxation as enjoyed by the Basque Country and Navarre. Negotiating such a Statute did not go as far as independence. But effectively it meant Home Rule for Catalonia within a Spanish state. But would Madrid accept such a compromise?

Zapatero and a new Statute of Autonomy

The 2004 Spanish general election took place days after the bombings of Madrid commuter trains that left 192 dead and scores more wounded. Prior to the bombings, polls showed the ruling PP on track to secure a narrow electoral victory. All that was to change. The retiring PP prime minister, Aznar, rushed to blame the killings on ETA, despite mounting evidence that they were the work of Islamist terrorists. The belief grew that, because the Aznar government had so vociferously backed the 2003 US-led invasion of Iraq, it was keen not to blame Islamists, as many would see the bombings as a consequence of this. The carnage also reminded people of the government's deeply unpopular decision to back Washington over Iraq.

The Socialists, led by José Luis Rodríguez Zapatero, had been trailing the PP in the polls. In the event they won, polling a record 11 million votes, the most garnered by any party in a Spanish political election up until then. Zapatero formed a minority PSOE government with the parliamentary support of the Catalan ERC and the ex-Communist United Left. This success opened the way for Pasqual Maragall's Catalan government, also in local coalition with the ERC, to press for a reform of the Statute of Autonomy. This unusual parliamentary geometry put the pro-independence ERC in a strategic political position for the first time since the Civil War.

Born in 1960 in Valladolid to a prosperous middle class family of Jewish descent, Zapatero's paternal grandfather had been executed by the Nationalists at the start of the Civil war. However, Zapatero represented a new generation, who became politically active after the fall of the Franco regime. Impressed by the leadership of Felipe González, Zapatero joined the PSOE in 1979 and soon became associated with its non-Marxist right wing, which identified with the German Social Democrats. With the help of another rising star – none other than Barcelona's charismatic mayor, Pasqual Maragall – Zapatero became party General Secretary in 2000. His centrist *Nueva Vía* (New Way) for the PSOE was consciously modelled on Tony Blair's *Third Way* in Britain. Zapatero's narrow defeat of Aznar in the 2004 general election was a reflection that many in the Spanish state wanted real change. But, like Tony Blair in the UK, they were soon to be disappointed.

Things began optimistically. Zapatero immediately withdrew all Spanish troops from Iraq and ordered the removal of the last remaining public statue of Franco in Madrid. On the constitutional front, he promised a 'second transition' to transform Spain's system of autonomous regions. That was code for giving Catalonia in particular a new deal. Historical baggage was involved. An earlier Statute of Autonomy for Catalonia had been approved in 1932. It was promoted by the then President of the *Generalitat*, Francesc Macià, and approved in a referendum by 99 per cent of Catalan voters. This draft Statute was then approved by the Spanish Parliament on 9 September 1932. One reason for Franco's coup had been to overthrow that particular democratic decision. Asking for a new Statute of Autonomy was merely a way of asking for this historic injustice to be rectified. Equally, it could be seen by the neo-Francoists and defenders of the 1978 regime as a provocation.

On September 30, 2005, the Catalan Parliament approved the draft of a new Statute of Autonomy by 120 votes to 15 (the opposition PP members). This majority in favour covered the entire Left-Right spectrum, including federalists, autonomists and pro-independence parties. In particular, the project was driven by Pasqual Maragall, who saw it as an opportunity to solidify local support for the PSOE/PSC, give himself more direct power, and perhaps launch himself on to the top job in Madrid. The draft then went to the *Cortes* in Madrid in November 2005. Every *Cortes* deputy voted in favour of considering the draft Statute except – the PP. In fact, the PP went further, appealing immediately to the Constitutional Court on the grounds that such a new Statute of Autonomy was unconstitutional in principal. The party also collected some four million signatures on a petition calling for a vote of all Spaniards on any new Catalan settlement. It even tried to organise a Spain-wide boycott of Catalan *cava*.

But the most worrying opposition came in January 2006, when the neo-Francoist Lieutenant-General José Mena Aguado, head of all land forces, made a speech to his troops in which he warned that passing the new Catalan Statute of Autonomy would trigger Article 8 of the 1978 constitution that tasks the army with defending Spain's 'territorial integrity and constitutional arrangements'. Aguado was also angry at Zapatero's removal of Franco's statue in Madrid and his negotiations with ETA. The Lieutenant-General was put under house arrest for eight days (a slap on the wrist) then transferred to the reserves, but the army had made its point: dismantling the existing constitutional arrangements was off limits. Aguado was still serving with the army reserves in October 2017, during the Catalan crisis.

Zapatero was clearly rattled by this resistance to a reformed Statute of Autonomy. He began to backtrack on original assurances that he would accept the draft submitted by the Catalan Parliament – where, after all, his friend Pasqual Maragall was Prime Minister. The original 2005 version recognised Catalonia as a 'nation' – anathema to the neo-Francoists. This was fudged and other references to 'sovereignty', 'independence' and 'self-determination of the people' were simply deleted. The major substantive reform proposed in the first draft was the granting of full financial autonomy to Catalonia along the lines already enjoyed by the Basque government. This too was struck out. Substantial new tax-raising powers were included but capital spending in Catalonia would still be controlled by Madrid, a point of friction that would intensify after the economic crisis of 2008. There was progress on the language front, giving Catalan the status of 'the preferred language' for Catalan administrations, public media and in education – another red line for the neo-Francoists.

Zapatero's backtracking had political consequences. The pro-independence ERC withdrew its support for Maragall, triggering elections in Catalonia a year ahead of schedule. Desperate to find a compromise, Zapatero struck a deal with the leader of the Catalan opposition, Artur Mas, who represented the traditional centre-right autonomism of the Catalan bourgeoisie rather than the ERC's left-wing independence stance. With approval from Mas, a final draft of the new Statute of Autonomy was passed by both Houses of the Spanish Parliament on 10 May, with only the PP voting against. ERC deputies abstained. The new Statute was then put to a referendum in Catalonia on 18 June 2006, where it was approved with 73.24 per cent in favour. But the turnout was only 48.85 per cent, reflecting a call from the ERC for a boycott. Unfortunately, this poor turnout undermined the credibility of the result, which was used later by the PP to claim the Statute was illegitimate even in Catalonia.

Despite these travails, the new Statute of Autonomy did bring substantial new powers to Catalonia, even if it failed to reform the 1978 constitution to any substantial degree. It strengthened the Catalan judiciary, allowed representatives of the *Generalitat* to join the Spanish delegation to the EU, granted the Catalan government control of half of income tax and VAT collected in the region and stated that Spanish investment in infrastructure projects within Catalonia would be based on its contribution to Spanish GDP over a seven-year period. The deal gave the gradualist centre-left at a Spanish level and the CIU traditionalists in Catalonia what they both wanted, without open rupture with the oligarchy or the neo-Francoist right. At the same time, it left intact the old 1978 structures, which placed strict limits of regional autonomy. The ERC in Catalonia now found itself losing ground as a result of its uncompromising stand on independence, which at the time seemed sectarianism. In the Catalan elections in November, the CIU under Mas increased their seats and share of the vote.

So why was the PP and the right in general unwilling to accept the new Statute? Why did it embark on a political and legal crusade to block the implementation of the new legislation – a crusade that turned pro-autonomy Catalans into supporters of full independence? One explanation is that the PP feared that even modest attempts to reform the 1978 settlement would lead inevitably to other interest groups or regions demanding the same, thus detonating a process that would bring down the oligarchy. This is precisely the view Rajoy would hold in 2017.

Furthermore, the PP calculated that taking a strong stand against the new Statute of Autonomy played well with its base in other, poorer parts of the Spanish state. The PP were desperate to find an issue that would undermine Zapatero, who was now well on his way to winning a second term in March 2008. As it was, a number of the autonomous communities – La Rioja, Murcia, Valencia, Aragon and the Balearic Islands – immediately lodged assorted challenges to the new Catalan Statute with Spain's Constitutional Court. Part of their motivation was a fear that Catalonia would pay in less into central resources. But this only reflects the need for a wholesale reform of the 1978 regime, which some of the autonomous communities may have been seeking. Others on the right were actually keen to sweep away decentralisation altogether and go back to a unitary form of government as a way of guaranteeing political and economic 'stability'.

For big businesses and the financial oligarchy, the struggle for the Catalan Statute of Autonomy was a dangerous diversion from the property and economic boom that was surging through Spain and the rest of the global economy in the first decade of the 21st century. With money cheap, Spanish groups were buying up foreign companies using debt, to create a multinational presence. Much of this effort was directed at Latin America, but the EU was also a target. For instance, in 2006, Basque-based Iberdrola bought Scottish Power for £12bn, as part of its strategy to become a global energy utility. Any hint of political destabilisation was therefore anathema. The major newspaper chains which reflected big business were vocal in opposing the new Statute. They included the right-wing Madrid daily *La Razón*, owned by the Barcelona-based Grupo Planeta. The anti-Statute position of the big bourgeoisie – inside and outside of Catalonia – is proof that the struggle for greater autonomy (and ultimately self-determination) is not a bourgeois project but a basic democratic demand of the mass of the Catalan people. In both 2006 and in 2017, the simple democratic struggle for Catalan self-determination soon threatened to take a radical and even anti-capitalist direction, because it instantly came up against the limitations of the 1978 constitution. And on each occasion, in the way stood that bastion and guarantor of the 1978 regime: the Constitutional Court.

The Constitutional Court strikes down the Statute of Autonomy

For the next four years, a battle was waged in and through the Constitutional Court to sabotage and undermine the new Statute of Autonomy. Finally, in 2010, after a contemptuously long deliberation, the Court struck down most of the key provisions of a piece of legislation that had been agreed by the Spanish Parliament and accepted in a legal referendum of the Catalan people. By a wafer-thin vote of six to four, the Court struck down 14 articles and amended many more. In an unprecedented response, the entire Catalan press published a joint editorial rejecting the Court's decision, under the title: 'Dignity!' The new Catalan Prime Minister, the conservative autonomist Artur Mas, called for a large protest rally under the banner 'We are a nation! We decide!' The opportunity for a Home Rule solution to the Catalan question had gone – outright independence was now on the agenda.

The Constitutional Court's deliberations took so long because massive political pressure was applied inside and outside the Court to influence the judges to reject the compact that had been agreed between the Catalans and the Socialist-led government in Madrid. Gerrymandering of the Constitutional Court during the proceedings was outrageous by any standards. The PP forced the retirement of one of the initial 12 judges claiming he had written a report for the Catalan Government several years previously. With this move, conservative and Spanish nationalist judges had a tacit majority of seven to four. But then a conservative judge died during the hearings. The 12-person Court limped on with only ten members, split six-four in favour of the conservatives. However, a quorum of eight was required to deliberate – liberal judges could, in effect, veto anything they disliked by declining to participate.

By November 2007, there were four judges whose term on the Court was due to expire. The PP and the PSOE deadlocked on fresh appointments, as both sides jockeyed to secure a majority of justices sympathetic to their political position. Zapatero used his parliamentary majority to modify the rules governing the Constitutional Court, to extend the expired mandates of the liberal President of the Court and the three other judges. If the Constitutional Court was not political to start with, it certainly was now. Inside the Court, sentence after sentence of the Statute of Autonomy was redrafted in search of a form of words that would carry a majority. There were widespread calls for the entire Court to resign. Meanwhile, as the years ticked by, the Statute was being implemented pro tem in Catalonia.

Finally, Court President Mari Emilia Casas produced a bizarre compromise. Instead of presenting a complete judgement to the court – for which there was no majority – she proposed voting in sections. Most constitutional experts cautioned against such a procedure, saying (rightly) it would result in a legally incoherent and possibly contradictory adjudication. But Casas, a former labour lawyer, was determined to proceed. Even then, the sections into which voting was split were decided pragmatically rather than on coherent legal grounds, to secure a majority at each stage. This was political compromise, not law-making.

Voting began on the contentious matter of Catalan nationhood. The new Statute, even in its watered-down form, implied that Catalonia was a nation in its own right. This was the real sticking point for the PP and its judicial lackeys, both because it compromised the idea of the indissolubility of Spain and because it opened the prospect of legal challenges by the Catalan government over Madrid's handling of taxation and revenue-sharing. By 6 votes against 4, the Court struck out the wording agreed by Zapatero and Mas. Their drafting noted that 'the Catalan Parliament has defined Catalonia as a nation' – a neat semantic way of actually staying within the boundaries of the 1978 constitution. The Court produced its own semantics, stating that Catalonia 'is a nationality' albeit within 'the only and indissoluble unity of the Spanish nation'. But legally a nationality is a population group. A nation is a political entity with legal rights. The Court also struck down a provision in the Statute ratifying the Catalan Supreme Court as the highest court for some kinds of civil law. This move actually represented an encroachment on traditional Catalan rights that had survived since medieval times and even under Franco. Catalan civil law has always been different from the rest of Castilian Spanish civil law – much as Scots law is different from English common law.

Next, the Court strayed into economic policy matters. It declared unconstitutional Catalonia's attempts to set up its own tax system. The Statute's provision that 'the [Spanish] state's investment in Catalonia should be on a level with the percentage of Catalan GDP in relation to the overall Spanish GDP' was deemed constitutional, but Madrid was not legally obligated to fulfil this provision. This ruling would be used by Madrid after the 2008 economic crisis to divert large sums of cash from Catalonia.

Last but far from least, the Court watered down provisions in the Statute covering the Catalan language. It removed the status of the Catalan language as 'the preferred language' for Catalan administration, public media and education. Furthermore, the court considered the provision calling upon the inhabitants of Catalonia to master the Catalan language to be of secondary importance to Catalans' constitutional duty to achieve proficiency in Castilian. The judges did not move immediately to threaten the Catalan linguistic model in which every pupil is immersed first in Catalan when they start school. But they had reaffirmed the primacy of Castilian. As a result, as soon as the Constitutional Court recovered a clear conservative majority in later years, it was able to move with a vengeance to obstruct the use of Catalan.

Spanish nationalists reacted with jubilation to the final Court ruling in 2010. The newspaper *ABC* carried an editorial by the ultra-conservative writer José María Carrascal, in which he thanked the Court for 'not becoming saboteurs of the constitution'. In Catalonia, a mass protest against the ruling was organised by Òmnium Cultural. It was supported by some 1,600 civic organisations, including four out of the six political parties represented in the Catalan Parliament. The two big trade unions (CCOO and UGT) took part, and also the main employers' federation (Cipec). And, of course, FC Barcelona. A million and a half Catalans demonstrated in the street under the slogan 'We are a nation! We decide!' [142]

In Madrid, Zapatero spoke of the 'end of political decentralisation'. He was correct. The Catalan autonomy project was dead – killed by the PP and the conservatives on the Constitutional Court. Since the end of the Franco regime, moderate Catalans had supported a constitutional arrangement, with Catalonia as a genuinely autonomous region within Spain. But the

Court ruling had shown this to be a chimera. Even middle-of-the-road Catalans now felt there was no possibility of reaching an agreement with the rest of Spain that would respect them or their identity.

Aftermath #1: the Language Wars

The aftermath of the battle for a second Catalan Statute of Autonomy was long and politically bitter. Far from returning to the pre-2006 constitutional status quo, the 2010 Constitutional Court ruling became the legal pretext for a major campaign to roll back *existing* Catalan rights, especially in language provision. This sotto voce repression would exacerbate tensions between Catalonia and Madrid. It would also help bring into being a new, grass-roots separatist movement. In conventional terms, Catalonia is an oppressed nation whose mother language is under constant threat from the Spanish political ruling bloc.

Catalan is one of the great European languages. It is spoken not only in Catalonia, but also in the Balearic Islands, in parts of Valencia, in Andorra, in the French province of Roussillon, and in the Sardinian city of Alghero. Catalan is now spoken by more than 10 million people, and up to 13.4 million understand it. Which makes Catalan the ninth language in Europe in terms of the number of speakers – more than Swedish, Danish, Finnish, or Greek. More than 150 universities around the world teach Catalan, and some 400 journals are published in the language. More than 80 television channels and 100 radio stations broadcast in the language. One sign of the times: more than 25,000 people have asked Netflix to introduce subtitles in Catalan.

During the Franco era, the Catalan language was banned in the school system. Castilian Spanish was promoted everywhere under the slogan: *Hable el idioma del imperio* – 'Use the language of the empire'. As a direct result, though more than half the population could speak Catalan at the time of the fall of the dictatorship, only 15 per cent could write it with any proficiency. As a result, after Catalonia recovered autonomy, teaching Catalan in schools became a cultural and national priority. This has proven an overwhelming success. According to the 2011 census, 73.2 per cent of the population can now speak Catalan fluently, and 55.8 per cent write it. In total, 95.2 per cent of the population say they understand Catalan for everyday use. Among those under 25, only 3 per cent do not speak Catalan. Catalan has also become the language of public administration government and business. Public sector jobs demand Catalan proficiency. There has been a successful campaign to promote product labels and signs in shops in Catalan. The majority of theatre productions are in Catalan. And Catalonia's biggest-circulation newspaper, *La Vanguardia*, started a Catalan edition in 2011, a sign of rising nationalism, which now accounts for 45 per cent of its print sales.

However, this cultural revival of Catalan in itself represents a threat to the foundations of the 1978 regime, which uses Castilian nationalism as a way of mobilising popular support. Spanish institutions remain wedded to the 'language of empire'. Catalan studies are weakly represented in Spanish universities, reflecting both the historical discrimination against Catalan and contemporary concerns about the drive for independence in Catalonia. Only seven Spanish universities outside Catalonia teach and research Catalan. That compares with 22 universities in the UK which offer courses in Catalan Studies, 20 in France and 24 in the United States.

The post-Franco attack on the Catalan tongue began in January 1981, when a group of 2,300 intellectuals and professionals in Barcelona published *Por la igualdad de derechos linguisticos en Cataluña* – 'Manifesto for the equality of linguistic rights in Catalonia'. This claimed that Castilian-speakers were being discriminated against and called on the Spanish state to intervene. Their particular animus was against the linguistic immersion of children in Catalan in the early years of schooling – though surely it is a norm in most nations for children to be taught initially in the national mother tongue. In Catalonia, which has a significant immigrant population, teaching primary school pupils initially in a common language also has an integrating function.

Within five days of the manifesto being published, Catalan cultural associations responded with the *Crida a la solidaritat en defensa de la llengua, la cultura i la nació catalana* – 'Call for solidarity in defence of the Catalan, language, culture and nation'. This was endorsed by 1,300 institutions and voluntary associations. The organisers set a vast mobilisation campaign in motion culminating in a festival-cum-demonstration in FC Barcelona's Camp Nou, which holds around 100,000 people. Throughout the 1980s, Crida organised campaigns in defense of the Catalan language. In March 1982, it organised a mass demonstration in Barcelona against the so-called LOAPA laws – a move by the main Madrid parties to roll back the Statutes of Autonomy in Catalonia, the Basque Lands and Galicia – particularly in regard to linguistic freedom.

Following the October 1982 coup attempt, LOAPA – the *Ley Orgánica de Armonización del Proceso Autonómica* – was introduced in the *Cortes* as a way of pacifying the right. It was supported by both the governing UCD and the PSOE opposition. The ostensible aim was to harmonise the devolution process – allowing Spain to claim thereafter it was one of the most 'decentralised' states in Europe. But its true purpose was to curtail the autonomy of the two main Autonomous Communities, Catalonia and the Basque Country, by standardising the menu of political power and representation allowed to each region. By deliberately extending devolution to a host of regions and cities (including Ceuta and Melilla in colonial Morocco) which had never had pretensions to self-government, the national and language demands of the Catalans and Basques could be diluted – even reduced to ensure 'harmonisation'.

Behind the smokescreen of LOAPA, the new PSOE government of Felipe González was able to delay the agreed transfer of powers to the *Generalitat* and place obstacles in the way of the launch of the first Catalan TV station. González would take Spain into EU membership in 1986 but he was also careful to deny Catalan and Basque recognition as working languages used by the EU. The result is that, in Catalonia, EU directives and regulations are published solely in Castilian, while under EU law food labels do not need to be in Catalan. These moves were not just politically petty, they helped undermine any success devolution might have had.

LOAPA also led to friction between Crida, the Catalan language rights organisation, and the new CIU government in Barcelona. In response to the LOAPA laws, Crida began calling demonstrations under the slogan '*not a l'harmonització, it autodeterminació*' – 'No to harmoniSATION, self-determination!' While Jordi Pujol's conservative *Generalitat* was against LOAPA, it was not in favour of raising the provocative demand for self-determination. Crida turned increasingly to direct action rather than mass protest, including painting the US Navy frigate Capodanno bright pink. Though Crida dissolved in 1993, some of its leaders would go on to figure in the independence struggle, including Jordi Sánchez, later head of the ANC. Many of Crida's best activists joined the ERC, speeding that party's leftward trajectory.

Meanwhile, the Spanish Constitutional Court continued to delegitimise the use of Catalan. School remained the flashpoint. In February 2014, now with a reliable conservative majority, the Court was finally able to rule against the Catalan school model and the linguistic immersion principle. Note that while teaching begins for everyone in Catalan, as a unifying principle, it also guarantees every pupil an equal knowledge of both Spanish and Catalan by the end of their schooling period; i.e. Catalonia guarantees bilingualism. However, the Court now mandated that classes be taught in Castilian from stage one, if demanded by parents. As a result, pupils are split as soon as they go to school – hardly a satisfactory state of affairs.

In fact, there is a rising tide of petty cases of Catalan language discrimination across Spain. People are routinely being fined or harassed by the Spanish state police for answering questions in Catalan, the Spanish Tax Agency has withdrawn VAT declaration forms in the Catalan language, and lawyers are often made to speak Castilian in court. The language rights NGO *Plataforma per la Llengua* ('Platform for Catalan') monitors these incidents and recently presented a report to the European Parliament, citing in detail cases where Catalan speakers were discriminated against in public institutions between 2013 and 2015. They include the case of a Chinese immigrant who had lived in Spain for 11 years and married a Spanish national yet who was denied citizenship because he could speak Catalan but not fluent Castilian. Another involved a mother who lost custody of her daughter because she moved to Catalonia. In March 2014, a Tenerife judge took away the custody of her child because he maintained that the Catalan language would pose 'a problem' for the girl. In yet another incident, during a misdemeanour trial in March 2015, defendant Mireia Fernández asked to testify in Catalan, as she would be able to express herself better. The judge replied: 'if you talk to me in Catalan, I'll call this trial off'.

As the independence struggle entered 2017, the Constitutional Court seemed to intensify its moves to roll back Catalan language rights. In July 2017, the Constitutional Court struck down a raft of Catalan language provisions in what many see as a pre-emptive strike ahead of the proposed independence referendum. A law passed by the Catalan Parliament obliging cinemas to show 50 per cent of films in Catalan was deemed 'disproportionate' and the quota arbitrarily lowered to a maximum of 25 per cent. Judges also ruled that new migrants in Catalonia should not receive their initial education in Catalan but in Spanish. The Catalan Consumer Code obliging private firms, if asked, to offer customer service in any of the official languages (including in Catalonia) was struck down. According to the Constitutional Court, companies cannot be held to the same degree of language regulation as the public administration.

Such discrimination against a major language group within a nation state is unheard of in Western Europe in recent times. It is, of course, a direct result of the legal framework that underpins the 1978 regime. But it is more than a legal abstraction. Living, breathing judges appointed by the PP and conservative bodies act in a political way, consciously interfering in the right of the Catalan people to determine their own laws and language, which explains the continuing desire of the Catalan nation for independence. Franco's body still lies inside the basilica at the Valle de los Caídos monument, built by Republican prisoners, outside Madrid. A shrine to the dictatorship and still a publicly-owned national monument, it is a shame on today's Spain. But the survival of Catalan as a great European language must mean that he is turning in his grave.

Aftermath #2 – the battle for economic autonomy

The failure of the Second Autonomy Statute also had an ongoing economic impact. If Catalonia were its own sovereign country, the GDP produced by its 7.5 million residents would measure some $314 billion, ranking it as the world's 34th largest economy. That is bigger than the economy of Portugal, Hong Kong or Egypt, to name but a few. Catalonia's GDP per capita, at $35,000, is greater than that of South Korea, Israel or Italy. The primary detonator of the recent upsurge in Catalan demands for independence is economic, even more so than linguistic. Ordinary Catalans feel they are being over-taxed and under-resourced by Madrid to pay for the implosion of Spain's debt-ridden financial elite after the 2008 banking crisis. Equally, Madrid refuses to let Catalonia go or risk losing Spain's most economically dynamic area. The Second Autonomy Statute was meant to alter this state of affairs by setting limits on the proportion of Catalan taxes which could be pre-empted by Madrid, imposing rules for revenue sharing, and introducing a mechanism for negotiations between the parties on fiscal decisions. But these provisions were struck down by the Constitutional Court in 2010, reinforcing economic centralism.

Since the days of Franco, Madrid has used the Catalan economy as a milch cow to fund the rest of Spain. The end of the dictatorship has not changed this situation. In fact, the imbalance actually worsened following the economic crisis of 2008, with Catalonia being used to underpin the huge debts run up by the central Spanish state during the unsustainable property bubble of the early 21st century. Catalonia cannot remain globally competitive if it has to carry such a heavy fiscal burden. Catalan companies pay high taxes, only to receive few public services and low infrastructure investment. High taxes make the region less competitive, and the low level of investment in infrastructure lowers productivity. Not only does it hamper economic growth and the modernisation of the Catalan economy, but it also impoverishes Catalan citizens and damages their social and territorial cohesion. As a result, Catalans want to control their own fiscal destiny – not because they are selfish but because, if they do not, their economic future is at stake.

Since the end of the Franco era, Spain's central government controls tax collection and decides how the fiscal revenues are distributed throughout the country – except in the autonomous regions of the Basque Country and Navarre. Catalans pay taxes to Madrid in exchange for public expenditure in the region. The difference between what is paid in by the region and what is received back from Madrid in revenue and capital spending is the fiscal balance, which can be positive (a 'fiscal surplus' for Catalonia) or negative (a 'fiscal deficit' for Catalonia). Calculating the exact fiscal balance is not an easy task given Madrid's reluctance to provide adequate data. However, the most recent studies show that Catalonia's fiscal deficit has been increasing and on average now runs at an unsustainable 8 per cent of Catalan GDP.

It is not the fact that Catalonia – the fourth biggest region of Spain by GDP per capita – contributes to the whole which causes local concern. Rather it is the unfair scale of these fiscal transfers. If we compare Catalonia to EU regions that have broadly similar levels of per capita GDP, we find that it has by far the largest fiscal imbalance. In fact, following the 2008 crisis, many similar regions in the EU now receive net inflows as a result of state borrowing at the centre. Scotland, for instance, has a net fiscal surplus. Another approach is to compare Catalonia to richer EU regions whose income per capita is 20 per cent or higher than the average of their respective state, as with Catalonia. These areas include the Ile-de-France, Bavaria, Baden-Württemberg, the South-East of England, Stockholm, and Emilia-Romagna and Lombardy. In this case, only the two Italian regions have a comparable fiscal imbalance.

Catalans do not reject the principle of keeping fiscal solidarity with the poorer regions of Spain or, indeed, of the EU. Rather, Catalans complain that – as a result of the way Catalonia has been treated by the political establishment in Madrid – many of Spain's other regions have more resources per capita to spend on essential services. The redistribution of tax money in Spain not only bridges the wealth gap between regions; it re-orders and increases that divide. Rather than the redistribution system giving every region in the Spanish state a common (average) spend per capita, the system reduces Catalonia to nearer 90 per cent of the average – while other regions get 110 or even 120 per cent.

Madrid tries to justify this arrangement by saying that it is merely an extreme form of redistribution from the richest to the poorest regions in a time of economic crisis. This argument does not stand up to scrutiny as other Spanish regions are not subject to the same grab on their tax revenues as the Catalans. The industrial Basque Country and Navarre have a different fiscal arrangement with Madrid that lets them keep almost all their tax receipts instead of forwarding them to the central government. This means that these regions have 40 to 60 per cent more in domestic resources per capita to spend than Catalonia.

Madrid disputes the scale of the fiscal drain on Catalonia but not the principle itself. Even then, Madrid puts the net fiscal drain at a hefty €8.5bn (£6bn) in 2011. Madrid also argues that the Catalan figures ignore national expenditure benefiting all of Spain, such as on defence. Centralists argue that the Balearic Islands and the Madrid region have even higher fiscal deficits than Catalonia. Such arguments obscure a central reality that no one disputes: the dire state of infrastructure investment in Catalonia compared to the rest of Spain. This is a direct result of decisions taken in Madrid. There is also a proven link between this infrastructure spending and the political corruption that has dogged Spain since Franco's time. Here economics and politics combine in a witch's brew that gives modern Catalan nationalism its central impulse.

Decisions on infrastructure investment in Spain are reserved mostly to the Madrid government – something the reformed Statute of Autonomy was originally meant to change. Madrid has used its control over infrastructure investment in a way that is heavily biased against Catalonian interests. One area in particular has been a constant source of political friction. In the early post-Franco years, the Catalan regional government funded its own network of motorways to help modernise the economy and create better communications with Europe. This motorway system was funded by tolls. In later decades, Madrid began building motorways in the rest of Spain which are toll-free – built in part with tax revenues diverted from Catalonia. As a result, Catalans are twice penalised: through local road tolls and by the tax burden placed on them to fund toll-free roads elsewhere.

However, there are limits to what Catalonia can invest in its own infrastructure. In recent decades the Catalan economy has needed new investment in transport and communications to remain globally competitive. In particular, it needs a modern urban train network to relieve congestion on the local suburban road system. And it needs a massive upgrade to the road connections with Europe. But Madrid has followed diametrically opposite priorities and used Catalan cash to fund them. In particular, Madrid concentrated on building a new and costly high-speed train system connecting the capital with southern Spain – a prestige project that remains underused. Meanwhile, better freight links between Catalonia and France were delayed.

The ticking clock

In 2010, ordinary Catalans could not grasp how the unelected Constitutional Court could strike down things they had voted in favour of only four years before. Economist Salvador Garcia-Ruiz grasped the significance of the court's decision:

> We followed the rules of the game. We got the Statute passed in the Catalan Parliament, in the Spanish Congress and Senate, and in a popular referendum... and then even though they had already 'whittled it down' as Alfonso Guerra, a high-level leader of the Spanish Socialist Party had boasted, the Constitutional Court finished it off by taking out some of its most important provisions. This was a turning point for a lot of people.[143]

This turning point saw the rise of a new Catalan independence movement. Autonomy had failed, self-determination beckoned. But there was also a new factor in play: the great Spanish property boom had imploded. Ironically, the Constitutional Court's decision to deny Catalonia greater economic powers virtually guaranteed that mass anger against austerity, youth unemployment and rising homelessness would turn into popular support for a Catalan Republic.

Chapter Ten: Austerity and Birth of a New Separatism

Two years ago the indignados *occupied the plazas of cities across Spain to protest against the crisis and demand a 'real democracy'. Now, it seems, indignation is becoming a generalised condition.*

Katherine Ainger

IN 2008, GLOBAL CAPITALISM suffered a near-death experience as the international financial system imploded. Spain would be caught up in the turmoil, unleashing new populist, political forces that – for the first time since the death of Franco – threatened the stability and very existence of the '78 Regime. In particular, the period gave birth to a new, left-wing Catalan independence movement that eclipsed the old bourgeois autonomist of the Convergence Party.

However, to outline these developments in so simplistic a fashion is to risk suggesting that the political process in Spain was both mechanical and inevitable. Neither is true. In other European states, the economic crisis produced no similar existential threat to the status quo, except in Greece or perhaps (in a more muted form) in the 2014 Scottish independence referendum. So we need to examine why precisely the anti-system reaction in Spain was so radical and why it ultimately took the form of demanding a new Republic in Catalonia.

Stage #1: *The financial bubble bursts*

The first thing that marks out the relative uniqueness of the Spanish reaction to the crisis is the horrendous quantitative impact on the domestic economy and society. Between 2008 and 2013, average household disposable income crashed by almost 10 per cent in real terms. In the poorest regions such as the Canary Islands, Andalusia and Extremadura, almost a third of the population fell below the poverty line. In 2011, the Zapatero government cut public sector wages by 5 per cent. The health and social services budget was cut by 13.7 per cent in 2012 alone. By 2013, a quarter of the national budget went on servicing public debt despite massive reductions in services and salaries. The social impact was devastating. The suicide rate in Spain rose by 20 per cent between 2008 and 2016, reaching double the number of deaths from road traffic accidents. The biggest rise in suicides was among middle-aged men. For millions of Spaniards, the years following the crash of 2008 were a return to the 'Hungry Years' of the late 1940s and early 1950s.[144]

What caused this? In any capitalist crisis, the bigger the investment bubble, the deeper the recession. In 2006, construction began in Spain of a staggering 800,000 new houses – more than in Germany, Italy, France and the UK combined. This was not rational investment in necessary infrastructure. This was a gigantic financial bubble based on high-risk lending by a uniquely corrupt banking system – a bubble facilitated by easy planning permissions granted by complicit politicians.

In July 2008, Martinsa-Fadesa, Spain's major property development company, went bust overnight, owing a mind-blowing €4 billion in debts to banks – chiefly to Caja Madrid, run by PP placeman Miguel Blesa. This was Spain's Lehman Brothers moment. Panic spread through the economy. Thousands of unfinished building projects were abandoned as other building companies crashed, throwing more than one million construction workers out of a job. Worse, as Spain's property boom imploded, the entire Spanish banking system teetered on the brink of insolvency. Spanish banks closed hundreds of branches and laid off thousands of employees.

This disaster was home made. It would then be compounded by the 2010 Euro Crisis which added further to the suffering of ordinary people in Spain by imposing austerity budgets on an already imploded economy. By March 2012, Spain's unemployment rate was 24.4 per cent – twice the eurozone average. Actual ghost towns appeared. Valdeluz, 65 kilometres from Madrid, was built for 30,000 people, but only 3,000 people now reside there. Houses, roads and infrastructure projects lie unfinished to this day. Vanity projects that were completed during the profligate years soon closed. They include the infamous Ciudad Real airport, in the central Castilla-La Mancha region. This cost €1.1 billion to construct, but no airline wanted to use it, and it was eventually sold to a group of British and Asian investors for £7,000.[145]

One reason why the global crisis struck Spain so harshly was due to the initial decision by the political establishment, including Zapatero's PSOE government, to try and hide the extent of the banking disaster. In the secretive, corrupt world of the Spanish oligarchy, self-protection came first. Rather than recapitalise the banking system immediately, which would have exposed the extent of their corruption and bad management, the Zapatero government (now at its fag end) organised a cosmetic restructuring of the caja system of savings banks – who were most damaged by the collapse of the property bubble. This delay and dissembling intensified the structural crisis inside the banking system, ultimately eroded international confidence in Spain and ensured that the county had to put itself in hock to the EU on a greater scale than necessary. Result: even more austerity.

Replacing Blesa as the new boss of Caja Madrid was Rodrigo Rato, a powerful member of the PP. Rato had been Economy Minister for eight years under Aznar, and for three years was head of the International Monetary Fund. With the connivance of the Spanish central bank, Rato merged Caja Madrid with six other failing regional savings banks, to create a giant called Bankia. It would be the largest holder of property assets in Spain – assets whose value was dropping like the proverbial stone. Bankia went public in July 2011, selling shares through its branches, after an aggressive marketing campaign. But Bankia was floated on the basis of unaudited accounts. When foreign investors shunned the offer, the Zapatero government called in the Spanish banks and fund managers and strong-armed them into buying 40 per cent of the €3bn of shares 'in the national interest'. Retail clients across Spain – 350,000 of them – were persuaded to buy the rest.

But Bankia was a sham. The merger had covered up massive liabilities. The bank quickly went bust and had to be nationalised and given a tax-payer-funded bailout of $30bn. Rato and 32 other bank executives were charged with fraud. In February 2017, the former head of Bank of Spain, Miguel Angel Fernandez Ordonez, was placed under investigation for his role in allowing the Bankia group to proceed with the 2011 rights issue. Typically, Ordonez was a political appointee and a card-carrying member of the then ruling Socialist Party. In February 2017, Rato was jailed for credit card embezzlement. In September 2017, Ordonez escaped prosecution on a technicality. Bankia's small shareholders, many of them retirees, lost everything.[146]

Stage #2: The euro crisis

Spain was now convulsed by a second economic tsunami – a crisis of the euro. As 2010 opened, the weakest Eurozone economies – especially Greece and Portugal, whose burgeoning national debt was foreign-owned – discovered that lenders were demanding higher interest rates in return for turning over loans when they fell due. Default loomed in the air – default that would undermine confidence in the euro and imperil lenders, among whom German banks were significant. At first Spain seemed less affected as its public debt level was comparatively low (at 60 per cent of GDP) and held domestically. But this was to ignore Spain's commercial and savings banks, which had run up foreign debts – mostly short-term – to fund their property lending. Profligate German bankers were only too happy to lend. At the height of the financial bubble in 2008, German exposure to Spanish banks, companies and governments amounted to €113 billion. Of course, interbank lending on this scale was reckless, but German financiers comforted themselves that the close relationship between the Spanish banks and the Spanish government would save their bacon if anything went wrong. The Germany government now made sure that happened.

The new PP government under Mariano Rajoy had no option but to bail out Spain's banks, to ensure they could repay their German loans. More than a dozen Spanish banks in total were bailed out by the state, costing the taxpayer €76.14 billion in capital injections and financial guarantees. But this gigantic bailout dramatically increased Spain's public debt and led to a substantial downgrading of its credit rating. The markets insisted on yet more austerity measures to guarantee interest payments. In June 2012, Spanish government 10-year bonds hit seven per cent and the prospect of default started to appear. This immediately rang alarm bells. As one of the largest eurozone economies – larger than Greece, Portugal and Ireland combined – the deteriorating condition of the Spanish public finances was of prime concern to Germany and the European Commission.

As a result, the EU agreed a rescue package for Rajoy's PP government, ostensibly to fund the bank bailout, and worth €100 billion. The cash would not go directly to Spanish banks – who were not trusted by the EU, for very good reason. Instead, the money went to a Spanish government fund dedicated to bank recapitalisations. This, of course, had the drawback that it counted as sovereign debt in Spain's national accounts. Rajoy would claim this was not a loan to Spain as such, but to the banks. No one else was fooled. Spain's public debt to GDP ratio shot up from 68.5 per cent to 90 per cent.

Spain received the largest financial aid of the five Eurozone countries bailed out. It should be noted that the cash did not involve any contribution from the IMF or non-Eurozone EU members, as was the case for Ireland, Greece, Portugal and Cyprus. The money came only from Germany and the rest of the Eurozone. This ensured that Rajoy did not have to suffer the sort of micro-management of the PP government's budget and economic reforms as was imposed on other bailed-out countries by the so-called Troika of the IMF, European Central Bank and European Commission. On the other hand, Berlin knew it could trust Rajoy to impose a super austerity on Spain without prompting.

This is exactly what Rajoy's PP administration would ensure over the next five years. The result was not just austerity but a massive attack on wages and employment regulations, which drove down Spanish labour costs. In the decade before 2008, wage costs had risen 30 per cent, as workers took advantage of the boom conditions. Now those gains were rolled back. After a decade of austerity, Spanish wage costs are well below the Eurozone average – helped along by the downward pressure on labour prices that has resulted from an unemployment rate of 17 per cent (2017). This in turn has created the conditions for an inflow of foreign investment and the creation of a new manufacturing export sector. In 2014, one third of Spanish goods and services were shipped outside of the country. Some 25,000 new jobs have been created in car manufacturing (mostly for export) by Opel, SEAT, Renault, Ford and Nissan.

Of course, much of this new, foreign-owned manufacturing sector is located in Catalonia (e.g. SEAT) or exports via the port of Barcelona. This explains the hostility of big business to Catalan independence. It is further proof, if needed, that the Catalan struggle is not some bourgeois plot to split Spain, as some on the international left have argued. Paradoxically, the emergence of this new export sector is not necessarily good news for the PP or the stability of the '79 Regime. It has certainly led to the recovery of economic growth and let Spain exit the European bailout mechanism early. But the rest of the Spanish economy – those sectors still in the hands of the old oligarchy – remains fragile, and under pressure from foreign competition.

Spain ranks only 32nd in the World Economic Forum Global Competitiveness rankings, on a par with Poland and the Czech Republic, but far below key Eurozone players such as Germany, France, the Netherlands and even Belgium – not to mention international threats such as Taiwan, South Korea and China itself. In other words, the PSOE and PP austerity offensive was not entirely successful in cowing the Spanish, Catalan and Basque working class. Instead, it met a rise in popular resistance stronger than anywhere else in Europe, reaching back into the memories of the anti-Franco resistance, but inventing new forms of organisation and struggle – a popular resistance that has challenged the very basis of the '79 Regime.

Constitutional amendment

Before looking at this popular resistance in detail, it is worth noting one interesting side-effect of the austerity policies introduced by the PSOE and PP: the only major change ever made to the 1978 constitution. This was implemented in September 2011, in the dying days of the Zapatero PSOE government. For 33 years the 1978 Constitution had been politically untouchable, modified only once in order to adapt its legal framework for EU membership. But under pressure from the international financial markets and Germany, Rajoy and Zapatero jointly agreed to fast-track a radical constitutional amendment that would mandate future Spanish governments to cap the national debt. The constitutional amendment was rammed through the Spanish Parliament, with 318 voting in favour and 16 against, on August 30th 2011, just before the general election. Voting for the amendment were Rajoy's PP members and the then ruling Socialists. Those against included nationalist and regionalist parties, including the Basque PNV and the ERC. One PSOE deputy abstained in protest – Antonio Gutiérrez, the ex-general secretary of the Comisiones Obreras (CC.OO). The CIU also abstained, trapped between its fiscal conservatism and unwillingness to court unpopularity back home in Catalonia.

The amendment had political repercussions. The cap does not come into operation fully until 2020, but it will affect the budgets of the autonomous communities as well as central government. So it represents a backdoor attack on the autonomy of both Catalonia and the Basque Lands. It also shows, if in a negative fashion, that it is perfectly possible to amend the 1978 constitution quickly – say to approve the right of Catalonia to hold a self-determination referendum. The passing of the debt-capping amendment was also the final death knell of the Zapatero administration. It drove working class supporters away from the party while, on the right, helping to burnish Rajoy's hardline reputation as someone who could handle the economic crisis.

The main trade unions, the UGT and CC.OO, organised a campaign against the constitutional amendment, including holding a token, one-day general strike. They demanded that the amendment be put to a national referendum, a procedure that can be triggered by 10 per cent of the deputies of either the upper or lower house of the Spanish Parliament. Predictably, both the PSOE and PP ignored this demand. This is worth remembering in the context of the 2017 1-O referendum, when Rajoy and the PP repeatedly claimed that no decision on Catalan self-determination could be made without a nationwide Spanish vote on the same.

Popular revolt: *the indignados*

On Sunday 15 May 2011, a 26-year-old Basque architectural student named Jon Aguirre climbed on to the back of a truck parked in Madrid's iconic Puerta del Sol square and addressed the waiting crowd. Later he would remark: 'That was the moment I thought "We're making history"'. The country was in the second year of harsh economic crisis. Youth unemployment had reached 40 per cent, and people were leaving the country in droves to seek work abroad. On that Sunday – it was the run-up to the Spanish local elections – around 150,000 young people took to the streets in 60 Spanish towns and cities to demand 'Real Democracy Now', marching under the slogan 'We are not commodities in the hands of bankers and politicians'. The protest was organised through web-based social networks without the involvement of the major political parties. If it had an inspiration, it was the Arab Spring of the year before. Using Twitter, people shared news and updates about the marches. Hashtags such as #15m and #democraciarealya were used to share thousands of links to photos and videos. The atmosphere was more carnival than political – a way of letting off steam, free from the conventions of normal, orchestrated demonstrations.

In Madrid, the march ended in Puerto del Sol, a normal occurrence. There were the traditional speeches. But these suggested a new indignation at the plight of young people under austerity. The speakers were not the usual suspects. This was the authentic voice of the oppressed. At the end of the speeches, some people decided to stay the night in the Puerto del Sol. Tents were erected. An impromptu occupation began. That, of course, ran foul of the equally traditional, heavy-handed attitude of the Spanish police. On the Tuesday, the police waded in with batons to clear the square.

As a result, young demonstrators returned to Puerto del Sol in even greater numbers. By the early hours of Friday, there was elbow-room only. Someone pinned a sign on the statue of King Carlos III: 'We are anti-idiots, not anti-politicians.' Other placards read: 'We aren't against the system, we

want to change it', and 'Take your money out of the bank!' 'I've been protesting for decades,' one 60-year-old passer-by was quoted as saying. 'I'm
glad to see so many young people here. The question is this: Is this another
May 1968 or are they just here for the party?' The answer was soon to
come.[147]

The call went out on social media across Spain for everyone to occupy
his or her local square. By the weekend, 65 public squares were occupied,
with support protests taking place in Spanish Embassies from Buenos Aires
to Vienna and London. A new movement had been born: 15-M, after the 15
May when it began, or, more popularly, *los indignados*. Not the mindlessly
angry but the righteously indignant.

In Barcelona, around 100 young people had started camping out in
Plaça Catalunya on the first Monday of the protest, on 16 May. Early in the
morning, Mossos tried to clear the square forcibly, arresting 19. However,
the Plaça was immediately reoccupied in even larger numbers. A general
assembly started to organise commissions to provide food, legal support, art
and entertainment, and political discussions. The nightly *cassolada* of pots
and pans summoned people to the general assembly of occupiers, which
soon reached into the thousands. The CNT lent a megaphone. Barcelona was
rediscovering its old revolutionary traditions. In the *Generalitat*, now controlled by the neo-liberal CIU of Artur Mas, this was disturbing news.

The new movement refused to set any political agendas, actively shun-
ning the established parties and trades unions. Instead it co-ordinated online
campaigns and targeted specific issues, such as banking and electoral reform.
15-M employed a bottom-up approach, in direct contrast to the vertical
power structures of the main parties that had dominated Spanish political
life since 1978. Through thousands of popular assemblies, 15-M created a
nationwide network that represented a serious challenge to the country's
vested interests.

The occupations and massive demonstrations petered out a month
later. The protest movement's influence, however, did not. Neighbourhood
committees formed across the country to discuss both local and national
issues. A myriad of co-operatives were set up around the country by a range
of professionals looking to barter their services with other groups, as well as
to sell them to the wider community. As the Spanish welfare state crumbled,
15-M offered practical solutions based on collaboration and co-operation.

The biggest impact was on housing. Between the very early stages of
the economic crisis, in 2007 and 2014, an estimated 600,000 evictions took

place. But under Spanish law, simply turning over your property to the bank does not cancel the debt. People found themselves both homeless and owing money to the bank. Barcelona was the hardest hit, accounting for 19 per cent of all evictions in Spain between 2008 and 2011. As a result, the 15-M movement threw its efforts into the Platform for Mortgage Victims (PAH), a grassroots organisation to help those evicted. Activists gathered outside properties due to be reclaimed by the banks, blocking the entrance and preventing the authorities from carrying out the foreclosure. Empty properties were also occupied. One of the crucial achievements of the PAH was the passing of the controversial 'Law of Urgent Measures against Evictions' (*La ley de medidas urgentes contra desahucios*) by the Catalan Parliament in 2015. This measure obliged landlords to let defaulting tenants stay in their property and rent it as social housing. It also prevented water, gas and electricity companies from cutting services to those unable to pay. The Constitutional Court later struck down many of these provisions – a move that added to support for independence.

Sociologically, the core supporters of 15-M were the children of the Spanish middle classes. Tens of thousands of young university students and ex-students took part – precisely the demographic impacted by the rising tide of youth unemployment. But they were also the offspring of the social sector on which the 1978 regime had based its stability – the professional middle class. The rage and frustration of the children soon transmitted itself to their frustrated parents, creating a crisis for the regime as middle-class voters fled the PP and PSOE. Working class organisations were sympathetic to the anti-system dynamic of 15-M but were only partially involved. Those sections of the white-collar professionals in the course of being 'proletarianised' – such as health workers – were more directly participatory. It is also true that the spirit of resistance of the 15-M movement propelled the official trades unions towards stronger action against government austerity measures, including general strikes in March and November 2012.

In political essence, 15-M was a democratic rebellion, as it tried to recover a sense of citizens' rights and popular justice in the face of neo-liberal austerity policies imposed by the PP and EU. But because it was not a political party as such, it studiously avoided analysis of the capitalist crisis (apart from denouncing corrupt bankers and politicians) nor did it advance any alternative set of structural reforms. Nevertheless, in counterposing popular democracy to neo-liberal austerity, it was both radical and anti-system.

As a movement, 15-M was not inevitable. It took advantage of the arrival of social media – Spain had 3 million twitter users in early 2011, mostly young and suffering from the economic crisis. The original Puerto del Sol occupation transmuted into a nation-wide protest because of the usual heavy-handed intervention of the riot police. Except in this case they beat up the children of the middle class who had smart phones and could tell the world. The lasting impact of 15-M was that it delegitimised the '79 Regime. The myth that the post-Franco settlement was either democratic or irreplaceable had been well and truly shattered. In no other European country, even Greece, were the ideological defences of the ruling order so comprehensively challenged. In Catalonia, it became possible to think the previously unthinkable: quitting the Spanish state altogether.

Podemos and Catalonia

Among those who took part in the 15-M protests in 2011 was a group of university professors from Madrid who harboured leftist sympathies. Led by Pablo Iglesias, they founded a new political party – Podemos – in 2014. As a party, they sought to penetrate the same institutions the *indignados* railed against. The birth of Podemos in January 2014 marked a significant strategic shift for the anti-system 15-M generation – a leap towards electoral activity. Podemos would attempt to embrace the methods of internal organisation invented by 15-M, particularly assemblies of members who could vote on key issues using social media. But its aim was political power through the ballot box.

Born in 1978, Iglesias came from a left-wing and Republican background. His paternal grandfather was sentenced to death in 1939 (but had the sentence commuted) while his father was a militant of the FRAP, a Maoist group that carried out armed action against the regime in the dying days of the Dictatorship. Iglesias himself was a member of the Communist Party youth wing (suggesting a somewhat Stalinist training). Something of an academic eclectic, Iglesias studied computing, film and political science (including a stint at Cambridge University's Centre of Latin American Studies) before finding his metier as a TV pundit and media advisor. His multi-faceted experience was the key to the creation of Podemos as a populist, activist election machine. Iglesias was elected to the European Parliament at the new party's first outing, in the European election of May 2014.[148]

Podemos emerged into a new, post-crisis political world. The traditional party of the left, PSOE, was decimated in the 2011 general election – punishment for the financial bubble, economic collapse and mass unemployment. Paradoxically, as a result, a right-wing PP government was returned to power, with 185 seats out of 350 in the *Cortes*. One explanation is that the PP, under the leadership of Mariano Rajoy since 2004, had abandoned its outward guise as a pro-globalisation, neo-liberal party and shifted opportunistically to a more Spanish nationalist stance. It was propelled in this direction by the need to distance itself from the collapse of the economy, which it blamed on the Socialists. At the same time Rajoy was also anxious to offset the 15-M protests and deflect public anger at the endemic corruption embedded in the post-Franco political settlement – corruption that went to the heart of the PP apparatus itself. Opposition to demands for increased autonomy by both the Catalans and Basque nationalists formed the main focus of the PP's campaign in the March 2008 general election. It was a tactic Rajoy would continue to use.

Podemos filled the vacuum created by the collapse of the PSOE, offering a genuinely radical alternative to the PP. In the 2015 general election, Podemos came from nowhere to win 21 per cent of the vote and 69 seats. It did so by appealing consciously to the legacy of 15-M. But there were other claimants to the 15-M mantle. Across Spain, Catalonia included, the grassroots *indignados* were combining local activism and civic politics. The results were spectacular. In the 2015 local elections, these local 15-M coalitions captured power in most of Spain's largest cities, including Madrid, Barcelona, Valencia, A Coruña, Palma, and Cádiz. Madrid and Barcelona elected charismatic female mayors, respectively Manuela Carmena and Ada Colau. In Zaragoza, an independent named Pedro Santisteve won the mayoralty in a municipality which is traditionally deeply conservative. These successful campaigns were conducted either under the Podemos banner or with national Podemos support. But they were essentially local, grassroots mobilisations – not traditional campaigns controlled by the centre.

Ada Colau's victory was in no small part a reflection of her work as the head of the PAH housing movement. This was a blow to CIU, which lost control of the city hall. Colau was anti-independence though supportive of Catalonia's right to choose. Her *Barcelona en Comú* movement represented local activists and was independent of Podem, the Catalan branch of Podemos. In contrast to the increasingly authoritarian Iglesias, Colau has maintained a democratic relationship with her activists. But since 2015, *Barcelona en*

Comú has functioned more as a complement to the city government, where many of its active members took positions, than a grassroots movement.

In the December 2015 Spanish general election, Podem/Podemos made an electoral pact with *Barcelona en Comú*, the Greens, and the Catalan branch of *Izquierda Unida*, the former Communist Party. This anti-independence (but largely pro-referendum) front actually won the largest share of the vote in Catalonia (16.6 per cent, 929,880 votes). In the June 2016 general election re-run, the alliance did almost as well.

But Podemos was changing. Once embedded in mainstream electoral politics, the party's anti-system positions began to moderate. At its launch Podemos had championed radical proposals that were popular in the movement: reforming the '78 constitution, refusing to pay the national debt, nationalising key sectors of the economy, and introducing a universal basic income. These radical positions were abandoned or watered down. Not that Podemos had entered the social democratic mainstream. Under the influence of Íñigo Errejón, who has close links to the Chavez regime in Venezuela, Podemos embraced the notion of a building a mass following by espousing a populist, but leftist, Spanish nationalism. Emulating left-populist parties in Bolivia and Venezuela, power would be won by blurring existing left-right ideological distinctions and challenging the PP on its home ground of representing Spanish national interests. The hostility of the mainstream media would be countered by a ruthless populism built around the personality of Pablo Iglesias.

This was a potent and novel political brew but a highly dangerous one. It sacrificed internal democracy in Podemos to the authority of Iglesias, wielded through internet plebiscites of the membership. And it created the potential for a split between the radical left in Spain and the growing separatist, anti-system mass movements in Catalonia and the Basque Lands. True, Iglesias and Podemos continue to argue for a multi-national Spanish state which could be a threat to the '78 constitution. And Podemos has supported the right of Catalonia to hold a self-determination referendum, unlike the traditional Spanish left parties. But in the end it led Iglesias to treat Catalonia as a political diversion. As events were to prove, Catalonia was anything but. Also, the trajectory of Podemos remains uncertain. Will it evolve into a reformist current, no matter how radical? Or is it prepared to break with the system? What gives the Catalan independence movement its historical importance is that it is prepared for a complete rupture with the '78 Regime.

Austerity and the crisis of traditional Catalan autonomism

On June 15, 2011 Prime Minister Artur Mas was forced to arrive at the Palau del Parlament by helicopter. The reason: the Catalan Parliament was being besieged by tens of thousands of *indignados* protesting against the austerity cuts being imposed by the CIU government in the 2011 Budget. Clashes with Mossos left 36 people injured, including 12 police officers.

The financial crash and the Constitutional Court ruling striking down much of the reformed Statute of Autonomy produced a political reaction in Catalonia. After two terms in the political wilderness, Artur Mas and the CIU regained power in the 2010 elections, winning 62 seats and forming a minority administration. This was their best score since 1992. Mas was the scion of a wealthy Catalan industrial family, his ancestors had made money out of the slave trade with Cuba, and today remains something of an enigma. He sat out the political turmoil of the Transition years, preferring to stick to his academic studies rather than build a new, democratic Spain and Catalonia. He is an ardent Zionist, often comparing his vision of Catalonia to Israel. On account of his technocratic abilities, Jordi Pujol (the godfather of the CIU) made Mas his protégé and right-hand man. When Pujol quit the leadership of CIU, Mas was able to see off the old man's sons and hangers-on and grab the reins of power. Emerging into the political limelight in 2003, Mas surprised many by taking to power like a duck to water. If nothing else, Artur Mas is a brilliant political operator. But he is also the embodiment of that wing of Catalan capital which relies on the art of manoeuvre to defend its material interests. Mas, though out of parliament, would be at Puigdemont's side throughout 2017.

But back in 2011, Mas was facing the *indignados* and their opposition to his own brand of austerity in Catalonia. Throughout the years of economic crisis and austerity there were repeated mass demonstrations on the streets of Barcelona protesting against poverty and unemployment. In February 2012, a crowd of 30,000 marched on the Barcelona stock exchange. This protest also saw violent clashes with Mossos as demonstrators occupied a downtown branch of Banco Popular and erected street barricades. In October 2012, Barcelona firefighters demonstrated against cuts outside the *Generalitat*, during a general strike against austerity – many of the same firefighters would be on the streets in 2017 supporting Catalan independence.

To have his 2012 austerity budget passed, Mas had to persuade the Catalan PP deputies to abstain. This was the same right-wing CIU whose representatives had supported the Aznar PP government in office in the 1990s and who had abstained on the Spanish constitutional amendment to cap the budget deficit in 2011. Yet in September 2012, only months after he had made this deal with the PP, Artur Mas declared in a speech to the Catalan Parliament that now was the time for the people of Catalonia to exercise their right of self-determination. The autonomist CIU had suddenly opened the door to independence. What had caused Artur Mas to change his mind and forsake autonomy?

The answer had everything to do with events on Catalan National Day, 11 September 2012, when over 1.5 million people took to the streets of Barcelona in the city's biggest-ever demonstration since the fall of Franco. They called for Catalan independence and control over the local economy. The demonstration was led by a huge banner with the Catalan slogan *Som una nació. Nosaltres decidim*: 'We are a nation. We decide.' This extraordinary outpouring of discontent from below was organised by a new civic group called the Catalan National Assembly. The ANC had been formed only the previous year, in the wake of the Constitutional Court ruling striking down the new Statute of Autonomy.

The sheer scale and enthusiasm of the 11 September mass protest had a marked impact on Artur Mas. For the first time, the traditionally conservative, devolutionist CIU was forced to acknowledge the demand for full Catalan independence, or face losing control of Catalan politics to new forces to the left brought into being by the anti-austerity protests. The seminal 15-M protests in May had transfigured the political landscape. Anything was now possible, including independence.

That evening, Mas welcomed the ANC leaders to the *Generalitat*, declaring somewhat theatrically: 'I have heard the voice of the people'. On the other hand, only two weeks later, Mas announced snap elections for the Catalan Parliament, arguing that 'the voice of the street must be heard at the polls'. Clearly, by calling the election, Mas and the CIU hoped to seize control of the new nationalist upsurge.[149]

But first Mas tried a classic diplomatic manoeuvre, prompting fears in the pro-independence wing that he was being opportunist (which he was). On September 20th, a week and a half after the demonstration, he went to Madrid seeking a new fiscal arrangement for Catalonia. He proposed to Rajoy a similar arrangement to that enjoyed by the Basques that would allow Catalonia to keep its own tax revenues. All too predictably, this was instantly rejected by the PP government, which was now desperate for

Catalan revenues. Rajoy resorted to a mantra that would be heard again in 2017 that any such fiscal renegotiation was simply 'contrary to the constitution' – this was barely a year after Rajoy had colluded with Zapatero to amend the constitution to include a cap on the public deficit. Five days after this abortive meeting, Mas called fresh elections, saying: 'The time has come for Catalans to exercise their right to self-determination'. It is arguable that he did not expect to get anywhere with Rajoy but was positioning the CIU to outflank the ERC and pro-independence parties in the upcoming election.

However, the result of the snap election was not what Mas had expected. Instead of gaining an absolute majority, the CIU lost 12 seats. The real victors were the parties supporting outright independence – the ERC and a new far-left group, Popular Unity (CUP), which won its first representation in the Catalan Parliament. The biggest loser was the Socialist Party, which paid the price for Zapatero's austerity policies. Mas stayed on as Prime Minister but only with support from the ERC, led by Oriol Junqueras. In return, he had to promise to hold a referendum on Catalan independence. Opinion surveys now showed for the first time since the fall of the Fascist regime that a majority of Catalans would vote Yes to independence, by 57 per cent to 43. Confrontation with Madrid was now certain. Artur Mas was left holding the tiger's tail.

The ANC continued to mobilise massive street demonstrations – partly to keep up pressure on Artur Mas, and partly to win international support for Catalan self-determination in the face of opposition from the PP government. On 11 September 2013, the ANC (now led by Carme Forcadell) organised the so-called Catalan Way. This was a 400-kilometre (250 mile) human chain in support of Catalan independence. An estimated 1.6 million people linked hands along the ancient Via Augusta, from Le Perthus in France to Alcanar on the Mediterranean, at the southern extremity of Catalonia. The inspiration for the project came from the Baltic Way demonstration of 1989, in which two million people in Lithuania, Latvia and Estonia linked hands to demand independence from the decaying Soviet Union. In a demonstration of internationalism, the Catalans invited two key organisers of the Baltic Way, Henn Karits and Ülo Laanoja, to come to Barcelona to advise on the mobilisation.

On 12 December 2013, Mas, together with the leaders of five Catalan parliamentary parties, announced the date for the Catalan self-determination referendum – Sunday 9 November 2014. In April 2014, the proposal to hold the consultative referendum was rejected by the Spanish Parliament, by 299 votes to 47. The Constitutional Court, in a series of judgements, declared that any referendum – even a non-binding 'consultation' – would be illegal.

Nevertheless, Catalan hopes were strengthened by the (legal) Scottish independence referendum in September 2014. Many activists went to Scotland to observe and take part in the referendum campaign. The UK Conservative government, in stark contrast to the PP, had agreed to give official recognition to the Scottish vote and abide by the result. As it was, the Scots voted narrowly against independence, but only after they had been promised complete Home Rule, including control over local taxes – a promise that was not kept. However, at the time, the Catalans drew the obvious conclusion that Madrid and the PP were isolated in their refusal to let Catalonia vote on its own future.

On Sunday 9 November 2014, the non-binding, popular consultation went ahead. There were fears that Madrid would order the Guardia Civil to intervene. In fact, there was a considerable and very public Guardia presence on polling day, but the paramilitaries did not interfere. Even if not recognised formally by Madrid, the plan was to use this de facto referendum to show Catalan determination to press for a legal vote in the near future. The ballot papers carried two questions: 'Do you want Catalonia to become a State?' and 'Do you want this State to be independent?' The second question could only be answered by those who had answered Yes to the first.

Some 2,305,290 votes were cast, with 80.8 per cent supporting the Yes-Yes option, 10.1 per cent Yes-No, and 4.5 per cent the No option. Clearly most of those opposed to independence abstained. It was also the case that young people aged 16 and 17, and non-Spanish EU residents, were allowed to vote – which would not have been the case had the referendum been officially sanctioned. Nevertheless, this was a clear indication of the momentum towards independence proper. A significant proportion of Catalonia had been radicalised and wanted to destroy the '78 Regime.

Madrid simply ignored the result. So on Sunday 27 September 2015 fresh elections were held for the Catalan Parliament. The old devolutionist CIU had finally ruptured – partly as a result of strains between its two wings over independence, and partly because Convergence was desperate to re-brand its image in the light of ongoing corruption scandals. In its place the main nationalist parties, including Convergence and the now powerful ERC, ran under a common *Junts pel Sí* ('Together for Yes') ticket. For the first time since Franco, pro-independence parties won an outright majority.

It would be only a matter of time before the countdown to independence would begin.

But it was a Catalan government without Artur Mas. *Junts pel Sí* was only able to form the administration with the tacit support of the far-left CUP. They were unwilling to accept Mas as government head because of his record as a neo-liberal and their suspicions regarding his real political motivations. In January 2016, after three months of infighting, Mas stood aside and Carles Puigdemont became President. Mas also resigned from his seat in the parliament, remarking that he would place his 'personal efforts' in rebuilding *Convergència*, soon to be rebranded PDeCAT.

Meanwhile, in Spain itself, the traditional party system of the '78 Regime was in deep crisis as a result of the economic meltdown. The December 2015 general election produced a hung parliament. The old voting blocs splintered, and new, populist political formations like Podemos and Citizens emerged. The scene was set for nearly two years in which Spain had no effective government. Only after a series of inconclusive general elections did Rajoy manage to form a new minority administration with the support of the pathetic rump of the old Socialist Party.

In order to cling on to power and fend off the corruption scandals engulf-ing the PP, Rajoy resorted to diversionary tactics. He unleashed a massive demagogic attack on the Catalan independence movement, pressuring the Constitutional Court to indict over 400 elected Catalan politicians for pro-moting the November 2014 non-binding referendum and for debating in the Catalan Parliament plans for another referendum. Included in these indict-ments were Artur Mas and Carme Forcadell, now Speaker of the Catalan Parliament. Madrid and Catalonia were now on collision course.

Conclusion

There is nothing inherent in Catalan society that makes it more left-wing than that of the rest of the Spanish state, though it helps that it can call on a long historical tradition of resistance and popular mobilisation. That historical memory, especially of the anarchist CNT, helped animate the 15-M move in Barcelona. Nor was there anything inevitable about Catalan society moving to the left simply as a response to austerity. But the combination of radical Catalan separatism, and its tradition of mass demonstrations, plus the street activism of the 15-M movement, marginalised the right influence of both the right and the soggy social democracy of the PSOE.

Above all, the Catalan nationalist project created a popular vehicle for anti-system mobilisation that went beyond electoralism (even of Podemos). This allowed activists a space to operate and influence events directly. (A similar process is found in Scotland with the Yes campaign for independence.) As a result, the anti-system left in Catalonia enjoyed a much more advantageous balance of forces than in the rest of the Spanish state, or indeed Europe. Levels of working class confidence and consciousness were higher there than elsewhere except perhaps the Basque Country. This would determine the march of events in 2017.

Meanwhile, in Barcelona, the new Catalan government now set the date for a new referendum for 1 October 2017.

Chapter Eleven: 1-0

Spain's northeastern region of Catalonia failed to hold an independence referendum on Sunday, Prime Minister Mariano Rajoy said, after more than 760 people were injured in clashes between police and voters...

Reuters report

On this day of hope and suffering, Catalonia's citizens have earned the right to have an independent state in the form of a republic. Hence, my government, in the next few days will send the results of today's vote to the Catalan Parliament, where the sovereignty of our people lies...

President Puigdemont

REFERENDUM DAY, Sunday 1 October 2017, opened with an unseasonal, pre-dawn, torrential downpour in Barcelona. In what would be a turning point for Europe as well as the Spanish state, tens of thousands of Catalans queued to cast their votes, despite the rain. Meanwhile, the Spanish state was mobilising, deploying everything in its power to stop them. Soon that would include the use of physical force unprecedented in a modern West European country – at least since the dying days of the old Franco regime.

The ballot paper was printed in two languages: Catalan and the Occitan spoken in the tiny Aran Valley, in the north-western province of Lleida. The question asked was effectively a two-in-one proposition: 'Do you want Catalonia to become an independent state in the form of a republic?' In this context, the word republic had a deep political resonance. It implied: 'We were a republic until Franco. We will be a republic again.'

On the night of Wednesday 6 September, the Catalan parliament finally passed into law the legislation needed to hold the 1-0 independence referendum. It passed by 72 votes after 52 opposition MPs walked out of the chamber at the end of an ill-tempered, 11-hour debate. The historic decision was instantly denounced by the PP government in Madrid, which repeated its intention to do everything in its political power to stop the vote from going ahead. Rajoy ordered government lawyers to file yet another complaint with the Constitutional Court so that the vote could be annulled – the

Court issued an injunction the next day which was duly ignored. Spanish prosecutors had already launched an official complaint against Puigdemont and members of his government, citing civil disobedience, misfeasance and misappropriation of public funds – the latter carries a potential jail sentence of eight years. The political die was now well and truly cast.

Preparations for and against the referendum taking place had been meticulous on both sides. In particular, this popular clash was dominated by a struggle to control the internet and social media. As well as prohibiting the national post office from mailing out any election materials, the Spanish authorities blocked 140 pro-referendum websites. The night before the vote, Guardia Civil units raided the Catalan government's data and digital communications hub. Their military objective was to take offline the Catalan census and voting rolls needed to process the voting. In addition, webpages advising voters which local polling station to attend were deleted. In anticipation, a smug Spanish government spokesperson in Madrid announced that the referendum had been 'nullified'.

Seizing the printed ballot papers and ballot boxes was a particular target for the Guardia in the lead-up to 1 October. On 12 September, the Spanish Public Prosecutor's Office instructed the security forces to seize any materials which it said could help with the 'consummation of the crime' – in other words, voting. Police proceeded to raid print shops and other businesses, confiscating literally millions of ballot papers and hundreds of ballot boxes. On 19 September, police seized documents from the offices of Unipost, Spain's biggest private delivery company, in the city of Terrassa, north-west of Barcelona. Guardia Civil officers scuffled with pro-independence protesters blocking the street outside. Among the materials impounded were boxes containing thousands of envelopes with the Catalan government's logo – in Spain, completed ballot papers are placed in envelopes before being put in the ballot box.

Eliminating the ability of the elected Catalan government to fund the vote was also a key goal. On Monday 11 September, Madrid took control of Catalonia's finances in order to prevent funds being used for the independence referendum, though the payment of essential services and public workers' salaries continued uninterrupted. Then on Wednesday 14 September, the Public Prosecutor in Madrid issued a court summons to more than 700 locally elected mayors in Catalonia who had agreed to provide facilities for the referendum. They were threatened with prison if they did not appear. The move backfired in a spectacular fashion: the following day the mayor of Barcelona, Ada Colau, dropped her reservations about allowing the city's schools to be used as polling stations – under pressure from daily popular demonstrations outside city hall.

Then on Wednesday 20 September – a bare 10 days before polling – Rajoy raised the political stakes significantly. That morning, Juan Ignacio Zoido, the PP Interior Minister, announced that he was cancelling leave for all Guardia Civil and National Police officers tasked with preventing the referendum. In a statement, the Interior Ministry said that these officers would have to be available between 20 September and 5 October. It added that this deployment would be extended if necessary. By the weekend of the referendum, some 10,000 Guardia Civil (out of a national Spanish total of 93,000) had been positioned in Catalonia, with 5,000 assigned to Barcelona. In a television address, Rajoy made it clear the referendum would be halted by all and any means. 'This referendum is a chimera,' he predicted.

So many paramilitaries had been transferred from other parts of Spain that there was no room for them in the barracks where the Guardia Civil normally live. To house the extra officers, the Spanish interior ministry chartered two large ferries from an Italian company called Moby Lines and anchored them in Barcelona's harbour. This move provided instant embarrassment for the Guardia and the Interior Ministry. One of the ferries, the *Moby Dada,* had been painted with giant pictures of characters from the world-famous Looney Tunes cartoon series, including Tweety Pie, the iconic yellow canary who always outwits Sylvester the cat. The Catalans, with their traditional sense of the absurd, instantly adopted Piolin (the local name for Tweety) as their mascot – and a perfect way to pour scorn on the hapless Sylvesters of the Guardia Civil stationed in their midst. Soon #FreePiolin was trending on Twitter, and posters and T-shirts appeared everywhere showing Tweety Pie caged or holding a Catalan flag in its beak. In a further twist, Warner Bros, the entertainment company that holds the rights to Looney Tunes, complained to Moby Lines, claiming that its characters were being used without permission. A rattled Spanish Interior Ministry turned embarrassment into downright farce by ordering the image of Tweety Pie to be covered up. It is possible that this satirical affront to military dignity was a factor in the conduct of the Guardia Civil on referendum day.

However, the events of Wednesday 20 September were not played out. For the first time, Guardia Civil officers raided Catalan government offices including those directing the economy, interior and foreign affairs, welfare, telecommunications and taxation. The operation was code-named Anubis, after the dog-headed Egyptian deity. As well as seizing 9.8 million ballot papers, 14 senior Catalan officials and business people were arrested and held, including Josep Maria Jove, the junior economy minister and member of the ERC. Puigdemont denounced the raids as 'a co-ordinated police assault' that showed that Madrid 'has de facto suspended self-government and applied a de facto state of emergency' in Catalonia. He also drew a direct parallel between the raids and the repression of the Franco dictatorship, tweeting: 'We will not accept a return to the darkest times.' The mayor of Barcelona, Ada Colau, called the raids 'a democratic scandal' while Podemos leader Pablo Iglesias warned: 'We are moving towards a situation in which there are going to be political prisoners in Spain'. The two leading civic movements supporting the referendum, the ANC and Òmnium, responded to the arrests by calling for thousands of protestors to demonstrate outside the offices of the economy ministry in central Barcelona.

Soon there was another twist. It transpired that these provocative arrests had not been ordered directly by the Madrid government or the public prosecutor's office – or at least this is what Madrid claimed. Instead, they had been ostensibly initiated at the personal direction of Juan Antonio Ramírez Sunyer, the investigating judge at Court N°13 in Barcelona. Ramirez was well known for his reactionary judgements, love of 'preventative detention' and general hatred of the left. He had been subject to at least one assassination attempt. Under the Spanish legal system, judges like Ramirez have extensive powers of investigation. But the politicised nature of the judiciary results in these powers often being used for political ends – as was the case here. In February 2017, criminal charges had been filed in the Catalan courts alleging that the Catalan government was making illegal use of citizens' tax records to prepare for the October independence referendum. The charges were brought by VOX, a small, ultra-right political party launched in 2014 by disgruntled former members of the PP. VOX plans to abolish the autonomy of Catalonia and the Basque Lands altogether, re-centralise the Spanish state, criminalise abortion, ban immigration and halt the spread of Islam in Spain. A serial litigant against the Catalan independence movement, VOX had no evidence for the charges against the Catalan government. But its politically-motivated complaint gave a green light to Judge Ramirez to use his investigative powers in a wholesale and disproportionate manner on 20 September.

Ramirez ordered the National Police and Guardia Civil to carry out searches in 41 separate premises in Catalonia, and even Madrid. Not only were Catalan government offices searched but also those of three IT companies and several private homes. Suspiciously, these searches were co-ordinated on the same day with a search of the CUP headquarters in Barcelona, on a supposedly unrelated matter. It is obvious that this was a gigantic 'fishing' expedition in which the Spanish state (in the person of Judge Ramirez) was looking for any evidence that could be used against the referendum project. It is also clear that – given the mass searches and arrests – Ramirez intended to disrupt the voting process itself. Those detained included some of the most senior IT staff in Catalonia, in both the public and private sectors. It is hard to believe that he could have mobilised such a police effort without the Spanish Interior Ministry in Madrid being in the know. Claims by the PP government that this was a purely local judicial initiative should be taken with a very large pinch of salt.

As the days and minutes to referendum day ticked by, many things were becoming clearer. First, the determination of the Spanish state apparatus to do anything it could to crush Catalonia's right to vote – a determination that would lead to naked violence on 1 October. Second, the equal determination of the radicalised Catalan people to press ahead. Every provocation by Madrid had been met by good-humoured, disciplined and dignified popular demonstrations. This was a mass movement, not some manoeuvre by Catalan politicians. The people wanted to vote!

Polling day: a carnival of democracy

The 1-o referendum was a vote unique in history by dint of the fact it had to be organised in secret. That it succeeded was down to the enthusiasm, discretion and discipline of literally tens of thousands of volunteers, in hundreds of districts, towns and villages across Catalonia. Humour played a part in the coded language used to phone and text: ballot boxes were called 'pizzas' and the ballot papers 'napkins'. The Catalan government representative who officially opened a voting centre was called 'la pizzera', the pizza maker. Volunteers who drove from polling station to polling station, to make sure each had enough 'pizzas' and 'napkins', were dubbed Telepizzas, after a local Barcelona delivery chain. Central Barcelona was divided into five Telepizzas.

The weekend before the referendum, Madrid ordered that all the schools, town halls and other potential polling stations should be sealed off. This task was assigned to the autonomous Catalan police – the *Mossos d'Esquadra* – who, though under the authority of the *Generalitat*, could be 'nationalised' by the Ministry of the Interior. Spontaneously, in a movement led by teen-age high school students radicalised by the pressure of events, these polling stations were occupied to prevent their closure. In big schools, students, teachers and parents arrived on the Friday night with sleeping bags and food, determined to stop the police from entering and preventing the voting on the following Sunday. At some schools a carnival atmosphere prevailed, with early occupiers programming a full weekend full of activities, talks and music, and inviting other local residents to join in. In one town, occupiers organised a tournament of rock-paper-scissors, advising likely participants that it would last till polling day. Other places were more direct – especially those under the influence of the CUP and ERC – calling for an organised 'ter-ritorial defence' of voting stations, complete with primitive barricades.

One problem remained: getting the bulky ballot boxes to literally hun-dreds of polling places under the noses of the Guardia Civil. After the ini-tial seizures of ballot boxes, the Catalan government had ordered new ones direct from China. These were made from clear plastic and ingeniously designed to stack inside each other – so many could be transported together discreetly, in the boots of ordinary cars. Initially, these boxes were stored at a secret location across the border in France, where they were safe from being discovered by the Guardia. As polling day approached, a huge delivery operation began. This was so well organised that all the ballot boxes were delivered unimpeded: another victory to the mass movement. In the former textile town of Sabadell, the fifth-largest city in Catalonia, the ballot boxes were ferried in refuse sacks. As one volunteer put it: 'They were disguised as bags of trash. But this was democracy we carried in our hands.'

Though voting was not scheduled to begin until 9.00am and despite heavy rain, crowds began gathering spontaneously much earlier. At many stations there were already long queues by 5.00 am, partly because people were too excited to sleep and partly because they were determined to prevent the polling places being closed by the police. It was known that Mossos were due to begin evicting people from polling stations from 6.00am. Plans were already in place to protect the ballot boxes and ballot papers in advance of the vote. In some schools the latter were being printed on the premises for greater security. Each polling station also made its own plans to protect the record of the people's democratic choice once polling had closed. At the *Foment Martinenc* community centre, in a middle-class district of Barcelona, they had a contingency plan to smuggle the ballot boxes out in trash bags and hide them in a nearby shop. At the Institut Menendez y Pelayo high school, in Barcelona's via Augusta, individual volunteers took completed ballot papers away in rucksacks to a secure location. At Tomás Moro, a school in the outskirts of Barcelona, poll workers hid the real ballot boxes and set out two boxes full of blank paper as decoys for the police to take.

The police strategy in disrupting the polling was two-fold. In Barcelona, they targeted polling stations at which the leaders of the independence movement were due to cast their votes early on. If the leaders could be stopped from casting their ballots, this would demoralise the mass of voters. In the rural small towns of the interior, where fewer independence supporters might be gathered, the plan was to use a massive Guardia Civil presence to shut down the polling stations completely. At first these tactics seemed to be working.

As Puigdemont went to vote, a Guardia helicopter followed his car to alert a police unit when he was close to his local polling station. But in a stunt worthy of James Bond, Puigdemont's convoy of cars stopped under a bridge so that the president could switch cars and cast his ballot in another town, without alerting the police hovering above. Faced with this deliberate targeting of certain polling stations, the Catalan government announced its own counter-strategy shortly before polling commenced. Any bona fide elector on the electronic census could chose to vote in any one of the still functioning polling stations. President Puigdemont himself eventually voted in Cornella del Terri instead of Sant Julià de Ramis where he was originally registered to vote, foiling the police operation to track him down.

There were immediate problems with registering voters. The Spanish authorities made every effort to disrupt the internet, making it difficult for polling clerks to access the online census data needed to identify voters. The local school WiFi system in Barcelona was turned off deliberately. Some polling stations used mobile phones to maintain access to the census database but voting remained subject to intermittent delays. Long queues of voters remained all day and were therefore vulnerable to police attack. Despite these difficulties, thousands of Catalan voters – many in wheelchairs, on crutches or with small children – waited patiently and good naturedly until they could cast a vote for their national freedom. Most took pictures on their mobile phones to mark the occasion. Meanwhile, news of police violence in Girona and parts of Barcelona started coming in through the mobile phone network. Although the voters were horrified, the queues remained solid. The atmosphere remained calm and dignified throughout the day. The only comparison could be with South Africa's first democratic election in April 1994.

In the afternoon, the Spanish Interior Ministry announced that the police had closed 79 of the 2,315 polling stations set up for the referendum – hardly a success rate. Earlier, the Catalan government had reported that, despite police violence, voting had proceeded in 96 per cent of the designated polling stations. Catalonia had voted.

Most polling stations closed at 8.00pm, though crowds remained to protect the count. For security reasons, counting was conducted inside each station or at a secure location nearby. Individual counting was monitored by authorised representatives of various political parties and by international observers. There were also media representatives at many of the counts. Voting papers were placed in sealed envelopes, which needed to be opened, so it was 9.15pm before the polling agents could phone in the final results. They then took away the ballot papers for a second count the following day. Where ballot boxes had to be moved, they were protected by large crowds, often chanting 'we voted'. There was a common expectation that the police would mount raids while the counting was in progress. However, by the evening, the violent police attacks of earlier in the day had resulted in a massive transformation of the political situation in Catalonia. As the world watched in horror, the old Francoist repressive apparatus suddenly reappeared dripping with blood. It was a miscalculation Madrid would regret.

Operation Copernicus

The operation to prevent Catalans expressing their democratic rights on 1-o was code-named 'Copernicus' by the Interior Ministry. The Interior Minister was Juan Ignacio Zoido, a former judge and ex-mayor of Seville, where he had been accused by civil rights activists of wilfully refusing to implement the controversial Law of Historical Memory which mandated the removal of Francoist symbols from public buildings and spaces. Appointed by Rajoy to the Interior Ministry in late 2016, Zoido introduced sweeping changes to the command structure of the security forces, placing the National Police and Guardia Civil under greater political control – ostensibly the better to fight Jihadist terrorism. He also 'retired' top Guardia Civil General Pablo Alonso, who was proving a thorn in the side of the PP by showing too much initiative in pursuing party officials in Madrid on corruption charges.

The individual to whom Zoido assigned primary responsibility for Copernicus was Diego Pérez de los Cobos, a 53-year-old Colonel in the

Guardia Civil. Pérez had served as a high-ranking official in the Interior Ministry in Madrid for 11 years prior to the referendum crisis; i.e. he was a key player in the Spanish security apparatus. Pérez comes from old pro-Franco stock. His father was a candidate for the ultra-Francoist Fuerza Nueva (FN) party in the 1977 Spanish general election. The FN's avowed aim was to 'keep alive the ideals of July 18th 1936', i.e. the ideals of Franco's coup against the elected Spanish and Catalan Republics. Pérez is also well connected. His brother Francisco was a member of the Constitutional Court from 2011 until 2017, and its actual President between 2013 and 2017. The records of the Spanish tax service show that in 2013 Judge Pérez was a member of the Partido Popular, a revelation that forced his recusal in several proceedings. As President of the Court, he issued the ruling declaring the 1-0 referendum process illegal. A referendum process which his brother Colonel Diego Pérez of the Guardia Civil was in charge of crushing.

After the Catalan regional parliament agreed on 6 September to hold a referendum on independence, Spain's central government lodged an urgent legal challenge at the Constitutional Court, which ruled on 8 September that such a poll was illegal and should not take place. Defiance of this order was ipso facto sedition against the state. The Attorney General, in co-ordination with his regional and municipal counterparts in Catalonia, instructed national and Catalan police forces to co-operate in halting the vote – with Colonel Diego Pérez in overall command. At his disposal were some 6,000 Guardia Civil and National Police stationed normally in the region, plus 5,500 rushed to Catalonia from other parts of Spain. These paramilitaries would be the cutting edge of the operation as the local Catalan Mossos could not be trusted. The Mossos would prove to be the Achilles' heel of the attempt to halt 1-0.

The composition of the forces under Pérez's command reveals exactly what was in the Colonel's mind as a way of halting the vote. The Guardia has special sections designated Police Intervention Units (UIP) – popularly known as anti-riot police. Three quarters of the 2,700 personnel making up all the UIP units were deployed to Catalonia. They were joined by about 500 members of other Guardia Civil groups charged with maintaining public order, and specialists capable of dealing with IT and computer systems.

However, Pérez and the Spanish Ministry of the Interior had a problem: the Guardia Civil drafted into Catalonia were not happy to be there, as they knew full well that they were seen by much of the local population as an occupying power. The angry, bitter mood of the Guardia Civil regarding

Catalonia was later given public expression in a demonstration in Madrid by Guardia members, the Friday after the referendum. Some 8,000 members of the National Police and Guardia Civil demonstrated carrying plastic ballot boxes similar to those used in the 1-0 vote (perhaps some of those 'liberated' from polling stations), waving Spanish flags, and blowing whistles. Ostensibly, they were demanding equal pay with the Catalan Mossos d'Esquadra, whom they accused of not doing their job. The chants included: 'Abandoned in salary, abandoned in Catalonia'.

Realising that it needed to retain the loyalty of the Guardia units drafted into Catalonia, the Interior Ministry tried bribery. According to documents leaked to the *El Pais* newspaper, these extra units were given special subsistence allowances for each day they remained in Catalonia. This amounted to €150 per day, three times the regular €49. However, that was not enough to mollify them. The vice president of the Spanish Guardia Civil Association, Raúl Lobato Esteban, denounced what he called 'the unjustified incitement to hatred from the *Generalitat* and some municipalities' towards the Guardia and demanded the 'absolute dissolution of the Mossos'.

The scene was thus set for confrontation on 1-0 between the Spanish state and Catalan democracy, and between an alienated paramilitary force and the civilian population it feared and despised. The result: police violence. On referendum day, Colonel Perez was determined to halt the voting before it had properly started. There was no question of mediation or crowd control. In full combat gear, Guardia Civil units moved into action, batoning those queuing to vote, smashing down doors to gain access, throwing polling staff to the ground, and grabbing ballot boxes without showing warrants or giving due cause. This was a military commando operation against an insurgent colonial people.

The worst incidents of unprovoked police violence took place in Girona (pop. 98,000), probably because the security forces felt that by picking on a smaller town they had more chance of shutting down the polls completely, thus demoralising voters in the rest of Catalonia. At the Collegi Verd primary school polling station, on Joan Maragall Street, police attacked at 9.00 am, just as the polls opened. National Police used batons and shields to charge repeatedly at a cordon of people who had linked arms to stop them entering through the school gate – hitting the protestors on their heads, arms, legs, and torsos. The police did not issue a warning before charging, and fired blanks into the air, frightening young children who were present. Camera-phone footage shows that once inside the school compound, police officers randomly struck people with batons. One parent who reported being hit was an off-duty policeman in the Mossos. Also in Girona, at the Sant Narcís polling station, Xevi Gil Rosdevall, a 47-year-old uniformed firefighter, had his arm broken by a police baton.

In Aiguaviva, near Girona, a detachment of around 50 police entered the village (pop. 763) at 3.45pm in the afternoon and attacked a crowd of between 70 and 100 locals who were gathered around their village hall polling station eating a communal meal. One villager, Jaume Mas, a 52-year-old engineer, asked the police for a copy of the judicial order authorising their entry. In response, the police began hitting the crowd with their batons. Video images show a police officer using a canister of irritant spray. When another villager started to film police carting off ballot boxes – clearly the aim of the raid – he was batoned. Footage shows a policeman hitting the arm holding the camera.

In Sabadell, police broke through the windows of the Escola Nostra Llar just as the polls opened. They used big hammers to smash their way in. A group of elderly people locked their arms together and tried to stop them. The police shouted: 'Where are the ballots? Where are the boxes?' Such scenes were repeated across Catalonia well into the Sunday afternoon. According to the *Generalitat*, 844 people requested the aid of the Catalan emergency health service following the Guardia Civil attacks. This number includes people with eyes irritated by gas and those suffering from anxiety attacks brought on by the violence. Most of the injuries were minor, but four people were hospitalised by the emergency health service and of those two were in a serious condition, one from the impact of a rubber bullet in the face.

The Interior Ministry responded by claiming that 431 Guardia Civil officers were injured, 39 of them requiring immediate medical treatment. The remaining 392 suffered bruises, scrapes, kicks and bites. There is evidence that some voters defended themselves after being attacked but any impartial viewing of the extensive video footage of 1-o clearly shows the Guardia encased in heavy protective gear deliberately assaulting unarmed civilians. On this evidence, the Ministry figures appear greatly exaggerated.

The violence against civilians might have been much worse but for the action – or rather inaction – of Mossos. Though tasked with closing polling stations, Mossos officers played a largely passive role and even, on occasion, intervened to protect the general public from attacks by the Guardia Civil and National Police. One of the authors witnessed Mossos activity at close hand. At the Institut Menendez y Pelayo high school, in Barcelona's via Augusta, some 500 people of all ages had arrived by 5.00am, hoping that sheer numbers would peacefully deter any police who turned up to interfere with the voting. The local Mossos police came twice, and each time asked for a named person to take responsibility for the school building. An older woman volunteered and signed the requisite paperwork. That satisfied the Mossos, who then left the voting undisturbed. At Vallvidrera, on the periphery of Barcelona, two Mossos officers were on duty outside the polling station all day. But they did nothing to halt proceedings and, indeed, intimated that they were there to 'protect' the citizens from the Guardia Civil. As a result, villagers had covered the windscreen of their car with red carnations. At the Foment Martinenc polling station in Barcelona, there were regular visits from the Mossos every two hours, but otherwise they took no action.

Were the Mossos obeying orders or was this passivity the decision of individual officers sympathetic to Catalan self-determination? Josep Lluís Trapero, the head of the *Mossos d'Esquadra*, had formally ordered his police to evict people from voting centres, following a court order. On the other hand, he told them not to use violence and not to disturb public order. Given the hundreds of people defending most individual polling stations, it is obvious that any two-person Mossos unit was in no position to evict. Also conspicuous by their absence on 1-0 were the Barcelona municipal police, who come under the control of the mayor. After the referendum, PP ministers were quick to criticize the Mossos for not acting more aggressively, and Trapero was immediately cited for sedition.

Even after the polls closed, police attacks continued. Some members of the Guardia Civil had been billeted at a hotel in Calella, a seaside resort town 36 miles north-east of Barcelona. Around 10.30pm on Sunday night, a group of local people gathered peacefully in front of the hotel chanting: 'Occupation forces out!' A group of Guardia – some carrying batons – suddenly emerged and attacked the protesters. According to the town's mayor, 14 people were injured and four taken to hospital.

The police violence against peaceful voters was instantly seen around the globe in all its horrific detail, thanks to social media. The result was an avalanche of criticism of the Spanish government and the paramilitaries. Spain is a party to the European Convention on Human Rights as well as the International Covenant on Civil and Political Rights, which impose specific obligations with respect to the right to peaceful assembly, freedom of expression, and the use of force by law enforcement agencies. While a government can impose restrictions on those rights in certain circumstances, any restrictive measures must be both necessary and proportionate. That was not the case in Catalonia on 1 October.

Human Rights Watch, the much-respected NGO, received numerous complaints regarding the behaviour of the security forces on 1 October. As a result, the organisation carried out on-site investigations to document specific incidents. Investigators spoke to victims and witnesses and reviewed video, photographic, and medical evidence from the city of Girona and two villages in Girona and Barcelona provinces. Human Rights Watch found that the Guardia Civil and National Police Corps had used excessive force in all three locations.

The British and foreign media were happy to trumpet a supposed 'apology' for the Guardia Civil violence issued by Enric Millo, the PP government delegate to Catalonia. However, Juan Ignacio Zoido, the PP Interior Minister, gave full support to his paramilitaries. The day after the referendum, he rushed to Catalonia to praise the Guardia on the ground and to dispel doubts about the government's support for the security forces. The following week he ordered the creation of a special legal team in the Interior Ministry dedicated exclusively to prosecuting or suing those whom he deemed to have 'harassed' the police or impugned their honour during Operation Copernicus. He announced that the first task for this new team would be to prepare a lawsuit against the mayor of Barcelona, Ada Colau, for accusing the police of incidents of sexual abuse during the 1-o referendum. Zoido claimed that the Ministry had catalogued some 107 cases of police harassment, which he vowed to prosecute as 'hate crimes'.

More sinister even, this new legal team will investigate the alleged passivity of the Mossos d'Esquadra, not only on referendum day but before and after. It will also take criminal action against Catalan schools where, according to Zoido, the children of members of the security forces have been 'segregated' from other pupils. The lawyers will also take action against Catalan hotels said to have cancelled bookings for Guardia and National Police members, and against mayors and local councillors who allegedly incited hotel owners to do so.

On 12 October the Council of Europe's Parliamentary Assembly formally condemned the actions of the Spanish police on 1 October. Afterwards, the Council's Commission for Democracy through Law (which sets European standards for human rights and the rule of law) contacted the PP Interior Minister. The Commission demanded a 'swift, independent and effective' investigation into allegations of the disproportionate use of force by the Guardia. But a truculent Zoido was unrepentant. He replied formally that the Guardia Civil had acted in a 'proportionate and appropriate manner'.

Zoido's actions can be seen as borderline paranoia. Alternatively, this is a PP politician desperately trying to maintain the allegiance of the state apparatus as Spain starts to fall apart. Above all, this is an unrepentant PP regime willing to use every form of repression in order to stop Catalonian self-determination.

Si! to the Republic

Tens of thousands of young Catalans gathered in Placa de Catalunya, Barcelona's main square, on the Sunday evening to hear the provisional results of the voting. The mood was joyful after the earlier police violence and tension. The entire crowd sat down when told to. They had not long to wait. Catalonia had voted 'Si' to independence as a republic.

The final, audited results published later in the week showed that 90.18 per cent of Catalans had voted 'Yes' in the referendum, while 7.83 per cent voted 'No', and 1.98 per cent cast a blank ballot. Despite the huge Spanish police crackdown on the vote, the turnout was 43.03 per cent. In absolute numbers, 2,044,038 people voted in favour of independence, while 177,547 voted against. The Catalan government estimated that polling stations representing up to 770,000 potential voters – 14.5 per cent of all registered voters – were closed down by the police in raids, any votes cast in those stations having been seized, lost or made inaccessible and therefore not counted. Certainly, some of these 'lost' voters cast their ballots at alternative polling stations using the 'universal census' system. However, given the level of police violence, it is reasonable to conclude that votes were lost, or willing voters intimidated. Catalan government officials have estimated that were it not for closures and police pressure, turnout could have been as high as 55 per cent.

How valid are these numbers as a test of the Catalan will? The 2,044,038 ballots for 'Yes' represented the highest-ever vote for independence in the post-Franco era. In the November 2014 non-binding referendum – which was free of police repression – some 1,861,753 voted for independence, with 104,760 against. In the 2015 Catalan parliamentary election, the parties supporting independence won 1,966,535 votes. So there has been a steady progression in the 'Yes' poll. It is impossible not to conclude that a vast majority of native Catalans desire self-determination as an independent republic.

Breaking down the votes on 1-o, the region with the biggest turnout was Central Catalonia, with 58.15 per cent, while the one with the lowest turnout was Tarragona, with 36.82 per cent. The highest percentage of ‹Yes› votes was among people voting from abroad (98.13 per cent), followed by Girona (94.86 per cent). In the metropolitan district of Barcelona, support for 'Yes' was the lowest in the country, at 87.8 per cent.

How trustworthy was the 1-o vote? The poll was monitored by a team of 17 accredited international observers who visited over 100 polling stations across Catalonia. This International Election Expert Research Team was led by Helena Catt, former chief executive of the New Zealand Electoral Commission and a former consultant to the Australian Electoral Commission. Her team had decades of collective experience garnered from carrying out over 300 election monitoring assignments all over the world. For 1-o, they monitored and recorded the referendum from 5.00 am until polls closed at 8.00 pm and then as ballots were counted. Dr. Catt concluded:

> Yesterday we witnessed events that no election monitors ought to ever witness. We hope never to witness scenes of this nature ever again. We saw numerous and repeated violations of civil and human rights. We are shocked that this happened at all. Even more so as it is clear to us that it was a centrally orchestrated, military-style operation carefully planned. We are stunned that armed masked officers entered polling stations with the purposes of preventing a peaceful democratic process.
>
> Despite these issues, and other difficulties people experienced trying to vote, I want to emphasise that we did see a day of voting yesterday... In the face of external interference there were improvisations and last-minute changes to the voting process that were not always consistent across Catalonia or with what was in the law or the manual and we will detail these in our final report. We repeatedly saw that those who worked in the polling stations did so in good faith, and we saw no sign of attempts to manipulate the vote. Everyone we saw was doing the best they could under difficult circumstances... The process should be respected.[150]

In addition, the voting was observed by a large international parliamentary team from around the globe, including representatives from 16 European countries plus Canada, Israel, Tunisia and Hong Kong. One of the delegation, the former Speaker of the Scottish Parliament, Tricia Marwick, commented: 'We have seen fascism from the Spanish state. Franco's ghost is at the table.'

Franco's ghost was indeed abroad on 1-o. But this time, Catalan democracy won.

Chapter Twelve: The Republic Is Born

General strike

THE MONTH IMMEDIATELY following the 1-0 referendum victory was dominated by mass protests in the streets of Catalonia intertwined with a diplomatic duel for popular and international support between the Catalan government and Madrid. Politics returned to the streets in the form of a pro-independence General Strike and increasingly angry demonstrations by the Spanish right. Stung by international outrage at the naked violence used by the Guardia Civil against referendum voters, Rajoy at first hesitated to use his nuclear option to suspend the Catalan parliament, under article 155 of the 1978 constitution. Puigdemont meanwhile played for time, desperately seeking European intervention to open a dialogue with Madrid that would sanction an orderly progression to independence. For several weeks in October the future of the Catalan Republic hovered in the balance.

The post-referendum crisis began on the Tuesday following the vote, when Catalonia went on General Strike in protest at the Guardia Civil violence. This was the first large-scale workers' strike against state repression in Western Europe since 1968. Hundreds of thousands of demonstrators participated in the mass protest – 700,000 in Barcelona alone. Guardia Civil barracks were focal sites of protests. Many who had voted 'No' in the referendum, or simply abstained, came on to the streets in disgust at the Guardia Civil tactics.

The strike had a number of important characteristics. Firstly, it was spontaneous, initially outflanking the Catalan government, main political parties and Spanish-led big trade union federations. The first calls for a general stoppage came in the wake of the 20 September police raids, led by a number of minor leftist (and pro-independence) unions in Catalonia – the Intersyndical, CGT, IAC and COS. This proposed strike was timed for the Tuesday following the referendum. The logic of the timing was quite sensible: to ensure that the mass movement returned to the streets after 1-0 itself, in order to forestall further state repression. It is surprising that the main pro-independence parties had not laid out a timetable for such an action. In fact, the General Strike proposal might have been lost in the tide of events. But circumstances were transformed by the Guardia Civil attacks on polling stations on the Sunday morning of the referendum. The resulting wave of popular anger found an outlet in the Tuesday General Strike and left the major unions and Catalan politicians rushing to catch up.

On the Sunday afternoon, Vice President Junqueras held an emergency meeting at the Barcelona offices of the CCOO, with the general secretaries of the two main Catalan unions, Camil Ros of the pro-Socialist UGT and Javier Pachero of Workers' Commissions (who was close to the ERC). Both men committed to supporting a stoppage on the following Tuesday in protest at the police violence now engulfing Catalonia – a stoppage many of their members were already going to hold anyway. Pacheco explained: 'An attack on democracy without precedent in recent times calls for a united response.' With 140,000 members, the CCOO remains the largest union in Catalonia, though its members are split between those who support independence and those who don't. The union locally has kept neutral while backing the right to hold a referendum.

However, local CCOO and UGT support for the Tuesday strike was qualified – under pressure from their Spanish national leaderships, who issued a joint statement simultaneously opposing any declaration of independence by President Puigdemont while urging Rajoy to agree to a dialogue with the Catalans. The national CCOO and UGT press release was also at pains to distance themselves from the initial General Strike call by the other Catalan unions. Instead, CCOO and the UGT would urge their members to join public or work-place demonstrations agreed with their employers. In other words, 3 October would become a street protest rather than a full-blown General Strike which – given the history of the Catalan and especially Barcelona workforce – had insurrectionary connotations the union leaderships in Madrid wished to suppress.

As calls for the General Strike gathered momentum in the hours after 1-o, there was growing tension between those (such as the far left CUP) who wished to see the Republic declared immediately and more cautious elements who were seeking to get Madid to the negotiating table. For Puigdemont and the main parties in the governing coalition, the tactical imperative was to make the demonstrations on the Tuesday as big and socially inclusive as possible. Their aim was to mobilise European and global opinion against Madrid's unwillingness to negotiate. At this point a new organising body entered the picture: the Taula per la Democràcia – literally the Democracy Board (or perhaps more elegantly, Round Table for Democracy).

The Democracy Board only came into being on 27 September, in the wake of the various alarming infringements of democratic and human rights by the Spanish government prior to 1-0. The Board brought together a vast array of Catalan civic organisations, including both trade unions and employers' organisations. Its stated aim was not independence but 'to provide a unified, peaceful and co-ordinated response in defence of Catalan institutions and fundamental rights'. The Board was launched with the support of over 40 organisations: all the workers' organisations (the Catalan federations of the CCOO and UGT, the Union of Peasant Farmers, the pro-independence Intersindical-CSC and the tiny syndicalist USOC); Omnium and the ANC, as the main civic organisations; plus a host of educational, sporting, LGBT, Green, anti-racist and cultural bodies, including the Catalan Scouts and Olympic Committee. Crucially, the Democracy Board included Cecot, the main employers' representative, and Pimec, the federation of small businesses. By any standards this was an extraordinary mobilisation of civil society around a common political purpose.

As its first major action, the Democracy Board effectively took over control of the 3 October General Strike, transforming it into a mass demonstration against police violence. It called on all Catalans – including business owners and the self-employed – to stop work and bring Catalonia to a halt. Nevertheless, by spearheading the call for a General Strike in the first place, the working class wing of the independence movement had finally taken the initiative, building on the earlier actions of the Barcelona dockers (led by the CNT union) to black the cruise liners acting as temporary barracks for the Guardia, and of local firefighters protecting protestors from the police. And while the intervention of the cross-class Democracy Board and the conservative CCOO and UGT leaderships had limited the strike to a one-day protest, more crucially the protest action spread to workers in the thousands of small factories and assembly shops that form the manufacturing base of the Catalan economy. In many places, workers occupied their factories and festooned them with Catalan flags.

By 9.30am on that Tuesday, the Barcelona municipal bus and subway systems had almost entirely halted. Catalonia's railway company suspended operations, while Spanish national railway services ran fitfully. The ports of Barcelona and Tarragona closed. So did shops, large stores and the Mercabarna wholesale food market. The tourist-magnet La Boqueria market in Barcelona remained virtually empty. Schools and universities cancelled classes. The strike was also joined by the staff of La Sagrada Família (which would have pleased Gaudi) and FC Barcelona, who quit training for the day. By midday, tens of thousands of people had already occupied the Catalonian capital's major streets – Avinguda Diagonal, Gran Via, Via Laietana – en route to the major demonstrations at the city's administrative center, Plaça Sant Jaume, and the intersection at Ronda de la Universitat, called for 6.00 pm. Similar mass protests took place outside town halls across Catalonia. A manifesto in the name of the new Democracy Board was read out. It called for withdrawal of Spanish security forces from Catalonia and dialogue rather than force from Madrid. Despite the high tension, the Tuesday protests were civil, festive, and largely without incident. In one case, a protester who threw a beer can into riot police was surrounded by fellow protesters who chanted 'We are a people of peace' and encouraged him to leave.

As always in mass confrontations, the 3 October General Strike gave rise to new forms of struggle and new tactics. One group of farmers tricked Spanish police with a simple ruse, in order to stop them disrupting the protest. Peasant farmers from La Jonquera loudly declared their intention to seal off the border with France, using tractors. In anticipation, hundreds of Guardia Civil rushed to the area to stop them. But once the police arrived, the farmers instead closed off the motorway behind the Guardia Civil units, trapping and immobilising the paramilitaries between their tractor road block and the French border. Joan Caball, president of Catalonia's farmer's union, later revealed that the initial plan had been to close down the railway line but as events unfolded they opted to close the roads, making a laughing stock of the Guardia Civil. Local media in La Jonquera reported that the police remained trapped for several hours and were not able to intervene during the peak of the General Strike.

What was the balance sheet of the 3 October General Strike?

While the mass demonstrations were impressive, the extent of the industrial action should not be exaggerated. Barcelona airport remained operational (perhaps so as not to inconvenience tourists) and most large industry, including the car plants, ran without disruption. The latter was almost certainly because of the CCOO and UGT intervention. Sections of the left, the CUP in particular, wanted to go further. In some places, road blocks were set up to stop transport deliveries and there were calls for the creation of popular committees to organise neighbourhood action in support of the Republic. It is certainly a valid point that Puigdemont and the main independence parties saw the Tuesday General Strike as a way of applying international pressure to Madrid, in the hope of securing negotiations. In itself, this was not an invalid tactic. But problems would arise if Madrid refused to play ball. In which case, turning the mass movement on and off might prove demoralising. Hence the perfectly valid argument that the General Strike should be pushed further, to begin to create 'dual power' in the neighbourhoods and workplaces, in preparation for Madrid suspending Catalan autonomy. On the other hand, given that General Strike was the first real independent move by sections of the Catalan working class, it would be sheer romanticism to imagine that such popular dual power was anywhere near at hand. Or that the strike could have been made indefinite, there and then.

The sheer scale of the demonstrations on that Tuesday did have a huge impact internationally, isolating the Spanish government even more than on 1-O. This led Rajoy to hold off arresting the Catalan leaders or making any precipitate moves to suspend Catalan autonomy. But the PP continued to bluster. Rafael Hernando, the PP's official spokesperson in the Spanish Parliament, vilified the 3 October protest: 'It is a political Nazi-style strike, where roads have been closed by a violent mob.' Mr Hernando might know a thing or two about being a Nazi, having been a member of the ultra-Francoist Fuerza Nueva in his youth. He is also a well-known climate change denier, and so is used to being blind to political reality. Hernando went on to call for President Puigdemont to be banned from public office. Puigdemont, in turn, charged the Spanish government with returning to the authoritarian methods of Franco. In this exchange, both sides crossed political lines not breached since the dictator died. The sham democracy that Spain had lived under since 1975 was being exposed for the world to see. Puigdemont announced that the Catalan government would declare independence within the week.

The King's Speech

The third of October was to produce one further dramatic turn: an ill-judged and ill-tempered public intervention by the monarchy. King Felipe VI suddenly appeared on Spanish national television – a rare event – to address the nation on the crisis. Coming from a supposed constitutional monarch, this was the political equivalent of Queen Elizabeth appearing on

UK TV during the Scottish referendum to urge a 'No' vote. Felipe gave no hint of reconciliation and made no attempt to defuse the political crisis. Instead he blamed Puigdemont and the 1-0 referendum for destabilising the Spanish nation and showing 'disloyalty towards the powers of the state'. Not once did Felipe mention the police violence during the referendum, the main cause for the General Strike. Barcelona's mayor, Ada Colau (an opponent of secession), instantly condemned the speech for its lack of solutions and failure to appeal for dialogue. Ordinary Catalans responded spontaneously with another *cassolada,* the traditional banging of pots and pans at sunset.

What had got into the King to make an intervention that could only inflame the delicate political situation? Felipe was new to the monarchy business. He ascended the throne in June 2014, following the abdication of his father, Juan Carlos. Felipe's mother, Sofia, is the sister of Constantine, the deposed ex-King of Greece, whose own democratic credentials were non-existent. Felipe was just eight when Juan Carlos was crowned King and successor to Franco as Spanish head of state. He was carefully educated for his role; not as constitutional guardian of democracy and human rights, but rather as protector of the unified Spain and settled order Franco had in mind when he revived the hereditary monarchy after a hiatus of 44 years. To fulfil this ordained role, Felipe was educated in all three branches of the military and is now their commander-in-chief. That did not stop him being a bit of a playboy as a young man, but he is no dunderhead, having gained a Masters in International Affairs from Georgetown University in Washington. He even speaks Catalan.

Felipe's TV intervention was no blunder in his own eyes. His speech's breathtaking arrogance is highly indicative of the political pathology of the neo-Francoist Spanish elite. In Felipe's mind, the role of the constitutional monarch is exactly what Francisco Franco created him for: to defend the status quo to the bitter end regardless of the popular will. The reactions to the King's speech were mixed. The PP and Ciudadanos lauded Felipe's 'commitment to legality' while, on the left, Podemos and Catalunya en Comú criticised it as 'unworthy and irresponsible' and laying the ground for direct intervention by Madrid. The PSOE, on the other hand, found itself in a dilemma. In public, the PSOE leadership supported the King's words but in private they intimated that they were troubled by Felipe's failure to call for dialogue or express any concern at the police action.

The King's speech had one dramatic effect: it gave a green light to the Spanish right and far right to mobilise on the streets in opposition to

Catalan calls for independence. On the weekend of Saturday 7 and Sunday 8 October, the right poured into the streets of Madrid and Barcelona – mostly bussed in from all parts of Spain. On the Saturday some 50,000 demonstrators gathered in Madrid's central Plaza de Colon, over which permanently flies a Spanish flag, 294 square metres in size. They chanted slogans in favour of Spanish unity and shouted 'Long live the Guardia Civil' and 'We're proud of our police'. There were also loud calls for Puigdemont to be jailed and 'no negotiations with the *golpistas*' – the traditional Spanish term for conspirators in a coup d'etat. The mood was defiantly nationalist and confrontational rather than seeking any reconciliation with Catalonia. Various ultra-right and Falangist splinter groups were noticeable, singing Civil War and Francoist songs and giving the fascist salute. Similar scenes took place in Barcelona on the Sunday. While the numbers taking part were large they were nowhere near the size of the big pro-Catalan demonstrations.

That weekend did see some 50 rather small gatherings across Spain, promoting dialogue and a political solution to the crisis. They were noticeable for attracting older people – comparatively few young people were involved. These events were called 'peace' demonstrations and participants were encouraged to wear white. But their comparatively small scale suggested that Spain was polarising. At one peace event held in the Catalan town of Hospitalet de Llobregat, the local mayor and PSC member Nuria Marin argued for talks: 'We should start from scratch with no pre-conditions.' But the PSC-PSOE had no concrete agenda for any such negotiations and its intervention in the pro-dialogue demonstrations appeared cosmetic. After all, the minority PP government in Madrid was only kept in office by the PSOE, which could easily have pushed for a new Statute of Autonomy for Catalonia, or vetoed any attempt to impose direct rule.

The real political tone of the weekend immediately following 1-0 was set by the Spanish Interior Minister, Juan Ignacio Zoido, who made a surprise visit to Catalonia. Far from seeking dialogue or to diffuse tensions, Zoido went out of his way to praise the Guardia Civil and National Police now stationed in Catalonia. Zoido trumpeted: 'There is not one person in the government who does not support the police actions'. He also announced the paramilitary units deployed to Catalonia for 1-0 would be staying longer. This was the language of confrontation, not peace.

Puigdemont declares the Republic – then puts it on hold

The original intention of the Catalan government was to meet on the Monday following the referendum to announce the official tally of votes and possibly declare independence and the Republic, as mandated under the referendum law passed on 6 September. But the Constitutional Court – responding to a challenge by the PSC – blocked the meeting from taking place. The Catalan Parliament finally convened on Tuesday 10 October. As the time came for Puigdemont to speak, thousands of people lined the *Passeig de Lluís Companys* ('the Promenade of Lluís Companys') in front of the parliament building, waiting to hear a declaration of independence. Tension built after Puigdemont's speech was delayed for an hour to allow hasty discussions with the CUP. Finally, at just after 7.00pm Barcelona time, President Puigdement addressed his people and the wider world.

But verbal fireworks were lacking. Puigdemont made a long, dry, technical speech practically devoid of emotion. After rehearsing the process that had led up to 1-0, and defending its legality, he finally announced: 'I want to follow the people's will for Catalonia to become an independent state.' The pro-independence deputies erupted into applause. But then Puigdemont added a swift coda – he was delaying a formal declaration for independence in order to press for negotiations with Madrid. He continued:

> We propose to suspend the effect of the independence declaration... in order to work towards putting into practice the result of the referendum... Today, we are making a gesture of responsibility in favour of dialogue.[151]

Independence had been declared and undeclared within seconds. The media and the listening Catalan public, not to mention Madrid, were confused to begin with. Just what had Puigdemont actually announced? It soon became clear he was playing for time. By announcing independence (sort of) he was seemingly keeping faith with the Catalan people who had struggled to the polls on 1-0 despite the truncheons of the Guardia Civil. But by instantly suspending the actuality of a unilateral declaration of independence, Puigdemont was making it difficult for Rajoy to respond by triggering article 155 of the Spanish constitution and suspending the Catalan Parliament. From one point of view, this was a diplomatic masterstroke that put all the pressure on Madrid to respond positively. It was also a clear message to the

EU and international community that Catalonia's leaders wanted dialogue and possibly some form of compromise.

But this strategy carried risks. It could be perceived as prevarication by independence supporters. And there was precious little proof that the international community was interested in mediation or promoting a deal with Madrid. That Tuesday, the new French president, Emmanuel Macron, had explicitly ruled out the EU getting involved. 'It is an internal Spanish matter,' Macron announced in Frankfurt, just before meeting Chancellor Merkel. Pressed by the media, he said he saw no way that he, as French head of state, could mediate in the affairs of a friendly neighbour.

Not everyone was happy with Puigdemont's tactical delay. A powerful current was emerging to Puigdemont's left in favour of declaring the Republic for real. First the ANC, the heart and soul of the popular movement for independence, urged him to 'unsuspend' the declaration of independence. This was followed by the far left CUP, on whose votes the Puigdemont's government depended. Responding to threats from Madrid to suspend Catalan autonomy, the CUP declared: 'if they [...] want to keep threatening and gagging us, they should do so with the Republic already proclaimed'.

A gap was starting to emerge between the CUP and ANC strategy of relying on mass pressure to secure independence and the parliamentary diplomacy being pursued by Puigdemont. The CUP was adamant: 'it was people who stopped this country [on 3 October] with a massive, unprecedented General Strike'. The party warned:

> People are the only solid structure this country has, faced with a lack of explicit international support... Our force is people and their needs, people and their hopes.

Former Catalan President, Artur Mas, was quick to defend Puigdemont's tactics. Testily, he informed Catalan public television that neither the ANC nor the CUP ran the Catalan government. However, one key component of the ruling coalition was not on message: Oriol Junqueras, Puigdemont's Deputy President and head of the ERC. Replying to a tweet from former Catalan education minister Ernest Maragall that 'It's time to assume the risk of freedom', Junqueras responded pithily: 'Totally agree'.

Puigdemont appeared to win the next round. Rajoy responded to the on-off declaration of independence by asking Puigdemont to clarify his position. Moves to suspend the Catalan Parliament were themselves suspended. On Monday 16 October, Puigdemont gambled again. He still refused to clarify whether the declaration of the Republic was in effect. Instead, he issued yet another call for dialogue with Madrid. Soraya Sáenz de Santamaría, Spain's deputy prime minister, responded saying Puigdemont now had until Thursday to change his stance or the government would 'take the next steps'. She cited article 155, coupling this with an explicit threat to call new elections in Catalonia.

The delay did result in some outside support for the Catalans. The First Minister of Scotland, Nicola Sturgeon, in a keynote speech to the Scottish National Party conference in Glasgow, explicitly called for EU intervention in the Catalan crisis:

> When the people of Catalonia – EU citizens – were violently attacked by police just for trying to vote, the EU should have spoken up, loudly, to condemn it. Friends, in Catalonia, I hope dialogue will replace confrontation. It is time for the Spanish government to sit down with the government of Catalonia.

The Belgian prime minister, Charles Michel, proposed an 'international and European mediation' if dialogue between the Catalan and Spanish governments failed. In an interview with the Belgian newspaper *Le Soir*, Michel said that the Catalan crisis was a test of the European Union because it was about 'fundamental issues such as freedom of vote and freedom of expression.' He stressed that 'there is no legal crisis in Spain, there is a political crisis', adding a 'political crisis must be resolved through political dialogue'. He called on Madrid and Catalonia to open new talks.

But these and a few other diplomatic initiatives were mainly from the political sidelines. It was soon apparent that the EU, far from brokering a settlement between Madrid and Catalonia, was backing Rajoy and the side of 'constitutional order' in Spain. Just as the EU had run roughshod over the Greek referendum in order to save the euro and wobbly German banks, so it was more concerned to support the Spanish state in its struggle with Catalan democracy. After all, Spain too had saved the German banks by imposing austerity on its people at the command of the EU. Now, post Brexit, German interests needed Spain more than ever as a loyal ally. No wonder Merkel called Rajoy personally the Saturday after 1-O, to stress her support for 'Spanish unity'. And Commission President Juncker went out of his way to warn that an independent Catalonia would have to apply to join the EU – which the residual Spanish state could obviously veto. Police violence? Barring some pro forma criticisms, Europe had done nothing to stop breaches of democratic norms in Poland or Hungary; why should Spain be any different?

Struggle for the loyalty of police and business

While Puigdemont manoeuvred publicly, the Spanish state was engaged throughout October 2017 in a behind-the-scenes struggle to subvert the very institutions an independent Catalonia would depend on. A gigantic effort was pursued to persuade or cajole Catalan-based companies to move their legal headquarters to other parts of the Spanish state – economic blackmail on a grand scale. Plans were set in train to purge the Catalan media of anyone deemed disloyal to Spain. Above all, the loyalty of the local Catalan police would be tested to breaking point.

On the business front, the exodus of Catalan-based firms to Madrid and the rest of the Spanish state was truly spectacular. Between the day after the referendum and 24 October, 1,501 companies moved their legal address to outside Catalonia, according to the College of Mercantile Registers of Spain. They included six of the seven Catalan-based companies listed on IBEX, the main index of Spanish shares. Caixabank, Spain's third biggest, said it would re-register in the Catalan-speaking Balearic Islands, though the final decision would have to be approved by shareholders. Banco Sabadell (which owns the British TSB) switched to Alicante. The big property group Inmobiliaria Colonial and the infrastructure firm Abertis both opted for Madrid.

Economically, these shifts were largely cosmetic. Actual HQ functions, company operations, production and – most importantly – jobs remained in Catalonia. Telecoms firm Cellnex said it would re-register in Madrid but only for as long as political uncertainty continued. However, even if no jobs were lost immediately, there was an element of political blackmail. The Spanish government was active in private, persuading firms to re-register. Volkswagen's SEAT operation in Catalonia was a key target. Matías Carnero, the head of the union committee at SEAT and Deputy General Secretary of the Catalan UGT, revealed to the media that the company's management had come under 'political and monarchical pressures' to move their registered office – which they declined to do. Not known for being pro-independence, Carnero likened the campaign by the PP government to move company registrations out of Catalonia a 'financial 155'.

This 'financial 155' had minimum impact on the independence process. More insidious was the attempt by Madrid to capture control of Mossos, the 17,000-strong Catalan police force led by Josep Lluis Trapero. If the Spanish government was ever to impose its writ over Catalonia it had to ensure it could at least neutralise Mossos, if not subsume it under the political direction of Interior Minister Zoido. The latter had directed huge quantities of riot control gear and water cannon to be deployed to Catalonia to quell civil disobedience, but he lacked manpower. The numbers of Guardia Civil and National Police available in the rebellious province were less than the Mossos could deploy if it came to a stand-off. Worse, the Guardia themselves were in a mutinous mood, disliking the fact they were badly paid (in their eyes) and far from home for an indeterminate period, in a Catalonia that despised them.

The solution, as far as Madrid was concerned, was to get rid of Trapero. The Catalan-born police chief, the son of a taxi driver, was known to be sympathetic to the nationalist cause, though he was punctilious at staying within the constitutional letter of the law. A career policeman, he also had a law degree and a postgraduate degree in public security. He had even attended the FBI academy at Quantico in the United States. Trapero had received national and international plaudits for the way the Mossos swiftly and surgically dealt with the Islamist terror attack in Barcelona on 17 August, only weeks before 1-O. Even then, there had been a clumsy attempt to undermine Trapero. This involved the publication, in the anti-nationalist *El Periódico* newspaper, of a bogus report which claimed the CIA had warned Mossos of a likely terrorist attack some two months before it occurred. The document was soon proved to have been a clumsy forgery. Trapero became a local hero who could handle a major crisis.

The move against Trapero began with an official Guardia Civil report claiming that the Mossos chief had been guilty not only of 'blatant inaction' on 1-O but had acted as part of a 'strategic plan for independence'. Most serious, Trapero was cited for failing to use his officers to rescue Guardia Civil police trapped inside the Catalan Economic Ministry by pro-independence protesters during the raids of 20 September. Trapero was quickly charged with sedition and called to appear in court on Friday 6 October. If found guilty, he faced 15 years in prison. But Madrid's immediate aim was to undermine Trapero's authority and prepare the way for 'nationalising' Mossos.

Two Jordis

Sunday 15 October was the 77th anniversary of the execution of Lluís Companys, iconic President of Catalonia during the Civil War. In ordinary times, a 77th anniversary would pass unnoticed. But these were not ordinary times. Puigdemont, Carme Forcadell and Barcelona mayor Ada Colau laid wreathes in memory of Companys at the Montjuic Castle. The ghost of the Catalan State declared by Companys from the balcony of the *Generalitat* in 1934 seemed very real. But even then the day might have passed quietly but for an intervention by Pablo Casado, the baby-faced rising star of the PP in Madrid. Commenting on the wreath-laying, Casado drew a parallel between Puigdemont and Companys, hinting the current president of Catalonia might share the fate of his illustrious predecessor, if he declared independence: 'We hope they don't declare anything tomorrow, because anyone doing so might end up like him [i.e. Companys].'

There was a storm of public indignation at a veiled threat to the life of Puigdemont coming from an official spokesperson of the Spanish government. Casado quickly backtracked saying he had only meant to imply Puigdemont would end up in prison if he declared independence – as if threatening an elected politician with incarceration for carrying out their mandate was anything other than a deliberate provocation. As ever, Puigdemont's response was measured. He announced that he was 'suspending' implementing the declaration of independence for two months, in the hope of securing negotiations with Madrid.

The Spanish response was instant. On Monday 16 October, state repression intensified when the *Audiencia Nacional*, the political court, ordered the arrest and detention of two key leaders of the national movement: Jordi Sánchez, president of the Catalan National Assembly; and Jordi Cuixart, president of Òmnium Cultural. Both men were held without bail pending trial for sedition against the Spanish state. They were kept apart and denied visits from their wives. Western Europe had its first political prisoners in many decades. Catalans took to the streets in huge numbers demanding the release of the pair – instantly christened 'the two Jordis'.

The *Audiencia* judge who incarcerated Sánchez and Cuixart was Carmen Lamela Díaz. Lamela was appointed to the bench with a specific political remit: to investigate lawyers allegedly connected to ETA. Despite a reputation for being close to the PSOE, she has taken a consistently hard line – some would say a paranoid line – against any crime she thinks is political or 'terrorist' related. She made a notorious ruling in the so-called Alsasua Affair concerning the beating up of two off-duty Guardia Civil officers – for which she gained the plaudits of the paramilitaries. In October 2016, in the small Basque town of Alsasua, two off-duty Guardia Civil and their girlfriends were beaten up in a bar-room brawl with some local youths. There is no doubt the Guardia officers received serious injuries – there is a long history of local animosity to the Guardia in the area. However, Judge Lamela ruled against a lower court and approved an indictment against the eight young defendants accusing them (literally) of terrorism. This absurd ruling let the public prosecutor seek prison sentences of 50 years and more for each of the Basque youths, triggering off mass protest demonstrations. Lamela's decision to jail the two Catalan civic organisers was in character.

Sànchez, an associate professor at Barcelona University, was elected head of the ANC in May 2015, when Carme Forcadell resigned to stand for election to the Catalan parliament on the list put forward by the Junts pel Si coalition. Sanchez beat the popular favourite, the writer Liz Castro, probably because he was seen as a consensus figure who would be able to keep the diverse strands of the ANC working together. Back in the 1980s, Sànchez was a member of *Crida per la Solidaritat*, a movement dedicated to protecting and promoting the Catalan language. He is also a leading member of the ICV, the Catalan green movement. Jordi Cuixart has a very different background, being an entrepreneur and small businessman – a social layer well represented in both the Catalan and Scottish independence movements. Cuixart has been associated with Òmnium since 1996 and held many senior positions within the cultural association, finally becoming president in December 2015.

Together, Sànchez and Cuixart organised all the big pro-independence mobilisations in the two years prior to 1-0. However, their jailing by Judge Lamela was specifically related to the mass demonstrations of September 20 that followed raids by the Guardia Civil and the arrests of individuals connected with organising the referendum. Some 40,000 people responded to a call made by the ANC and Òmnium to protest outside the Catalan department of economic affairs in Barcelona, where the junior economics minister had been arrested. According Judge Lamela's written decision, both Jordis were 'the main instigators and directors of the protests of September 20 and 21'. Lamela claimed that these were not peaceful demonstrations but called deliberately to 'protect' those pro-independence officials and institutions targeted by the Guardia Civil. According to Lamela's writ, the actions of Sanchez and Cuixart constituted sedition – a felony under article 544 of the Spanish Criminal Code carrying a potential 15-year prison sentence for those who 'publicly and tumultuously rise up to prevent, by force or outside the legal channels [any]... public officer from the lawful exercise of their duties'. Practically any anti-government demonstration could be construed to be illegal under this catch-all definition – another example of how the post-Franco Spanish state retains the methods of the dictatorship under a thin veneer of democratic respectability.

As to the specific events of 20 September, it is true that a massive crowd surrounded the Catalan Ministry of Economic Affairs following an appeal from the ANC and Omnium. As a result, a court official overseeing the search could not physically leave the building and had to make an ignominious exit using the rooftop. It is also the case that three Guardia Civil patrol cars parked in the street had their windows smashed and were covered in pro-referendum stickers – though this hardly amounted to the €135,600 of damage the Guardia claimed. However, the demonstration was overwhelmingly peaceful. And when the press of numbers became unmanageable, threatening the crowd's own safety, Jordi Cuixart called on them to disperse – a moment caught on video. None of this suggests a reason – other than political bias – to physically detain the two Jordis without bail.

Also appearing in the *Audiencia* court with the two Jordis was the Mossos police chief, Josep Lluis Trapero. But with political deftness, Judge Lamela released Trapero on bail rather than incarcerating him as she had the two civic activists. Jailing Trapero at that point might have guaranteed that Madrid would lose the sympathies of much of Mossos. And without the triggering of Article 155, the Interior Ministry in Madrid still lacked the legal mandate to take over the Catalan police force directly.

In retrospect, the incarceration of the two Jordis was the turning point in the march towards the declaration of the Republic. Jailing Mas, Puigdemont or Junqueras would have been inflammatory, but they were professional politicians. The Jordis were civic leaders and making them political prisoners indicated to the mass of Catalans that there could be no turning back from a declaration of the Republic. Once again multitudes of demonstrators took to the streets across Catalonia to protest the detention of the Two Jordis. Equally, in Madrid a turning point had arrived. In not deposing police chief Traperos, the Spanish state was indicating its uncertainty over its ability to dictate events. To control Catalonia there was no alternative now but to trigger Article 155 and impose direct rule.

Declaration of the Republic

Triggering 155 was always a nuclear option for Rajoy. Imposing central rule could set off a chain of events destabilising Spain and awaking the sleeping dog that is Basque nationalism. True, calling fresh elections in Catalonia might split and depose the bloc of parties favouring independence. On the other hand, after the police violence of 1-0, it might consolidate their position. This is one reason why Rajoy was rumoured to favour engineering a split between the Catalan government and the CUP, so that the government would fall of its own accord. But with the popular movement in Catalonia pushing Puigdemont towards a full declaration of the Republic, there was now no alternative to 155 in the eyes of the PP ultras.

A glance at the official English language translation of article 155 shows just how broad a law it is:

> If a Self-governing Community does not fulfil the obligations imposed upon it by the Constitution or other laws, or acts in a way that is seriously prejudicial to the general interest of Spain, the Government, after having lodged a complaint with the President of the Self-governing Community and failed to receive satisfaction therefore, may, following approval granted by the overall majority of the Senate, take all measures necessary to compel the Community to meet said obligations, or to protect the above mentioned general interest.[152]

In Catalonia itself, the PP's local leader and firebrand, Xavier García Albiol, was only to ready to demand the maximum direct intervention, including not just the jailing of Puigdemont but the banning of the pro-independence parties outright. Pablo Casado, another PP ultra, went as far as suggesting the 'Parties Law', drafted during the conflict with ETA, should be invoked to ban all the main independence parties. Meanwhile, to his left, Rajoy had to ensure that the PSOE would support any triggering of Article 155, to ensure its swift passage through the Spanish Senate. The new PSOE leader, Pedro Sánchez, had no love of Catalan separatism but equally he had no desire to write the PP a blank cheque. Given the fact that Rajoy depended on PSOE acquiescence to stay in power, now was the time for Sanchez to extract some commitment from the PP to reintroduce an agreed Statute of Autonomy for Catalonia, or even to review the existing constitution and move towards a genuine form of Spanish federalism. In the end though, Sanchez capitulated to Rajoy without extracting any real concessions – a testimony to how weakened a political force the Socialists had become.

With the arrest of the Two Jordis, Catalonia was on cruise control towards a declaration of the Republic. The only question was when. In Madrid, moves towards the imposition of 155 and direct rule were equally public. With the PSOE and Citizens squared, Rajoy announced that he would take 155 to the Senate. Within the pro-independence bloc, the timing of the next step depended on whether to declare the Republic at the moment 155 was voted on, or try one last time for dialogue with Madrid. Backchannels were available through the Basque President, Íñigo Urkullu. One option was to keep the independence declaration in the freezer, provided Madrid held off on triggering 155. That would allow time for new Catalan elections as a quid pro quo. However, Puigdemont also wanted guarantees from Madrid that the Jordis would be released and the Guardia Civil withdrawn. In private, Madrid was intransigent; in public the PP was pressing on with a vote on 155 in the Senate. But could they be bounced into an agreement if the Catalan government unilaterally called an election?

Thursday 26 October was a day of nerves and high tension. After a marathon 7-hour meeting on the previous evening, which only ended at 2.00am, there was still no agreement on the way forward. The Catalan cabinet resumed at 10.00am joined by Artur Mas, the PDECAT éminence grise. Announcing the declaration of independence was favoured by a majority. But at noon came a surprise: Puigdemont announced he was going to dissolve parliament and call an election, in return for the Spanish government abandoning the threat of 155, releasing Cuixart and Sànchez, and withdrawing the Guardia Civil deployed to Catalonia. This plan was briefed to the waiting media.

This unilateral announcement caused consternation in the independence movement and came close to splitting it. The ERC let it be known they would quit the government if Puigdemont called elections. Even inside Puigdemont's own party, there was an outcry and demands for independence to be ratified. In the streets, where striking school and university students were demonstrating, the mood was for calling the Republic. Confusion seemed to reign as Puigdemont cancelled a scheduled press conference.

Behind the scenes, the intercession by Íñigo Urkullu had come to nothing. It appeared that the PSOE in the Cortes was sympathetic to suspending 155 if Puigdemont called an election. But Rajoy and the PP remained implacable, knowing they had a majority in the Spanish Senate and could push through 155. Finally, several hours later than expected, Puigdemont appeared in front of the cameras to say there would be no elections because the Spanish government would not back down on dissolving the Catalan parliament and imposing direct rule. For once there was an emotional edge to Puigdemont's normal technocratic style of delivery:

> It is an abusive and unfair application of the law when it seeks to eradicate not only sovereignty, but all the historic tradition of Catalanism that has brought us here. I do not accept these measures [i.e. 155]. Not just because of their unfairness but because they hide, almost without concealing, the vindictive intention of a [Spanish] State that was defeated on 1-0.[153]

The next day, Friday 27 October, the Catalan Parliament would vote for independence. The Second Catalan Republic was born. Or was it?

Chapter Thirteen: Into the Unknown

Virtual Republic or serious bid for power?

THE POLITICAL SITUATION at the close of Friday 27 October was one where two different governing bodies claimed sovereignty over Catalonia: the new Republic and the Spanish 1978 state. A dual power like this could not endure for long. One of the two social contestants had to prevail over the other. Rajoy and the Spanish courts immediately initiated measures to enforce Article 155. What did the leaders of the Catalan Republic do?

Basically, nothing, other than issue vague statements talking of 'democratic resistance'. On the Monday morning, every Catalan minister was dismissed under Article 155. They could go to their offices on Monday morning but only to pick up their personal effects. Josep Rull, the PDeCAT Minister for Sustainability, posted a Twitter photograph of himself in his office, with a copy of Monday's edition of the newspaper *El Punt Avui* visible on his desk. But this was only for show. Having posted his Twitter message, Rull duly went home. The Republic was an empty symbolic shell; perhaps a very potent symbol, but a shell nevertheless.

As it turned out, this would not be one state (albeit in embryo) competing with another for the allegiance of the police, civil service, public workforce and loyalty of its citizens. This was not July 1936. Instead, the 27 October declaration of Catalan independence led only to a 'virtual' Republic, a statement of intent and nothing more. The most positive construction is that the Catalan leadership embarked on a strategy of what was, in effect, public political martyrdom through incarceration by the Spanish state, – hoping thereby to convince a reluctant EU to intervene. But the most negative construction is that Puigdemont, Junqueras and the Catalan Cabinet simply had no idea what to do next. A massive political vacuum then opened up which Rajoy filled by calling fresh Catalan elections for 21 December – much more quickly than anyone anticipated. Meantime, the popular movement was both disappointed and disoriented, recovering only because of the need to mobilise against the mass arrests of Catalan ministers which soon followed.

Puigdemont fled to Brussels with five other cabinet members. They drove across the border into France undetected and made for Marseilles. From there they boarded a plane to Brussels. In the group were the ministers for social affairs, education and agriculture. At first sight this looked like a plan to set up a government in exile, paralleling the exiled *Generalitat* administration that persisted through the long Franco years. Included in the group were Education Minister Professor Clara Ponsati, the ex-director of the School of Economics and Finance at the University of St Andrews; Culture Minister Lluis Puig, a renowned musician and Catalan folklorist; and Health Minister Toni Comin, a gay dad and prominent member of the Jesuit-run Centre for the Study of Christianity and Justice. They hardly sounded like a gang of desperados.

However, setting up a government in exile was the last thing Puigdemont had in mind. Rather, he wanted to embarrass the European Union, in the hope of an external intervention. The mass movement was neither consulted nor informed, while the pro-independence political parties were left scrambling to decide whether or not to contest the elections. The first weeks after the declaration of the independence were politically chaotic. This telegraphed that UDI and the Republican project supported by the mass of the independence movement meant something different in practice to Puigdemont and those around him. The mass movement was seeking a genuine rupture with the 1978 Spanish settlement while Puigdemont still wanted to negotiate with it.

The ill-preparedness of the Catalan political leadership was in stark contrast to that of the Spanish government. At 4.00 am on the Saturday morning, Interior Minister Zoido (using Article 155) sacked Josep Trapero, head of the Catalan police. This was the key move. If Trapero refused to go, there would be an open confrontation between Barcelona and Madrid, not to mention the possibility of violent clashes between the Guardia Civil and Mossos. But Trapero went meekly and was replaced instantly by an acquiescent deputy willing to take orders from the Spanish Interior Ministry. The civilian director of Mossos, PDeCAT member and lawyer Pere Soler, also accepted Trapero's dismissal. For his pains, Zoido sacked him too. Petty as ever, Zoido's first move was to order the removal of all photographs of President Puigdement from Catalan police stations.

Two weeks later, ERC spokesperson Sergi Sabrià would argue that the reason why the Catalan government did not implement independence was due to threats from the Spanish authorities:

> We were not ready to face an authoritarian State with no limits when it came to using violence. Perhaps we were not prepared enough, but even if we had been, we would never have overcome this situation, putting the public in danger.[154]

It is understandable that the Catalan government was reluctant to engage in any course of action that risked more violence and potentially the loss of innocent lives. It was always committed to a peaceful road to independence. To that end, on being fired, both Trapero and Soler issued a statement to Mossos officers directing them to follow the orders of their new Spanish bosses. There would be no insurrection in its literal sense. But this misses the point. After a referendum process that had lasted all of five years, why were PDeCAT and the ERC leaderships so unprepared? Why did Puigdemont announce a Republic in quite such a dramatic fashion, knowing he was unprepared for the likely confrontation this would produce, and then flee to Brussels? Why was the mass movement left in the dark as to what was going on?

In retrospect, 27 October revealed a seismic gap between the wishes and aspirations of the mass of ordinary Catalans and their government – a government committed to work inside a very narrow parliamentary framework and with extraordinary illusions regarding the willingness of the EU institutions and European governments to intervene.

First, consider the class and political interests represented by Puigdemont's PDeCAT, the linear descendant of Pujol's old, autonomist CIU. Ideologically, PDeCAT is, at heart, a party of the centre-right – if not neoliberal in its vison of a future Catalan society. In many respects, Puigdemont is not representative of PDeCAT or its real leader in exile, Artur Mas. Puigedemont comes from comparatively modest origins, outside the Catalan elite which for years dominated CIU. He became Catalan PM only because the anti-capitalist CUP refused to endorse Mas for the post, in the aftermath of the 2015 elections. Puigdemont supported independence in the 1980s when it was still a fringe view – a consistency that the CUP respected. In other words, Puigedemont was always likely to be more susceptible to pressure from the mass movement pushing him towards the referendum and UDI. But that personal position was not fully reflective of PDeCAT or its centre-right constituency.

In office, PDeCAT ministers and local councillors carried out austerity cuts in the face of opposition from CUT and ERC representatives from the left. Between 2008 and 2016, under Mas and Puigdemont, social spending in Catalonia was cut by 17 per cent, education by 17 per cent, health by 14 per cent, and housing a massive 60 per cent. Indeed, Mas scandalised public opinion in Catalonia, especially on the left, by appointing Boi Ruiz i Garcia, head of the business association representing private medical care companies, as Health Minister. One reading of the willingness of Mas and the CIU/PDeCAT establishment to go along with the referendum project was that it was a tactic designed to counter the rising tide of opposition to such austerity policies – and to stop the left-wing ERC from becoming the largest party in the Catalan Parliament at the next elections. Indeed, the PDeCAT leadership, under pressure from Mas, vetoed Puigdemont's proposal of a joint slate with the ERC in the 21 December elections, in a bid to reassert the party's traditional hegemony of the self-determination movement.

Of course, PDeCAT's tactical shift towards an outright independence stance lost it the confidence of big business, Catalan-based banks and the main media voice of Catalan bourgeois opinion, the *La Vanguardia* newspaper. The Catalan big bourgeoisie – while seeking a degree of social and economic autonomy from Madrid, sufficent to feather their own financial nests, corrupt or otherwise – were nevertheless scared witless by the anti-austerity and anti-capitalist demands being unleashed by the independence project. So were some PDeCAT ministers, such as Santi Vila who resigned from the government in protest at the decision to declare UDI. Vila is close to Artur Mas and is vocal on the need for PDeCAT to change tack and re-embrace the legal, autonomist stance of the old CIU, thereby winning back business support.

In the present circumstances, the PDeCAT machine knows that it has no option but to ride the independence tiger until it can reassert control over the mass movement. However, riding that tiger meant fighting a series of delaying tactics in the run-up to 1-0 and UDI, hoping against hope that Rajoy would enter negotiations, or the EU intervene to impose a dialogue. Either result could have allowed Puigdemont, Mas and the PDeCAT establishment to open up a discussion leading to a reform of the '78 constitution, some recognition of Catalan sovereignty, and a return to normality for the business community and the Catalan middle class.

Evolution of the mass movement

The ERC, on the other hand, has always been in favour of independence. Its traditional class base was among the petty bourgeois, farmers and small business class of rural Catalonia. In recent times it has moved leftwards, embracing a clear social democratic ideology under the influence of public sector workers, especially teachers, who have underpinned its electoral base as austerity worsened. As a result, PDeCAT has found itself steadily losing seats to the ERC. Their electoral alliance in 2015 was a desperate attempt by PDeCAT to remain the dominant force in the government. But this alliance came at the cost of PDeCAT having to accept the ERC timetable for a new referendum, and a commitment to founding a new Republic if there were a 'Yes' vote. Which begs the obvious question: why was the ERC, with its long political history, not better prepared for UDI on 27 October?

The answer lies in its conception of winning independence, its parliamentary electoralism and its top-down relationship with the mass movement. For the ERC leadership, establishing its own Catalan state was an objective separate from defeating anti-austerity and defending democratic rights. Certainly, the ERC as a party (and in government) was anti-austerity. But it viewed the solution to austerity and mass unemployment as achievable only through winning a Catalan state. It saw that as possible only by maintaining maximum unity with conservative Catalan forces led by PDeCAT. Though PDeCAT and ERC deputies in the Catalan parliament were known to vote in different ways on social and economic issues, the ERC's plan for a short-term referendum kept them bound to the coalition. That precluded – whether ERC leaders such as Oriol Junqueras realised it – formulating a set of policies for post-independence. Instead, the ERC spent its time pushing PDeCAT towards 1-0 rather than reaching out to broader anti-austerity layers who might be won to the independence cause. ERC simply assumed (erroneously) that these other social forces would see the light some day.

This strategy was down to Oriol Junqueras. The burly, soft-spoken Junqueras is a strange combination of the super intellectual (he has authored numerous serious works on Catalan history) and the emotional (he has been known to get teary-eyed speaking about independence). He became ERC leader in 2011 only 18 months after officially joining. His forte lies in his ability to network and broker deals. Under Junqueras, the ERC has managed to avoid the internal feuding that characterised the previous leadership of Josep Lluís Carod-Rovira. On the other hand, it is difficult to divine where Junqueras really stands ideologically. His commitment to Catalan independence is absolute: he refused to join Puigdemont in exile because he would not abandon fellow Catalans under threat from the Spanish legal system. But his political ambiguity between left and right, not to mention a steely personal ambition, suggests he is less a charismatic leader and more of an apparatus man.

The tool the ERC used to keep up pressure on PDeCAT was, of course, the mass movement embodied in the ANC and Omnium grassroots organisations. These were heavily penetrated by ERC militants. Since 2012, the independence process has taken the form of an unprecedented mass movement under the leadership of the ANC. But a mass movement that was under the strict management of the ANC itself, with its 45,000-strong membership organisation – many of whom were ERC members in their own right. The ANC's direction has been vertical with control from above – a culture of top-down representation and delegation rather than bottom-up self-organisation.

The ANC's policy was to pressure the Catalan government (i.e. the CIU and then PDeCAT) to move forward to a referendum. But the ANC had no policy dimension. Its job was to bring millions on to the streets, a job it did magnificently. Thus the ANC pressured a reluctant President Artur Mas to carry out the 9 November 2014 referendum after it was banned by the Constitutional Court. It returned to the streets after the elections of 27 September 2015, to back a second referendum. But at each stage, the mass movement retreated and waited on the politicians to determine the agenda. Without the initiative of the mass movement on 1-0 – occupying the polling stations and defending them from the Guardia Civil – the referendum itself would never have taken place. The disconnection with political reality was that the Catalan Government was responding to events, not leading them.

The sheer scale of the multi-million events organised by the ANC hides the fact that it was not reaching out to social layers that were still agnostic (or hostile) to independence, but who could be won over. These dramatic protests were also so stage-managed and media-focused, that they presented little real threat to the status quo unless they delivered independence. On the other hand, the ANC and Omnium did not become involved in any other key social protest movements such as the housing rights struggle organised by the PHA, *La Plataforma de Afectados por la Hipoteca*. Nor was the independence movement good at penetrating the large immigrant community, especially in the Barcelona suburbs. Catalonia has around 280,000 Moroccan immigrants, nearly 120,000 Romanians, and 80,000 Ecuadorians. While the SNP in Scotland has made a point of recruiting in the immigrant population and guaranteeing their citizenship, the Catalan movement has been less focused.

The point when the mass movement overflowed these limits to its self-organisation came in the month between 1-0 and the declaration of the Republic. The General Strike of 3 October and the mass protests against the arrest of the Two Jordis caught the ERC and ANC off guard, generating worries that they might lose control of the situation to the new neighbourhood Committees for the Defence of the Referendum. These CDRs were often initiated by the far-left CUP but soon developed their own leadership and momentum. It was these fears – plus the headiness and intoxication of the moment – that led the ERC leadership to embrace UDI. Unfortunately, the ERC was no better prepared for running an independent Republic than Puigdemont and the PDeCAT.

The Spanish state showed no such inertia. The Monday following UDI, Spain's chief prosecutor José Manuel Maza – nominally independent of the executive but nevertheless a political appointee – charged Puigdemont and every minister in his government with rebellion, sedition and misuse of public funds, for organising the 1-0 referendum. It was a move he only felt able to make now that Article 155 had been implemented. Six members of the Bureau, Speaker Forcadell's forum for organising parliamentary business, were also indicted on similar charges, linked to the vote on independence. The accused all faced 30 years in prison. In the following weeks, most of those ministers still in Catalonia were imprisoned, pending trial. They included the ERC leader Oriol Junqueras, and Foreign Minister Raul Romeva.

The pro-independence mass movement soon switched focus to mounting huge protests against these imprisonments, including a second general strike on 8 November and a march in Brussels on 7 December, to which 45,000 Catalans travelled. Meanwhile, the Spanish right had learned the lesson of popular mobilisation. Some 300,000 marched in a wholly reactionary demonstration in Barcelona in defence of Spanish unity. The march was called by the SCC, a shady body whose founders had links with the far right. It had the full backing of the PP and Ciudadanos, as well as the Catalan branch of the Socialist Party. The march was supported by half a dozen openly fascist and racist organisations which afterwards attacked the *Generalitat* and carried out a number of racist and fascist outrages in Barcelona. The Catalan capital felt once more like an occupied city.

The most significant development has been the growth of the grass-roots organisations, now re-christened as Committees for the Defence of the

Republic. A plenary meeting held in Manlleu on 4 November, represented 172 CDRs from across Catalonia pledged to 'to defend the Republic in a peaceful but radical way'. They were primarily responsible for the success of the second general strike, on 8 November. The country was paralysed by widespread blockades of transport, roads and railways organised spontaneously by local CDRs. Raging with impotence, Interior Minister Zoido denounced what he termed 'radicalised pickets', calling the blockades 'sabotage' and promising arrests. On 10 November, a representative of the CDR in Sabadell, Helena Vazquez, claimed there were now 280 committees in existence – one hundred created in response to the strike action. The new development in the CDRs was the bringing together of pro-independence forces with others who were responding to the need to defend democratic rights or merely protect their neighbourhoods from the state security apparatus. This organic political process was taking place separate from and in partial opposition to Rajoy's attempt to channel the crisis back into an electoral straighjacket. The plenary meetings of the CDRs have opened a debate on the possibility of a 'constituent process from below' leading perhaps to the creation of a 'Catalan Social Assembly'.

Catalonia's crisis is Spain's crisis

Regardless of how the immediate crisis in Catalonia pans out, it is safe to conclude that nothing is really resolved for the long term. For the heart of the crisis lies not in Catalonia itself but in the rotten state of the Spanish 1978 regime – in its corruption, centralisation, authoritarian direction and political fractures. All these tendencies have been exacerbated by the October crisis. Triggering Article 155 and arresting Catalan ministers and civic leaders has created a serious anti-democratic precedent in the heart of Europe. It implies that Madrid can now move against any autonomous community it does not like. The de facto alliance of the PP, PSOE and increasingly populist Ciudadanos may have underpinned the repression in Catalonia, but this is a desperately unstable bloc – and one of such breathtaking opportunism that it can only reinforce the historical decline of the traditional Socialists. As for the Bourbon monarchy that lies at the centre of the 1978 regime, it has emerged weakened from the crisis as a result of Felipe's crass intervention, and his unwillingness to act the role of mediator. In other words, the Catalan uprising has set in motion the final disintegration of the post-Franco compromise political settlement.

It is certainly true that the disappointment and confusion that followed the Declaration of the Republic, the successful implementation of Article 155, and Spain's imposition of fresh elections have combined to pass the political initiative to Rajoy. But only within limits. In no sense does this resolve the deep structural crisis of the Spanish 1978 regime exposed by the 2008 financial crash.

The Spanish economy is characterised by a series of structural problems that have accumulated over a long period, and which were not only disguised but exacerbated by the financial and property bubble. This includes the dominance of the construction and tourism sectors, with low value added and low productivity. Internationally competitive industries and innovation capacity are lacking, except perhaps in the high-tech sector emerging in Catalonia. The financial sector still boasts a number of leading international banks, such as Santander and Sabadell. However, much of the indigenous credit system has been so severely weakened by the bubble that it lacks the capacity to finance a modernisation of the Spanish economy as a whole. It is also doubtful if the tourism industry has much more spare capacity to exploit. Corporate structure is another problem. Medium-sized enterprises which, especially in Germany, play a key role in competition and innovation are almost non-existent in Spain.

None of this has been addressed by the austerity policy pursued under Zapatero and Rajoy. If anything, Rajoy's attempt to hunker down and preserve the privileges of the oligarchy have delayed capitalist modernisation. Indeed, one aim of Rajoy's intransigence towards the Catalans is to mobilise the PP base to fend off the political force which does represent this modernising agenda – the centre-right Ciudadanos. The PP are only in government with the support of Ciudadanos, a staunch advocate of neo-liberal spending and tax cuts. But it is becoming increasingly clear that Rajoy has little enthusiasm for implementing the list of economic and anti-corruption reforms agreed with Ciudadanos in return for this backing – a point the PSOE is using to claim that the Ciudadanos are, in effect, acting as cover for the PP's defence of the oligarchy. Opposition to Catalan self-determination is about the only thing holding together the PP-Ciudadanos marriage of convenience. If that shatters, Spain's political crisis will go from bad to worse.

The inability of Spanish capitalism to find a political formula to stabilise the national government apparatus, and move towards German-style structural economic reforms, is ultimately connected with the obsolete 1978 regime, and the latter's role as a bulwark against social modernisation.

Ciudadanos does want to democratise the 1978 constitution. But it is caught in the contradiction that equally it does not want such a reform process to unleash separatism in Catalonia and the Basque Lands, which account for so much of Spanish GDP. Especially if this separatism threatens to take an anti-capitalist direction. All of which means that the Catalan and Basque independence struggles will remain central to the course of Spanish politics for years to come, even if the current crisis is defused in the short-run.

This conclusion exposes another weakness of the Catalan leadership, who have been negligent in inserting themselves directly into the Spanish national debate, other than calling for a new Statute of autonomy, or latterly to declare UDI. With the exception of the CUP, both PDeCAT and the ERC have failed to advance concrete reassurances to the rest of Spain that an independent Catalonia would be a good neighbour and join in a financial-pooling arrangement, to ensure that the poorer regions were not immediately affected by the loss of Catalan revenues.

Meanwhile, the rickety nature of the PP minority government and Spanish capitalism explains the limits to Rajoy's scope for action. While he could trigger Article 155 and arrest Catalan ministers, it was impossible for the PP to engage in any prolonged period of direct rule, hence the calling of an election almost immediately. Prolonged direct rule – including the closure of the Catalan state television and radio – threatened to provoke a major popular backlash in Catalonia, with the prospect of more violence. Even Rajoy could see that would have a negative impact in international circles and send Spanish share prices into a nosedive, all of which suggests the Catalan situation will remain on a political knife edge. Rajoy bought time with the elections and certainly quashed any question of who controls Catalonia. But this does not imply that he has managed to defeat the independence movement in a deeper sense.

Impact on the Basques

The declaration of the (virtual) Catalan Republic and the massive repression unleashed by the Spanish state against the independence movement has also had dramatic implications for smouldering Basque aspirations for self-determination. For decades, the ETA military campaign made Catalans unwilling to seek common ground with the Basques. But the end to the armed struggle in the Basque Lands has opened up – for the first time since the end of the Franco era – the possibility for joint pressure on Madrid by the Basques and

Catalans for political change. This new axis will help shape the future of Spanish politics.

Madrid has always pursued a divide-and-rule approach to the nationalities. A key strategy pursued by Rajoy throughout the October referendum crisis was to isolate the Catalans politically by offering – or seeming to offer – major concessions to the Basques. In July and August 2017, there was what the Spanish media described as a 'discreet' contact between Rajoy and the head of the Basque government, Iñigo Urkullu, to discuss the transfer of more powers to Euskadi. These included the transfer of responsibility for social security and prisons, two 'priority' issues for the Basques. Rajoy has also soft-pedalled on demands for a bigger Basque contribution to central government budgets and offered more cash for infrastructure investment.

These brazen attempts to buy off the Basques while repressing the Catalans are now backfiring. In late October, Basque PM Urkullu responded to Madrid's repression in Catalonia by issuing his own blueprint for the future of Spain. In it he denounced the current 'imposed unity' of the 1978 post-Franco constitution, which he said quashed the previous 'voluntary union' model and the historical rights of the Basque people. But he went further and – for the first time since the end of the ETA military campaign – linked the political fortunes of the Basques with those of the Catalans:

> I cannot understand or share Madrid's approach to the decade-long crisis regarding the Basque country, which has now extended to Catalonia. Even less so when, in the Catalan case, the government refuses to address politically a conflict that is political by its very nature and seeks purely legal answers. I completely reject the extreme measures taken with regard to Catalan civil society and institutions in the past month. These actions will make solving the present impasse even harder.[155]

He went on to call for 'a plurinational Spanish state' which would recognise the Basque and Catalan nations 'along with the Spanish' based on 'co-sovereignty, or shared sovereignty'. Urkullu finished by saying that the way forward now required 'setting up legal channels to allow political communities who wish to consult their citizens on their future to be able to do so'.

Urkullu and the PNV now find themselves under increasing pressure from the left and a new mass movement for Basque independence. The declaration of Article 155 in Catalonia brought about major street protests in the Basque Lands. These were used by the BH Bildu (the main front representing pro-independence, left-wing Basque forces) to step up pressure on the ruling PNV to break its pact with the PP in the Madrid Parliament. Arnaldo Otegi, the leader of Sortu (the linear descendent of the old Herri Batasuna, but anti-violence) demanded that Urkullu and the PNV join with other Basque parties in a common front against Rajoy.

So far, Urkullu's response has been lukewarm, despite his pro-Catalan rhetoric. His line reply was: 'I must defend the well-being of the Basques, regardless of who is in La Moncloa'. But the ground is shifting under Urkulla's feet. The conservative PNV only won back control in the Basque Country in 2016, on the basis of strong economic growth and a feeling among much of the population that they wanted a rest from politics now that ETA had de-mobilised. However, the intensity of the repression against Catalonia has indicated to many in the Basque Lands that the Madrid leopard has not changed its spots. Any concessions being offered to the Basques by Rajoy are a cynical ploy and can be withdrawn any time. Besides, the implementation of Article 155 shows that Madrid cannot be trusted not to interfere in the Basque Lands in the future. All of which suggests that the dynamic in the Basque Country is following the same path as in Catalonia, with the mass movement and pro-independence socialist parties forcing the traditional autonomists to the left and a break with Madrid.

Catalonia's crisis is Europe's crisis

Whether an independent Catalonia emerges from the crisis precipitated by the October 2017 referendum, or whether it is subsumed back into the Spanish state pro tem, either outcome will have a transformational effect on the European Union. If the concurrent and acrimonious Brexit negotiations between the UK and Europe are added in, we can say that the autumn of 2017 marked a turning point for the post-war history of the European 'project'.

All through the Catalan crisis, the President of the European Commission, Jean-Claude Juncker, was quick to defend Rajoy's intransigence and unwillingness to negotiate. 'I do not want a situation where, tomorrow, the European Union is made up of 95 different states,' said Juncker, a former Prime Minister of tiny Luxembourg (population one third of Barcelona's). Angela Merkel was just as supportive of Rajoy. After a meeting between the Spanish and German government leaders, Merkel's spokesperson Steffen Seibert reported: 'In her conversation with Mariano Rajoy, the Chancellor ratified her support for the unity of Spain.' Just to underscore where matters stood, an EU Commission statement bluntly told the Catalans that they would have to leave the EU and re-apply to join, if they went ahead with UDI. Alex Salmond caught the public mood in both Catalonia and Scotland when he said:

> I think the EU are in the dock on this. My regret is their unwillingness to condemn outright the violence that we saw from the Spanish state on the people of Catalonia who were merely trying to exercise their right to vote.[156]

The hostile position to Catalan self-determination taken by Juncker, Merkel and Donald Tusk, the President of the European Council, cannot be explained in terms of EU consistency. Ostensibly, they opposed Catalonia's declaration of independence because they did not want to see Spain (an EU member state) disintegrate. Yet in the early 1990s, EU members were to the fore in encouraging the breakup of Yugoslavia. Nor is the record any better when it comes to EU institutions staying out of the affairs of individual members. The manner in which the bailout programmes for Greece, Ireland, Portugal, Cyprus and Spain itself were imposed during the euro crisis is a glaring example of heavy-handed, anti-democratic intervention by the Commission, the European Central Bank and the German Bundesbank. In Greece and Italy, democratically elected European governments were actually forced to resign under pressure from the EU and replaced by non-elected administrations run by technocrats.

All of which leads to the conclusion that the EU's tacit decision to back Rajoy's crackdown in Catalonia – a decision supported by Germany, France and the UK – was sui generis and premeditated. In Germany's case, there is a worry about the economic uncertainties resulting from the Catalan crisis – around 1,000 German companies have invested in Catalonia, including Volkswagen-SEAT, and the chemical giants Bayer and BASF. And the German political establishment felt sufficiently worried about a rise in support for the autonomist Bavarian Party, for the Federal Constitutional Court to rule in January 2017: '...there is no room under the constitution for individual states to attempt to secede. This violates the constitutional order.' But these worries hardly explain the vehemence with which Germany and the main EU institutions have supported Rajoy, or their readiness to ignore human rights violations that most people thought modern Europe had long since turned its face against.

The best explanation is that the Catalan people are expendable in EU eyes as the Union struggles to hold itself together politically in the face of a surge in anti-EU populist parties, the continuing structural failures of the common currency, and the British Brexit. The EU is essentially a mechanism for protecting the property and trading interests of large, multi-national companies and of the international banks that service them. This mechanism is now under severe strain, not just politically but economically. European capitalism is foundering in the face of competition from American and Chinese rivals. None of the world's biggest and most successful technology companies are European. US investment banks have recovered from the 2008 financial crisis and now direct global investment, while their European counterparts remain in trouble.

Holding the EU together is a sine qua non for protecting European capitalism from greater foreign competition. For this to succeed, Merkel and Macron have calculated that they need the Spanish state on their side politically. The problem is that by backing the Spanish PP crackdown in Catalonia, the EU has succeeded only in alienating the most pro-European community in the Spanish state. Worse, by watching from afar as Guardia Civil truncheons battered the heads of European citizens trying to vote, the European Commission has triggered a massive crisis of legitimacy for the organisation.

Besides, the Commission's fanciful declaration that it would summarily expel a Catalan Republic from the Union is patently against the economic interests of the Union. All the main surface transport links between the rest of Spain and France go through Catalonia. How could the EU single market and common customs union operate between Spain and France if Catalonia is ejected from the Union? Most of Spain's exports and imports run through Catalonia. The 'nuclear' option of exiling Catalonia from the European economic family would be disastrous for the remaining Spanish economy in terms of tariff barriers. Besides, over 6000 multinationals have facilities located in Catalonia, most of which are French, German, British and Italian. It is hardly in the interests of these firms for Catalonia to be isolated by the EU. Catalonia is also home to some 300,000 citizens from other EU nations, who benefit from free movement rights.

Yet these rational arguments are not being heard in Brussels, Paris and Berlin, despite Puigdemont's vocal exile at the heart of Europe. The big EU states have calculated that Rajoy can see off the Catalans while the

Commission deals with the Brits. This will buy time for Europe to stabilise and reboot capital investment, in a bid to take on the American and
Chinese. But the truth is that the present EU system is no more fit for purpose than the Spanish 1978 regime. Over-centralisation, harsh pro-austerity
policies designed ultimately to protect insolvent German banks, high youth
unemployment, and an immigration crisis caused by Western destabilisation
in the Middle and Near East, have combined to de-legitimise the post-war
European project.

From this perspective, Catalan self-determination is potentially part of
the solution to Europe's democratic deficit. Suppose a free Catalonia successfully retains its EU membership. That does not mean business as usual.
Catalonia is unlikely to accept the present domination of the EU by Germany or the imposition of the austerity policies that have been imposed by
the European Commission and European Central Bank. The path would
be open for an alliance between Catalonia, left-wing Portugal and perhaps
Greece – and possibly Scotland, if it achieves independence in the wake of
Catalonia – to reject the imposition of austerity policies and demand a more
expansionist EU budget. Even if this met resistance from Merkel's Germany
and Macron's France, a new, progressive axis would have emerged inside the
EU – one that is bound to shift the internal debate towards decentralisation,
anti-austerity and action against the multinationals.

Far-fetched? We have been here before, albeit briefly. In the late 1980s
and early 1990s there was a popular movement inside the EU to create just
such a 'Europe of the Regions' in an attempt to address the same democratic
deficit and mobilise popular support for the EU project at a time of sharp
economic crisis. In 1994, a Committee of the Regions was created as a new
EU body to give political substance to the new concept. The fly in the oint-
ment was the introduction of the euro as a common currency, at the start
of the 21st century. This led to a re-centralisation of economic policy led
by Germany, as the euro was essentially the old Deutsche Mark with a new
name. The emergency policies to 'save the euro' imposed by Germany had
disastrous effects in Portugal, Ireland, Italy, Greece and Spain.

On the other hand, given the present balance of forces, the prognosis for
a rejuvenated, progressive European Union composed of new states such as
Catalonia must be largely negative. However, there are signs of a movement
on the left which aims to reform the present EU, and if that is not possible
then to create some progressive alternative. In October 2017, Europe's main
radical, anti-austerity political parties met in Lisbon to discuss such a 'Plan

B' option for the EU. Taking part were key parliamentary representatives of Die Linke from Germany, the Red-Green Alliance in Denmark, the Left Bloc in Portugal, Podemos and Jean-Luc Melenchon's La France Insoumise. They concluded that if the EU and the common currency arrangements prove incapable of reform 'due to the predictable hostility of the European institutions' then that 'should open the way for a breakup with the Eurozone and the EU Treaties' and the launch of 'a new system of European co-operation based on the restoration of economic, fiscal and monetary sovereignty, the protection of democracy and social rights and social justice'. Their collective declaration went on:

> The European Union must not have the monopoly over Europe.
> The Plan B offers new perspectives with our neighbours. New spaces for co-operation exist.[157]

The insouciant, negative reaction of the EU institutions to the Catalan crisis has exposed all the political fault lines of the Union. The traditional project of CIU/PDeCAT to seek EU protection for Catalan sovereignty has been seriously undermined if not totally destroyed. Faith in the democratic bona fides of the EU has been shaken not only in Catalonia, but across Europe. All of which suggests that, as the Catalan crisis unfolds, the EU will find it difficult to remain insulated from the political fallout.

Crossroads for the Spanish and international left

The Catalan crisis represents a crisis of perspectives for the left, first in Catalonia itself, but also in Spain as a whole, and across Europe. In Catalonia itself, the left split three ways between pro-independence forces (ERC, CUP); those parties which supported 1-0 and the right to choose, but who were against independence (Podemos, United Left); and the discredited PSOE/PSC which had turned into a mouthpiece for the 1978 regime. The strategic problem is that the Catalan pro-independence parties failed to build strategic alliances with those anti-austerity forces led by the pan-Spain radical left, around social and economic campaigns. That had two results. First, it limited the ability of the independence movement to win over and mobilise support outside the traditional, indigenous Catalan population – especially in the immigrant working class in Barcelona. Second, it limited the ability of the Catalan independence forces to mobilise popular support in the rest of Spain, thus restricting Rajoy's room for manoeuvre. In other words, it made it difficult to transform a political crisis inside Catalonia into a general social and political crisis for the whole regime.

Though the CUP made huge efforts to work outside the parliamentary arena, building popular support in the neighbourhoods through local campaigning, it was often sectarian towards the non-independence left in Catalonia, including *Catalunya en Comú*. The latter alliance (dominated by Podemos but involving the Greens and the Communist United Left) was not opposed to the referendum, as it respected the democratic right of the Catalan people to decide their own future. But neither was en Comú supportive of independence, concentrating instead on popular anti-austerity measures and local housing campaigns. As a result, there was a divide between the two parts of the radical left.

The Catalan October had a huge impact on Podemos and Podem, its main Catalan wing. The party's official position on the national question favours a 'plurinational' Spanish state. But the Catalan crisis upended this policy, splitting the party. When the Catalan parliament declared independence on 27 October, Pablo Iglesias, the party's charismatic founder, called the move illegal and illegitimate. At the same time, Iglesias denounced Article 155, saying that it would 'do a lot of damage to Catalonia and to Spain.' He tweeted: 'We are against repression and for a negotiated referendum, but the declaration of independence is illegitimate' and only played into Rajoy's hands.[158]

But under pressure from the mass movement, Podem deputies in the Catalan Parliament had voted for the enabling motion that paved the way for declaring the Republic. And the influential Podemos current known as Anticapitalistas quickly recognised 'the new Catalan republic'. Led by MEP Miguel Urban and Podemos Andalusia general secretary Teresa Rodriguez, this group saw the crisis and mass participation unfolding in Catalonia as the start of a political revolution that could lead to the dissolution of the 1978 regime. In a statement, they argued:

> On 27 October, in fulfilment of the mandate of the referendum of 1 October in which, despite police repression, more than two million people participated, the Catalan Parliament proclaimed the Catalan Republic. In a Spain with a monarchy that is a direct successor of the dictator Franco, a Republic that opens up a constituent process is without doubt a proposal that breaks with the 1978 regime, with its political consensus and with a constitutional order that serves the elites.[159]

Albano Fachin, the leader of Podemos-Podem in Catalonia, publicly split with Pablo Iglesias after the latter attempted to purge his Catalan supporters of pro-independence heretics. Fachín went so far as to say that 'Pablo Iglesias has intervened in Podem Catalunya in the same way as Mariano Rajoy has intervened in Catalonia'.[160]

The split in Podemos, and the shift by the Anticapitalista faction towards embracing Catalan independence as part of a wider process of social change in Spain, suggests the beginning of a process of realignment on the left. The PSOE has also been impacted. In the wake of the repression, PSOE leader Pedro Sánchez has been forced to distance himself from Rajoy and call for the PP government to introduce constitutional reform. This turn may be politically cosmetic but it shows the traditional Spanish left is being forced to respond to Catalan demands for self-determination.

Electoral impasse

The political forces described above came to a confluence in the 21 December election for a new Catalan Parliament. Not surprisingly, the crisis produced a record voter turnout of 82 per cent. Equally unsurprisingly, the three pro-independence parties collectively retained a majority of seats in the Palau del Parlament: 70 out of 135. This result was a blow to Rajoy: his gamble in forcing an early election patently had failed to defeat or isolate the independence movement. On the contrary, the vote was a popular democratic endorsement of the Catalan Republic and the leaders of the independence movement, including Puigdemont and the imprisoned Junqueras.

The biggest loser in the election was, in fact, the PP, which saw its vote share halved, keeping only three seats. This suggested that while Rajoy's intransigence had rallied the Spanish hard right, it offered no lasting political solution to the crisis of the post-1978 constitutional settlement in the eyes of more moderate, middle class opinion. This explains the success in the election of the pro-unionist, centre-right Ciudadanos, which became the largest single party in the chamber, with 37 seats. However, it remains to be seen if Ciudadanos (perhaps in conjunction with the Spanish Socialists) has the capacity to dislodge Rajoy from government and offer a new constitutional arrangement. Rajoy and the PP have the experience and will to run rings round Ciudadanos. Their immediate response was to intensify court action against the Catalan leadership with the aim of stopping Puigdemont from returning from exile and being re-elected as the Catalan President.

The strong showing of the Catalan pro-independence parties on 21 December was a tribute to the mass mobilisation of the civil movement in the days following the declaration of the Republic on 27 October. During November and December, the independence movement had been driven forward only by the grassroots Committees for the Defence of the Republic. But following the election, the focus of activity shifted back to the Catalan Parliament, leaving the mass movement drifting.

The election also saw Puigedemont's PDeCAT win the most seats inside the pro-independence bloc, unexpectedly overtaking the ERC. Undoubtedly, PDeCAT won support because of the popularity of Puigdemont. But this doomed the ERC's plan to make Oriol Junqueras the Catalan president. With Junqueras under lock and key in a Madrid prison, Puigdemont was now in supreme charge of the independence movement from his Belgian exile. There he continued with his increasingly futile efforts to persuade the European Union to mediate with Madrid. He even rented a £4,000-per-month house in Waterloo, promting jibes from Madrid that he would never return home.

The biggest losers in the independence camp were the far left CUP, who lost six of their 10 seats. Their lesson was clear: separating independence from the social struggle will not work. In Barcelona, the old Socialists and the new left Podemos won nearly a quarter of the vote. This came from trades unionists in the big multinational plants in the Barcelona suburbs, and from disaffected youth and immigrants in the Barcelona slums. Neither group much supported the independence parties largely because those parties – CUP especially – had failed to mobilise them. Yet the continuation of direct rule by Madrid had rolled back many of the progressive social measures introduced by the previous Puigdemont administration under pressure from the CUP and ERC.

Into the unknown

El Mundo, the conservative Spanish newspaper, summed up the post-election situation in a cartoon depicting Puigdemont a bumblebee, buzzing around the head of Rajoy, who is haplessly pointing an insect gun in the wrong direction. Puigdemont in exile remains a nuisance to Rajoy but little more. Rajoy himself maintains his repressive grip on Catalonia while Spain drifts politically. Something will have to give. At some point, the pro-independence parties will have to sieze the initiative in the Catalan parliament, form a new government and re-engage with the Catalan people – with or without Puigdemont.

The Catalan Republic declared in the Palau del Parlament on 27 October proved more virtual than real. But that does not make it irrelevant by any means. The Catalan leadership were making a declaration for the history books – a political down-payment which, they hoped, would open a process that would lead eventually to national self-determination. The whole sweep of Catalan history suggests that process will continue. Whatever the strengths and weaknesses in the present strategy pursued by Puigdemant, no one can deny that the independence process is, at heart, driven by the popular will of ordinary Catalans to end Madrid's long legacy of repression and cultural oppression, and to change society for the better. There is a fashionable view that ordinary citizens everywhere have become cynical about democratic politics or fallen prey to populist demagogues. On the contrary, the Catalan October proved once again that the common people make revolutions. Whatever happens next, they will have the last word.

NOTES

1   William Booth and Pamela Rolfe, Spain's Senate gives central government unprecedented powers to take over Catalonia, *Washington Post*, 27 October 2017
     http://www.princegeorgecitizen.com/washington-post/international/spain-s-senate-gives-central-government-unprecedented-powers-to-take-over-catalonia-1.23076936.

2   *Financial Times*, 27 October 2017.

3   Sam Jones, Stephen Burgen and Emma Graham-Harrison, Spain imposes direct rule as Catalan parliament votes for independence, *The Guardian*, 28 October 2017
     https://www.theguardian.com/world/2017/oct/27/spanish-pm-mariano-rajoy-asks-senate-powers-dismiss-catalonia-president.

4   https://weegingerdug.wordpress.com/2017/10/27/the-catalan-declaration-of-independence-in-english/.

5   https://news.gov.scot/news/statement-on-catalonia-1.

6   Liz Castro, Colm Tóibín: "It's very difficult to dilute a national identity under pressure", Vilaweb, 11 2014
     http://www.vilaweb.cat/noticia/4203144/20140711/colm-toibin-its-very-difficult-to-dilute-national-identity-under-pressure.html.

7   Hannah Strange, *The Telegraph*, They Banned Us Speaking Catalan: Now They Want Us To Disappear, 26 September 2015
     http://www.telegraph.co.uk/news/worldnews/europe/spain/11893734/They-banned-us-speaking-Catalan.-Now-they-want-us-to-disappear.html.

8   Spanish Civil War victim's 91-year-old daughter finally buries her father, Reuters, 2 July 2017 https://www.reuters.com/article/us-spain-civilwar-burial-idUSKBN-19N0QS.

9   Guy Hedgecoe, Anger at plans for guided tours to show 'greatness' of Franco, Irish Times, 15 August 2017 https://www.irishtimes.com/news/world/europe/anger-at-plans-for-guided-tours-to-show-greatness-of-franco-1.3187585

10   https://www.amnesty.org/en/countries/europe-and-central-asia/spain/report-spain/.

11   R. Tremosa-i-Balcells, Catalonia An Emerging Economy, *Sussex Academic Press*, 2010, P117.

12   Isambard Wilkinson, King starts row over the use of Spanish, *The Telegraph*, 26 April 2001 http://www.telegraph.co.uk/news/worldnews/europe/spain/1317352/King-starts-row-over-the-use-of-Spanish.html.

13   J.H. Elliott., *Imperial Spain 1469-1716*, Penguin, 1990, p.24.

14   X.M. Núñez Seixas, X.M., (2001) 'What is Spanish Nationalism Today? From Legitimacy Crisis to Unfulfilled Renovation (1975–2000)', *Ethnic and Racial Studies* 24(5): 2001, p.719-752.

15   S Harris., Catalonia Is Not Spain, available at http://www.barcelonas.com/right-to-decide.html.

16   J. Friend, Stateless Nations: Western European Regional Nationalisms and the Old Nations, Springer, 2012, P74.

17   M.Tree., 'Catalan language literature: What's Going On?', in L. Castro (ed.), *What's Up With Catalonia*, Catalonia Press, 2013, p.150.

18   Robert Brenner, 'Agrarian Class Structure and Economic Development in Pre-industrial Europe', in TH Aston and CHE Philpin (Editors), *The Brenner Debate: Agrarian Class Structure and Economic Development in Pre-industrial Europe*, Cambridge University Press, 1987, P40.

19   M. Rovira-Martínez., 'Our September 11th (1714)', in L. Castro (ed.), *What's Up With Catalonia*, Catalonia Press, 2013, p.209.

20   J.H. Elliott., *Imperial Spain 1469-1716*, Penguin, 1990, p.378.

21   R. Hughes., *Barcelona*, Harvill, 1992, P374. This effervescent and extraordinary book captures the social and cultural dynamic of one of the world's greatest cities. Curiously, it runs out of steam towards the end.

22   Frederick Engels, The Bakunists At Work, Marxist Internet Archive https://www.marxists.org/archive/marx/works/1873/bakunin/.

23   P. B. Radcliff., *Modern Spain: 1808 to the Present*, John Wiley & Sons, 2017, p.10.

24   M. Vicente, *Clothing the Spanish Empire*, Springer, 2006, p.71.

25   R. Grau., 'The Foundation of the Spanish State', in R. Grau and J. M. Muñoz (eds.), *Catalonia, A European History*, Generalitat de Catalunya, 2006, p.84-85.

26   J. F. Coverdale., *The Basque Phase of Spain's First Carlist War*, Princeton University Press, 1984, p.7.

27   Jeremy MacClancy, The Decline of Carlism, University of Nevada Press, 2000, p.116.

28   Michael Eaude, *Catalonia: A Cultural History*, Signal Books, 2007, p.76.

29   A. Carreras., *The Strengths and Limitations of an Industrial Revolution*, in R. Grau and J. M. Muñoz (eds), *Catalonia, A European History*, Generalitat I, Catalunya, 2006, p.80.

30   F. Engels., *The Bakunists At Work*, Marxist Internet Archive https://www.marxists.org/archive/marx/works/1873/bakunin/.

31   Pelai Pagès i Blanch, *War and Revolution in Catalonia, 1936-1939*, Brill, 2013, p.7.

32   A. Smith., 'Spain', in S. Berger and D. Broughton (eds), *The Force of Labour: The Western European Labour Movements and the Working Class in the Twentieth Century*, Berg, 1995, p.174.

33   R. Carr., *Modern Spain, 1875-1980*, Oxford University Press, 1980, p.32.

34   S. Balfour and A. Quiroga., *The Reinvention of Spain: Nation and Identity Since Democracy*, Oxford University Press, 2007, p.22-23.

35   F. J. R. Salvadó., *Spain (1914-1918) Between War and Revolution*, Routledge, 1999, p.1.

36   S. Balfour., *The End of the Spanish Empire, 1898-1923*, Clarendon Press, 1997, p.16.

37   Borja de Riquer i Permanyer, 'The Catalanist Project and the Crisis in Spain', in R.Grau and J. M. Muñoz (eds), *Catalonia, A European History*, Generalitat de Catalunya, 2006, p.116-117.

38   S. Ben-Ami, 'The Catalan and Basque Movements for Autonomy', in Y. Dinstein (ed), *Models of Autonomy*, Transaction Publishers, 1981, p.70.

39   S. Balfour and A. Quiroga., *The Reinvention of Spain: Nation and Identity Since Cuba*, Oxford University Press, 207, p.29.

40   J. Moreno-Luzón and X. M. Núñez Siexas, 'The Flag and the Anthem: The Disputed Official Symbols of Spain', in J. Moreno-Luzón, X. M. Núñez Seixas (eds), *Metaphors of Spain: Representations of Spanish National Identity in the Twentieth Century*, Berghahn Books, 2017, p.35.

41   T. Kaplan., *Red City, Blue Period: Social Movement's in Picasso's Barcelona*, University of California Press, 1992, p.7.

42   M.V. Montalban, *Barcelonas*,Verso, 1992, p.90.

43   R. Hughes, *Barcelona*, Harvill, 1992, p.523.

44   M. V. Montalbán, *Barcelonas*, Verso, 1992, p.33.

45   The Events of Cu-Cut! November 25 1905 https://www.barcelonas.com/events-of-cu-cut.html.

46   T. Kaplan, *Red City, Blue Period: Social Movements in Picasso's Barcelona*, University of California Press, 1992, p.141.

47   Borja de Riquer i Permanyer, 'The Catalinist Project and the Crisis in Spain', in R. Grau and J. M. Muñoz (eds), *Catalonia, A European History*, Generalitat I, Catalunya, 2006, p.116-117.

48   J. Moreno-Luzón and X. M. Núñez Siexas., 'The Flag and the Anthem: The Disputed Official Symbols of Spain', in J. Moreno-Luzón, Xosé and M. Núñez Seixas (eds), *Metaphors of Spain: Representations of Spanish National Identity in the Twentieth Century*, Berghahn Books, 2017, p.40.

49   A. Smith., 'Spain', in S. Berger and D. Broughton (eds), *The Force of Labour: The Western European Labour Movements and the Working Class in the Twentieth Century*, Berg, 1995, p.177.

50   A. Smith, 'The Catalan Employers' Dirty War', in F. J. Romero, Romero Salvadó and A. Smith (eds), *The Agony of Spanish Liberalism: From Revolution to Dictatorship 1913–23*, Palgrave MacMillan, 2010, p.155.

51   A. Smith, 'The Catalan Employers' Dirty War', in F. J. Romero Romero Salvadó and A. Smith (eds), *The Agony of Spanish Liberalism: From Revolution to Dictatorship 1913–23*, Palgrave MacMillan, 2010, p.185.

52   M. Cabrera and F. del Rey Reguillo, *The Power of Entrepreneurs: Politics and Economy in Contemporary Spain*, Berghahn Books, 2007, p.22-23.

53   C. Humlebæk, *Spain: Inventing the Nation*, Bloomsbury Publishing, 2015, p.36.

54   C. Fonserè., *Memoirs of a Spanish Civil War Artist*, Pensódromo, 2016, p.16.

55   C. Ealham., *Class, Culture and Conflict in Barcelona, 1898-1937*, Routledge, 2004, p.90.

56   C. Ealham., *Class, Culture and Conflict in Barcelona, 1898-1937*, Routledge, 2004, p.97.

57   A. Dowling., *Catalonia Since the Spanish Civil War*, Sussex Academic Press, 2013, p.26.

58   C, Fonserè., *Memoirs of a Spanish Civil War Artist*, Pensódromo, 2016, p.58-59.

59   C. Ealham., 'Revolutionary Gymnastics and the Unemployed: The Limits of the Spanish Anarchist Utopia 1931-1937', in K. Flett and D. Renton (eds), *The Twentieth Century: A Century of Wars and Revolutions? Rover Oram Press*, 2000, p.140.

60   N. Rider., *The New City and the Anarchist Movement in the Early 1930s*, in A. Smith (ed.), *Red Barcelona: Social Protest and Labour Mobilization in the Twentieth Century*, Routledge, 2003, p.79-82.

61   R. Vinyes., 'The Republic, A Democratic Reference Point', in R. Grau and J. M. Muñoz, *Catalonia, A European History*, Generalitat de Catalunya, 2006, p.130 and R. Fraser, *Blood of Spain*, Penguin, 1981, p.535.

62   Pelai Pagès i Blanch, *War and Revolution in Catalonia, 1936-1939*, Brill, 2013, p.15-16.

63   G. Brennan., *The Spanish Labyrinth*, Cambridge University Press, 1971, p.277.

64   S. Giner, *The Social Structure of Catalonia, The Anglo-Catalan Society 1984*, p.34
     http://www.anglo-catalan.org/downloads/acsop-monographs/issue01.pdf.

65   A. Dowling., *Catalonia Since the Spanish Civil War*, Sussex Academic Press, 2013, p.31.

66   J. Peirats., *The CNT in the Spanish Revolution*, Vol. 1, p.132.

67   C. Ealham., *Class, Culture and Conflict in Barcelona, 1898-1937*, Routledge, 2004, p.173.

68   C. Ealham., *Class, Culture and Conflict in Barcelona, 1898-1937*, Routledge, 2004, p.173.

69   V. Alba and S. Schwartz, *Spanish Marxism Versus Soviet Communism: A History of the P.O.U.M. in the Spanish Civil War*, Transaction Publishers, 2008, p.117-118.

70   C. Ealham., *Class, Culture and Conflict in Barcelona, 1898-1937*, Routledge, 2004, p.159-160.

71   A.Durgan., *The Spanish Civil War*, Palgrave Macmillan, 2007, p.93.

72   A. Smith., 'Spaniards, Catalans and Basques: Labour and the Challenge of Nationalism in Spain', in A. Smith and S. Berger (eds), *Nationalism, Labour and Ethnicity 1870-1939*, Manchester University Press, 1999, p.84-85.

73   C. Fonserè., *Memoirs of a Spanish Civil War Artist*, Pensódromo, 2016, p.346.

74   Paul Preston, Franco A Biography, Fontana Press, 1995, p.245.

75   M. V. Montalbán., *Barcelonas*, Verso, 1992, p.130.

76   A. Beevor., *The Battle for Spain. The Spanish Civil War 1936–1939*, Penguin, 2006. p.411-412: H. Graham, *The Spanish Civil War. A Very Short Introduction*, Oxford University Press, 2005, p. 117; P. Preston., *The Spanish Civil War*, Reaction, Revolution & Revenge, Harper Perennial, 2006, p.315.

77   M. Eaude., 'Notes from Barcelona's dark side', *The Guardian*, 18 May 2002
      https://www.theguardian.com/books/2002/may/18/crimebooks.

78   R. Fraser., *Blood of Spain*, Penguin, 1981, p.484-485 and C. Fonserè, *Memoirs of a Spanish Civil War Artist*, Pensódromo, 2016, p.333.

79   C. Mir., 'The Francoist Repression in the Catalan Countries', *Catalan Historical Review*, 1: 133-147 (2008), p.143.

80   L. C. Engel., 'Policy as Journey', in C. McCarthy, *Globalizing Cultural Studies: Ethnographic Interventions in Theory, Method, and Policy*, Peter Land, 2007, p.398; R. Hughes, *Barcelona*, Vintage, 1993, p.8-9.

81   M. V. Montalbán., *Barcelonas*, Verso, 1992, p.143.

82   D. Conversi., *The Basques, the Catalans and Spain: Alternative Routes to Nationalist Mobilisation*, University of Nevada Press, 2000, p.113.

83   S. Giner., *The Social Structure of Catalonia*, The Anglo-Catalan Society 1984, p.55
      http://www.anglo-catalan.org/downloads/acsop-monographs/
      issue01.pdf.

84   C. Güell., *The Failure of Catalanist Opposition to Franco (1939-1950)*, CSIC Press, 2006, p.67-68.

85   M. Eaude., *Barcelona: The City That Re-invented Itself*, Five Leaves, 2006, p.171.

86   S. Harris., *Catalonia Is Not Spain*, available at
      http://www.barcelonas.com/catalan-culture-under-franco.html.

87   M. Eaude., *Catalonia: A Cultural History*, Signal Books, p.153.

88   M. V. Montalbán., *Barcelonas*, Verso, 1992, p.170.

89   M. Eaude., *Catalonia: A Cultural History*, Signal Books, p.115.

90   M. Eaude., *Barcelona: The City That Re-invented Itself*, Five Leaves, 2006, p.172.

91   A. Smith., 'Spain', in S. Berger and D. Broughton (eds.), *The Force of Labour: The Western European Labour Movements and the Working Class in the Twentieth Century*, Berg, 1995, p.195.

92   M. Eaude., *Barcelona: The City That Re-invented Itself*, Five Leaves, 2006, p.176.

93   C. Harman., *The Fire Last Time*, Bookmarks, 1988, p.322 and A. Smith., 'Spain', in S. Berger and D. Broughton (eds.), *The Force of Labour: The Western European Labour Movements and the Working Class in the Twentieth Century*, Berg, 1995, p.194.

94   M. V. Montalbán., *Barcelonas*, Verso, 1992, p.175.

95   L. Castro, Colm Tóibín: 'It's very difficult to dilute a national identity under pressure', Vilaweb, 11 2014
      http://www.vilaweb.cat/noticia/4203144/20140711/colm-toib-in-its-very-difficult-to-dilute-national-identity-under-pressure.html.

96   Salvador Cardús i Ros., 'Politics and the Invention of Memory: For a Sociology of the Transition to Democracy in Spain', in Joan Ramon Resina (ed) Disremembering *the Dictatorship: The Politics of Memory in the Spanish Transition to Democracy,* (Amsterdam and Atlanta: Rodopi), p.18-19.

97   C. Harman, The Fire Last Time, Bookmarks, 1988, p.328.

98   E. Rodríguez and I.Lopez, Franco's Afterlife, Jacobin, 12 August 2016 https://www.jacobinmag.com/2016/12/spain-franco-dictatorship-psoe-podemos-pp-democracy-austerity.

99   P. Preston, Juan Carlos: a people's king, HarperCollins, 2004, p.416.

100   Michael Eaude, Barcelona: The City That Re-Invented Itself, Five Leaves, 2006, p.185.

101   G. R. Páez., *Counter-hegemonic Movements in the Era of Liquid Modernity: Building a Third Way: A case study of the Spanish indignados,* MA thesis, 2014.

102   M. Eaude., *Catalonia: A Cultural History*, Signal Books, p.15.

103   M. Eaude., *Barcelona: The City that Re-invented Itself*, Five Leaves, 2008, p.177.

104   http://www.parliament.am/library/sahmanadrutyunner/ispania.pdf.

105   C. Hill, The Role of Elites in the Spanish Transition to Democracy (1975-1981): Motors of Change, Edwin Mellen Press, 2007 p.51.

106   C. Freeman, King Juan Carlos I of Spain: elephant-hunter, biker, and dictator's protege who helped deliver democracy, *The Telegraph*, 3 June 2014 http://www.telegraph.co.uk/active/10870371/King-Juan-Carlos-I-of-Spain-elephant-hunter-biker-and-dictators-protege-who-helped-deliver-democracy.html.

107   Fiona Govan, Juan Carlos was 'sympathetic' to 1981 coup leaders, *The Telegraph*, 9 February 2012 http://www.telegraph.co.uk/news/worldnews/europe/spain/9072122/Juan-Carlos-was-sympathetic-to-1981-coup-leaders.html.

108 Carsten Humlebæk, *Spain: Inventing the Nation*, Bloomsbury Publishing, 2015, p.166.

109 *The Economist*, 4 February 2006.

110 Ashifa Kassam, Spanish authorities arrest 51 top figures in anti-corruption sweep, *The Guardian*, 27 October 2014
https://www.theguardian.com/world/2014/oct/27/spanish-authorities-arrest-51-anti-corruption-sweep.

111 Spain losing €26bn in tax revenue due to fraud, says economists' report, *El Pais* (English), 15 June 2017
https://elpais.com/elpais/2017/06/15/inenglish/1497545884_038119.html.

112 Spain Needs Urgently To Deal With Systematic Corruption, Transparency International Secretariat, 18 May 2017
https://www.transparency.org/news/pressrelease/spain_needs_urgently_to_deal_with_systemic_corruption.

113 P. Haywood, 'From Dictatorship to Democracy: Changing Forms of Corruption in Spain', in D. D. Port and Y. Mény (eds.), *Democracy and Corruption in Europe*, A & C Black, 1997, p.68.

114 A. Cazorla-Sanchez., *Franco: The Biography of the Myth*, Routledge, 2013, p.101.

115 Richard Eder, Spain's Parliament Gets Scandal Data, New York Times, 1 July 1970
http://www.nytimes.com/1970/07/01/archives/spains-parliament-gets-scandal-data.html?mcubz=2.

116 P. Preston, 'Spain feels Franco's legacy 40 years after his death', BBC News, 20 November 2015
http://www.bbc.co.uk/news/world-europe-34844939.

117 Mariano Sánchez Soler, Los Franco, S.A.: Ascensión y caída del último dictador de Occident, Oberon, 2007.

118 Obituary: Miguel Blesa de la Parra The Times, 6 October 2017
https://www.thetimes.co.uk/article/miguel-blesa-de-la-parra-obituary-d75kv3csx.

119   P. Haywood., 'From Dictatorship to Democracy: Changing Forms of Corruption in Spain', in D. D. Port and Y. Mény (eds), *Democracy and Corruption in Europe*, A & C Black, 1997, p.74.

120   V. P. Díaz., *Spain at the Crossroads: Civil Society, Politics, and the Rule of Law*, Harvard University Press, 1999, p.28 and C. P. del Campo., 'A Spanish Spring?' *New Left Review* 31, January-February 2005
https://newleftreview.org/II/31/carlos-prieto-del-campo-a-spanish-spring.

121   BBC News, Heads roll in Spanish finance scam, 21 September 2010 http://news.bbc.co.uk/1/hi/business/1556372.stm.

122   J. Pique, Catalan nationalists are just like other separatists – they feed on division and fantasy, *The Telegraph*, 30 September 2017. http://www.telegraph.co.uk/news/2017/09/30/catalan-nationalists-just-like-separatists-feed-division-fantasy/.

123   F. Jiménez and M. Villoria., 'Political Corruption in Spain', in J. Mendilow (ed.), *Money, Corruption, and Political Competition in Established and Emerging Democracies*, Rowman & Littlefield, 2012, p.122.

124   D. Torres, *Spain's kickback culture on trial*, Politico, 17 October 2016
https://www.politico.eu/article/spains-cash-corruption-and-construction-trial-caso-gurtel/.

125

126   F. J. Peréz., 'Manuel Moix dimite como fiscal jefe Anticorrupción tras conocerse su sociedad en Panamá', *El Pais*, 1 June 2017. https://politica.elpais.com/politica/2017/06/01/actualidad/1496304595_239167.html.

127   I. Mount., 'Ex-IMF chief sentenced over Bankia card scandal', *Financial Times*, 23 February 2017
https://www.ft.com/content/7f93082e-f9ed-11e6-bd4e-68d53499ed71.

128   D. Torres., 'Spain's never-ending corruption problem', *Politico*, 18 May 2017
https://www.politico.eu/article/spain-corruption-pp-rajoy-never-ending-problem-graft-ignacio-gonzalez/.

129   D. Torres., 'Spain's never-ending corruption problem', *Politico*, 18 May 2017
https://www.politico.eu/article/spain-corruption-pp-rajoy-never-ending-problem-graft-ignacio-gonzalez/.

130   http://www.omct.org/monitoring-protection-mechanisms/urgent-interventions/switzerland/2016/08/d23900/.

131   European Court of Human Rights Press Release, 31 May 2016, issued by the Registrar of the Court
https://www.globalgovernancewatch.org/library/doclib/20160603_ECtHRBeorteguiMartinezvSpain.pdf.

132   Incommunicado detention and torture in Spain, Part I: The Istanbul Protocol Project in the Basque Country, Istanbul Protocol Project in the Basque Country Working Group
https://irct.org/assets/uploads/Vol%2026%20No%203%20Incommunicado%20detention%20by%20Istanbul%20Protocol.pdf.

133   R. Fraser., *Blood of Spain*, Penguin, 1981, p.191.

134   Teresa Whitfield, *Endgame for ETA: Elusive Peace in the Basque Country*, Oxford University Press, 2014, p.39.

135   Jerrold M. Post, *The Mind of the Terrorist: The Psychology of Terrorism from the IRA to al-Qaeda*, St. Martin's Press, 2007, p.57.

136   D. Muro., *Ethnicity and Violence: The Case of Radical Basque Nationalism*, Routledge, 2013 p.97.

137   M. Simons., 'Spain Is Haunted by Basque Death Squad Scandal', *New York Times*, 4 February 1996
http://www.nytimes.com/1996/02/04/world/spain-is-haunted-by-basque-death-squad-scandal.html.

138   R. P. Clark, *Negotiating with ETA: Obstacles to Peace in the Basque Country, 1975-1988*, University of Nevada Press, 1990, p.55-56.

139　D. Muro., *Ethnicity and Violence: The Case of Radical Basque Nationalism*, Routledge, 2013, p.179 and T. Whitfield, *Endgame for ETA: Elusive Peace in the Basque Country*, Oxford University Press, 2014, p.25-26.

140　G. Hedgecoe., 'Calls for 'independentzia' revived in Basque Country', *Politico*, 18 March 2016
http://www.politico.eu/article/basque-country-independence-calls-revived-arnaldo-otegi-prison-release/.

141　Amnesty International,Spain: Puppeteers Accused of Glorifying Terrorism, 12 February 2016
https://www.amnesty.org/en/documents/eur41/3428/2016/en/.

142　Kevin Mermel, The End of the State of Autonomies? An Analysis of the Controversy Surrounding the 2010 Spanish Constitutional Court Ruling on Catalonia's 2006 Statute of Autonomy, University of Colorado, Boulder, CU Scholar Undergraduate Honors Theses, p.30.
http://scholar.colorado.edu/cgi/viewcontent.cgi?article=2312&context=honr_theses.

143　S. Garcia-Ruiz., 'To my Spanish friends', in L. Castro (ed.), *What's Up With Catalonia*, Catalonia Press, 2013, p.195.

144　D. Vampa., *The Regional Politics of Welfare in Italy, Spain and Great Britain*, Palgrave, 2016, p.131.

145　K. Abbey-Lambertz., 'There's A Lesson In Spain's Surreal, Unfinished Cities', *Huffington Post*, 2 November 2016.
https://www.huffingtonpost.com/entry/spain-empty-cities_us_56ba6221e4b0b40245c47dff.

146　G.Hedgecoe., 'Jailed Rodrigo Rato is the poster boy for ills of Spanish banks', *Irish Times*, 25 February 2017
https://www.irishtimes.com/business/financial-services/jailed-rodrigo-rato-is-the-poster-boy-for-ills-of-spanish-banks-1.2987897.

147　G. Tremlett., 'How corruption, cuts and despair drove Spain's protesters on to the streets', *The Guardian*, 21 May 2011.
https://www.theguardian.com/world/2011/may/21/spain-reveals-pain-cuts-unemployment.

148 A. Dawber., 'Pablo Iglesias: How the leader of the leftist Podemos party upset Spain's elites to reach the brink of power', *The Independent*, 25 December 2015
http://www.independent.co.uk/news/people/pablo-iglesias-how-the-leader-of-the-podemos-party-upset-spains-elites-to-reach-the-brink-of-power-a6786291.html.

149 R Minder., 'Catalan Leader Boldly Grasps a Separatist Lever', *New York Times*, 5 October 2012
http://www.nytimes.com/2012/10/06/world/europe/in-catalonia-spain-artur-mas-threatens-to-secede.html.

150 http://www.cataloniavotes.eu/wp-content/uploads/2017/10/RESEARCH_GROUP_STATEMENT_ON_CATALONIA_REFERENDUM-1.pdf.

151 Patrick Greenfield, Catalonia: Puigdemont to reveal independence plans – as it happened, *The Guardian*, 10 October.
https://www.theguardian.com/world/live/2017/oct/10/catalan-parliament-discusses-independence-referendum-live.

152 https://www.boe.es/legislacion/documentos/ConstitucionINGLES.pdf.

153 http://catalangovernment.exili.eu/pres_gov/government/en/news/303862/president-puigdemont-parliaments-duty-proceed-application-article-155-catalonia.html.

154 Catalan Government Not Ready For Republic Says ERC, Catalan News, 13 November 2017
http://www.catalannews.com/politics/item/catalan-government-not-ready-for-republic-says-erc.

155 I. Urkullu., 'Only political dialogue can bring stability to Catalonia – and the EU must help', *The Guardian*, 23 October 2017.
https://www.theguardian.com/commentisfree/2017/oct/23/dialogue-stability-catalonia-eu-madrid-basque-autonomy-catalan-crisis.

156 J. Rankin., 'EU silence over Catalan leader's call for action speaks volumes', *The Guardian*, 1 November 2017.
https://www.theguardian.com/world/2017/nov/01/eu-silence-over-catalan-leaders-call-for-action-speaks-volumes.

157　Lisbon Declaration: 'Our Europe, for and by the people!', Esquer-daNet, 13 November 2017
https://www.esquerda.net/node/51894.

158　Independence: Communique on Situation in Catalonia, Global Justice and Equality Project, 1 November 2017
https://globaljusticeecology.org/independence-communique-on-the-situation-in-catalonia-anticapitalistas/.

159　Anticapitalistas, Communiqué on the Situation in Catalonia, The Bullet, 1 November 2017
http://socialistproject.ca/bullet/1505.php.

160　Pablo Iglesias Orders Take Over Of Podemos Catalonia After Anti-capitalist Sector Recognises Catalan Republic, *The Spain Report*, 30 October 2017
https://www.thespainreport.com/articles/1250-171030121434-pablo-iglesias-orders-take-over-of-podemos-catalonia-after-anticapitalist-sector-recognises-catalan-republic.

Homage to Caledonia
Scotland and the Spanish Civil War

By Daniel Gray
ISBN 978-1-906817-16-9 PBK £9.99

 The Spanish civil war was a call to arms for 2,300 British volunteers, of which over 500 were from Scotland. The first book of its kind, Homage to Caledonia examines Scotland's role in the conflict, detailing exactly why Scottish involvement was so profound.

Using a wealth of previously-unpublished letters sent back from the front as well as other archival items, Daniel Gray is able to tell little known stories of courage in conflict, and to call into question accepted versions of events such as the 'murder' of Bob Smillie, or the heroism of 'The Scots Scarlet Pimpernel'.

Homage to Caledonia offers a very human take on events in Spain: for every tale of abject distress in a time of war, there is a tale of a Scottish volunteer urinating in his general's boots, knocking back a dram with Errol Flynn or appalling Spanish comrades with his pipe playing. For the first time, read the fascinating story of Caledonia's role in this seminal conflict.

Daniel Gray has done a marvellous job in bringing together the stories of Scots volunteers - in [this] many-voiced, multi-layered book.
SCOTLAND ON SUNDAY

Book of the week - Gray deserves applause for shining a light on a lesser-known aspect of the nation's character of which we should all be proud.
PRESS & JOURNAL

Small Nations in a Big World
What Scotland can Learn

By Michael Keating and Malcolm Harvey
ISBN 978-1-910745-89-2 PBK £9.99

 Small northern European states have been a major point of reference in the Scottish independence debate. For nationalists, they have been an 'arc of prosperity' while in the aftermath of the financial crash, unionists lampooned the 'arc of insolvency'.

Both characterisations are equally misleading. Small states can do well in the global market place, but they face the world in very different ways. Some accept market logic and take the 'low road' of low wages, low taxes and light regulation, with a correspondingly low level of public services. Others take the 'high road' of social investment, which entails a larger public sector and higher taxes. Such a strategy requires innovative government, flexibility and social partnership.

Keating and Harvey compare the experience of the Nordic and Baltic states and Ireland, which have taken very different roads and ask what lessons can be learnt for Scotland. They conclude that success is possible but that hard choices would need to be taken. Neither side in the independence debate has faced these choices squarely.

This study throws up all sorts of illuminating questions about the character of government, state and social partners in an independent or more self-governing Scotland.
GERRY HASSAN, THE IRISH TIMES

McSmörgåsbord
What post-Brexit Scotland can learn from the Nordics

By Lesley Riddoch & Eberhard Bort
ISBN 978-1-912147-00-7 PBK £7.99

The Nordic countries have a veritable smörgåsbord of relationships with the European Union, from in to out to somewhere in between. So, what does that mean for Scotland?

Well, somewhere in this incredible diversity of relationships with Europe is an arrangement that's likely to be good for Scotland too – strangely enough, maybe more than one. Inside or outside the UK, Scotland wants to keep trade and cultural links with Europe – that much is clear. But is the EU really the best club in town for an independent Scotland? Or would Scots benefit from 'doing a Norway' – joining the halfway house of the EEA and keeping the Single Market but losing the troublesome Common Fisheries and Agriculture Policies? Would an independent Scotland need the support and shelter of another union – or could the nation stand alone like the tiny Faroes or Iceland?

These tough questions have already been faced and resolved by five Nordic nations and their autonomous territories within the last 40 years. Perhaps there's something for Scotland to learn?

The unique combination of personal experience and experts' insights give this book its hands-on character: pragmatic and thought-provoking, challenging and instructive, full of amazing stories and useful comparisons, enriching the debates about Scotland's post-Brexit future as a Nordic neighbour.

Scotland's response to Britain's divided Brexit vote has been positively Nordic – Scots expect diversity and empowerment to be entirely possible – whilst Westminster's reaction has been decidedly British. One singer – one song. One deal for everyone – end of.
LESLEY RIDDOCH

A Utopia Like Any Other
Inside the Swedish Model

By Dominic Hinde
ISBN 978-1-910745-32-8 PBK £9.99

Does a utopia really exist within northern Europe? Do we have anything to learn from it if it does? And what makes a nation worthy of admiration, anyway?

Since the '30s, when the world was wowed by the Stockholm Exhibition, to most people Sweden has meant clean lines, good public housing, and a Social Democratic government. More recently the Swedes have been lauded for their environmental credentials, their aspirational free schools, and their hardy economy. But what's the truth of the Swedish model? Is modern Sweden really that much better than rest of Europe?

In this insightful exploration of where Sweden has been, where it's going, and what the rest of us can learn from its journey, journalist Dominic Hinde explores the truth behind the myth of a Swedish Utopia. In his quest for answers he travels the length of the country and further, enjoying July sunshine on the island of Gotland with the cream of Swedish politics for 'Almedalan Week', venturing into the Arctic Circle to visit a town about to be swallowed up by the very mine it exists to serve, and even taking a trip to Shanghai to take in the suburban Chinese interpretation of Scandinavia, 'Sweden Town', a Nordic city in miniature in the smog of China's largest city.

Arguing for Independence
Evidence, Risk and the Wicked Issues

By Stephen Maxwell
ISBN 978-1-908373-33-5 PBK £9.99

Independence: a nation's right to effective government by its people or for its people
Evidence: interpretation of facts
Risk: likelihood that outcomes will not be as predicted
Wicked issues: problems perceived to be resistant to resolution

What sorts of arguments and evidence should carry the most wight in assessing the case for and against Scottish independence? Given the complexity of the question and the range of the possible consequences, can either side in the argument protend to certainty, or must we simply be satisfied with probability or even plausibility? Are there criteria for sifting the competing claims and counter-claims and arriving at a rational decision on Scotland's future?

By offering an assessment of the case for independence across all its dimensions, Arguing for Independence fills a longstanding gap in Scotland's political bookshelf as we enter a new and critical phase in the debate on Scotland's political future.

Stephen Maxwell has a positive, left-wing case for independence.
SCOTTISH LEFT REVIEW

Maxwell was an intellectual, a thinker, a writer, a civic activist, and a dedicated servant of Scotland's voluntary sector.
JOYCE MCMILLAN, THE SCOTSMAN

Tackling Timorous Economics
How Scotland's Economy Could Work

By Stephen Boyd
ISBN 978-1-910021-37-8 PBK £9.99

Timorous: adj, 1) shy, not bold 2) easily frightened.

Economics: n, social science concerned with the production and consumption of goods and services.

What is the best way to run a country? How long should a person be obliged to work every day? What will the economy look like after Brexit?

In this new take on the Scottish economy, experts Trebeck, Boyd and Kerevan address how our economy can serve us, as opposed to the people serving the economy. They believe that current economic policies are not aligned with what we as people need in these times of rampant inequality and inequitable distribution, advocating an increased focus on the quality of Scotland's economy. Using Scotland as an example for the economic workings of any country, Tackling Timorous Economics shows a better way of how economics could work for us.

...of interest well beyond Scotland's borders ... it will challenge you to reflect on your own views on big issues like inequality and economic policy.
DAVID MCCAUSLAND, THE CONVERSATION

Luath Press Limited

committed to publishing well written books worth reading

LUATH PRESS takes its name from Robert Burns, whose little collie Luath (*Gael.*, swift or nimble) tripped up Jean Armour at a wedding and gave him the chance to speak to the woman who was to be his wife and the abiding love of his life. Burns called one of the 'Twa Dogs' Luath after Cuchullin's hunting dog in Ossian's *Fingal*. Luath Press was established in 1981 in the heart of Burns country, and is now based a few steps up the road from Burns' first lodgings on Edinburgh's Royal Mile. Luath offers you distinctive writing with a hint of unexpected pleasures.

Most bookshops in the UK, the US, Canada, Australia, New Zealand and parts of Europe, either carry our books in stock or can order them for you. To order direct from us, please send a £sterling cheque, postal order, international money order or your credit card details (number, address of cardholder and expiry date) to us at the address below. Please add post and packing as follows: UK – £1.00 per delivery address; overseas surface mail – £2.50 per delivery address; overseas airmail – £3.50 for the first book to each delivery address, plus £1.00 for each additional book by airmail to the same address. If your order is a gift, we will happily enclose your card or message at no extra charge.

Luath Press Limited
543/2 Castlehill
The Royal Mile
Edinburgh EH1 2ND
Scotland
Telephone: +44 (0)131 225 4326 (24 hours)
email: sales@luath. co.uk
Website: www. luath.co.uk